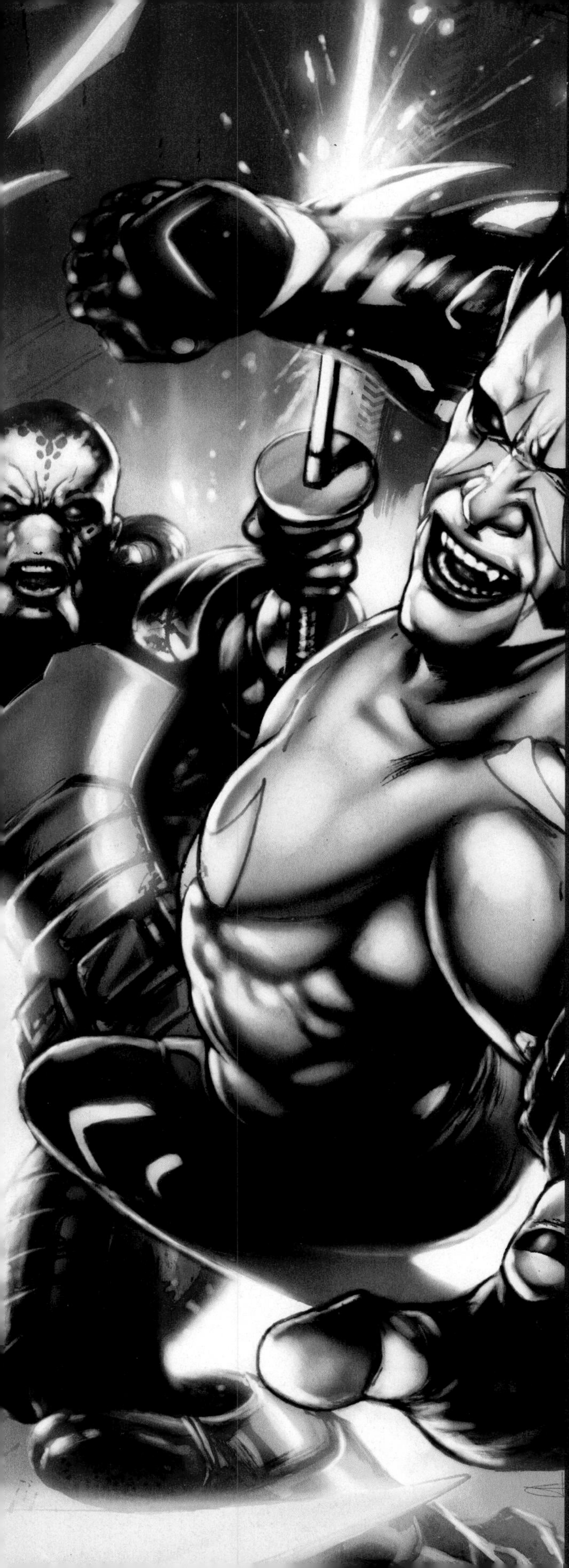

LOBO

VOLUME 2

BEWARE HIS MIGHT

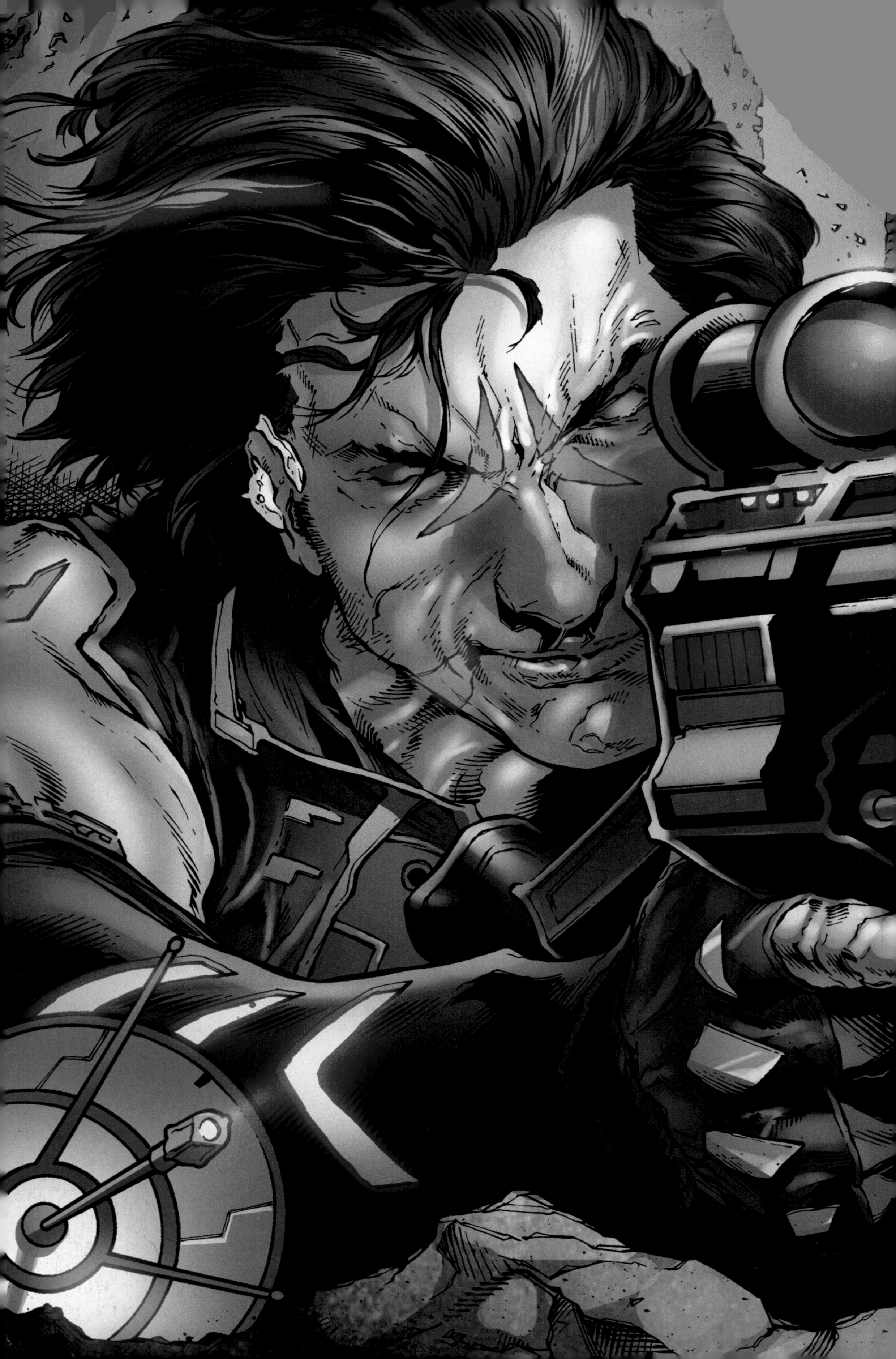

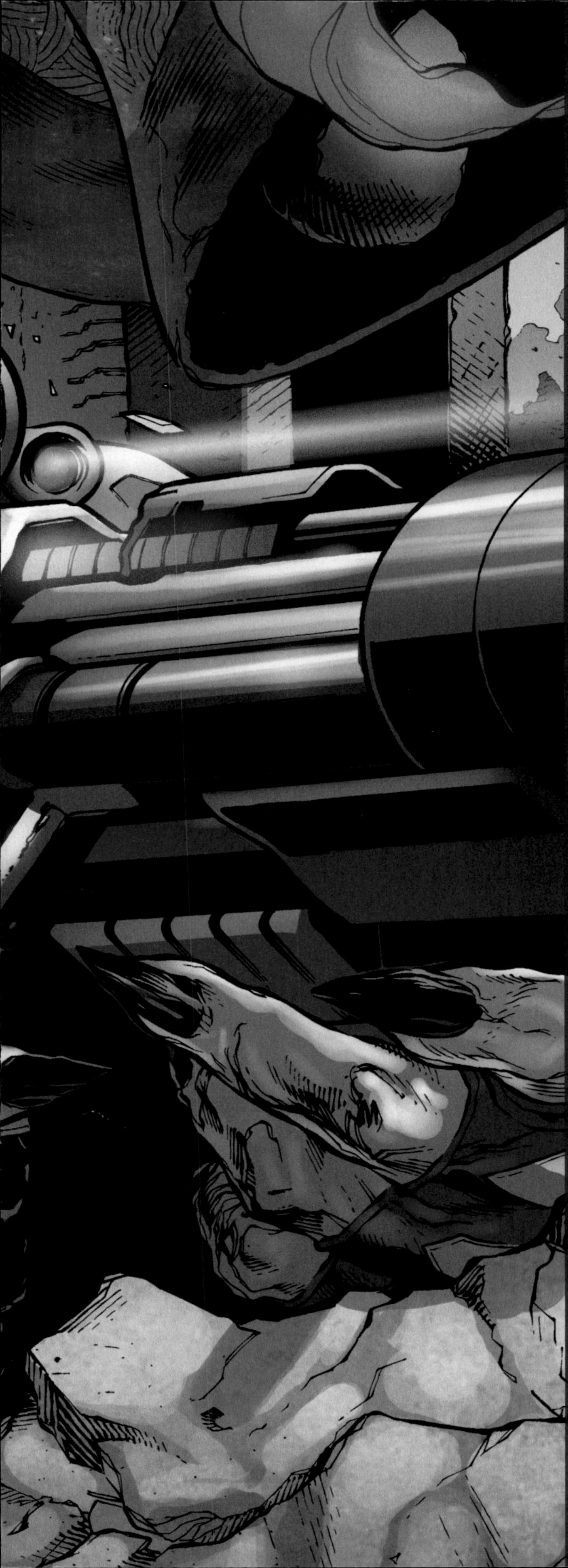

LOBO

VOLUME 2
BEWARE HIS MIGHT

WRITTEN BY
CULLEN BUNN
FRANK BARBIERE

ART BY
CLIFF RICHARDS
SZYMON KUDRANSKI
ROBSON ROCHA
GUILLERMO ORTEGO

COLOR BY
MIKE ATIYEH
BLOND

LETTERS BY
TRAVIS LANHAM

COLLECTION COVER ART BY
LEONARDO MANCO

LOBO CREATED BY
ROGER SLIFER AND
KEITH GIFFEN

THE CITADEL CREATED BY
MARV WOLFMAN &
GEORGE PÉREZ

MIKE COTTON Editor – Original Series
PAUL KAMINSKI Associate Editor – Original Series
JEREMY BENT Assistant Editor – Original Series
JEB WOODARD Group Editor – Collected Editions
LIZ ERICKSON Editor – Collected Edition
STEVE COOK Design Director – Books
DAMIAN RYLAND Publication Design

BOB HARRAS Senior VP – Editor-in-Chief, DC Comics

DIANE NELSON President
DAN DIDIO and JIM LEE Co-Publishers
GEOFF JOHNS Chief Creative Officer
AMIT DESAI Senior VP – Marketing & Global Franchise Management
NAIRI GARDINER Senior VP – Finance
SAM ADES VP – Digital Marketing
BOBBIE CHASE VP – Talent Development
MARK CHIARELLO Senior VP – Art, Design & Collected Editions
JOHN CUNNINGHAM VP – Content Strategy
ANNE DEPIES VP – Strategy Planning & Reporting
DON FALLETTI VP – Manufacturing Operations
LAWRENCE GANEM VP – Editorial Administration & Talent Relations
ALISON GILL Senior VP – Manufacturing & Operations
HANK KANALZ Senior VP – Editorial Strategy & Administration
JAY KOGAN VP – Legal Affairs
DEREK MADDALENA Senior VP – Sales & Business Development
JACK MAHAN VP – Business Affairs
DAN MIRON VP – Sales Planning & Trade Development
NICK NAPOLITANO VP – Manufacturing Administration
CAROL ROEDER VP – Marketing
EDDIE SCANNELL VP – Mass Account & Digital Sales
COURTNEY SIMMONS Senior VP – Publicity & Communications
JIM (SKI) SOKOLOWSKI VP – Comic Book Specialty & Newsstand Sales
SANDY YI Senior VP – Global Franchise Management

LOBO VOLUME 2: BEWARE HIS MIGHT

Originally published in single magazine form in LOBO 7-9, LOBO ANNUAL 1 and online as DC SNEAK PEEK: LOBO 1
Copyright © 2015 DC Comics. All Rights Reserved. All characters, their distinctive likenesses and related elements featured in this
publication are trademarks of DC Comics. The stories, characters and incidents featured in this publication are entirely fictional.
DC Comics does not read or accept unsolicited ideas, stories or artwork.

DC Comics, 2900 West Alameda Ave., Burbank, CA 91505
Printed by RR Donnelley, Salem, VA, USA. 3/18/16. First Printing.
ISBN: 978-1-4012-6150-4

Library of Congress Cataloging-in-Publication Data is available

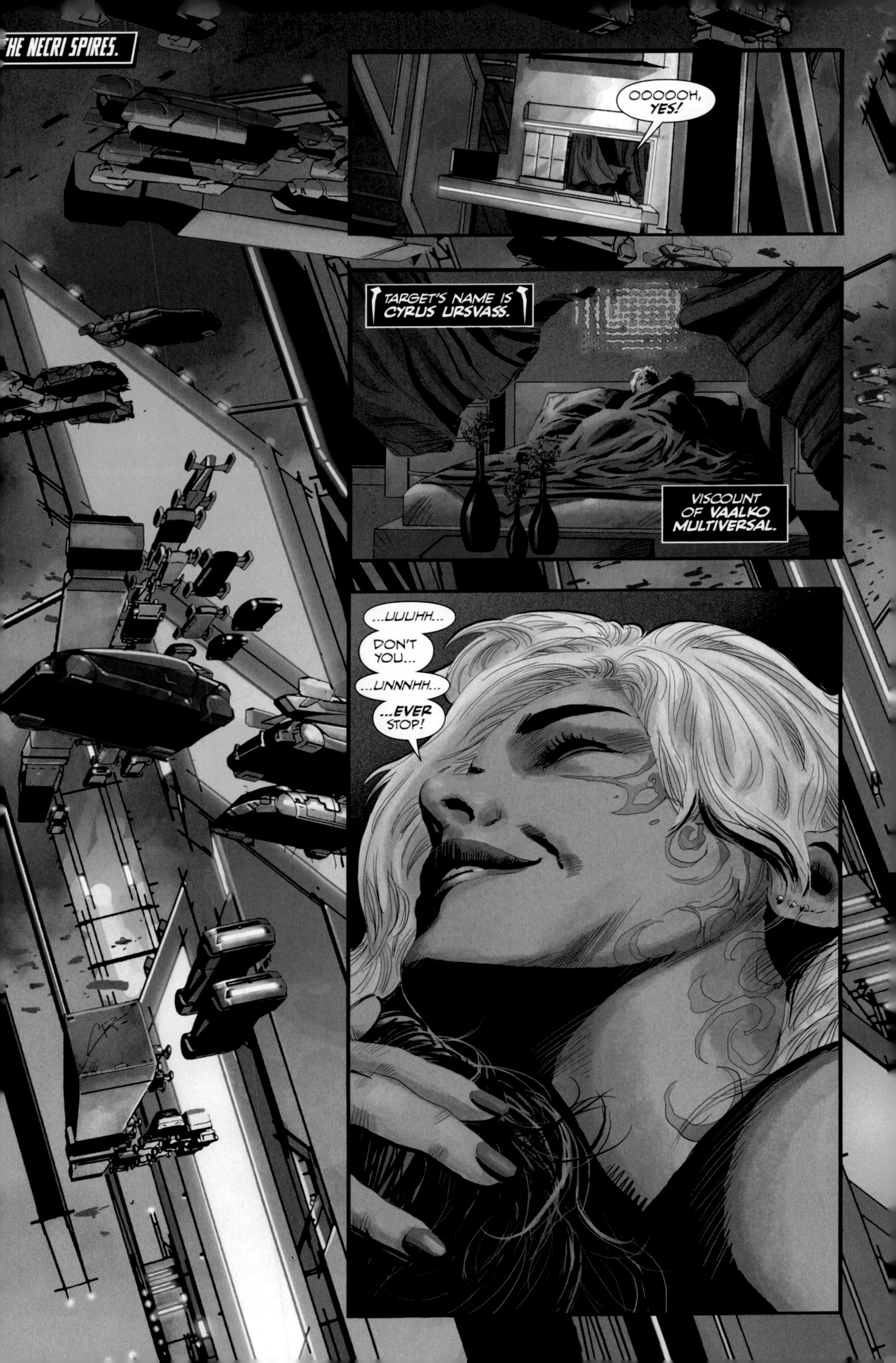
THE NECRI SPIRES.
OOOOOH, YES!
TARGET'S NAME IS CYRUS URSVASS.
VISCOUNT OF VAALKO MULTIVERSAL.
...UUUHH...
DON'T YOU...
...UNNNHH...
...EVER STOP!

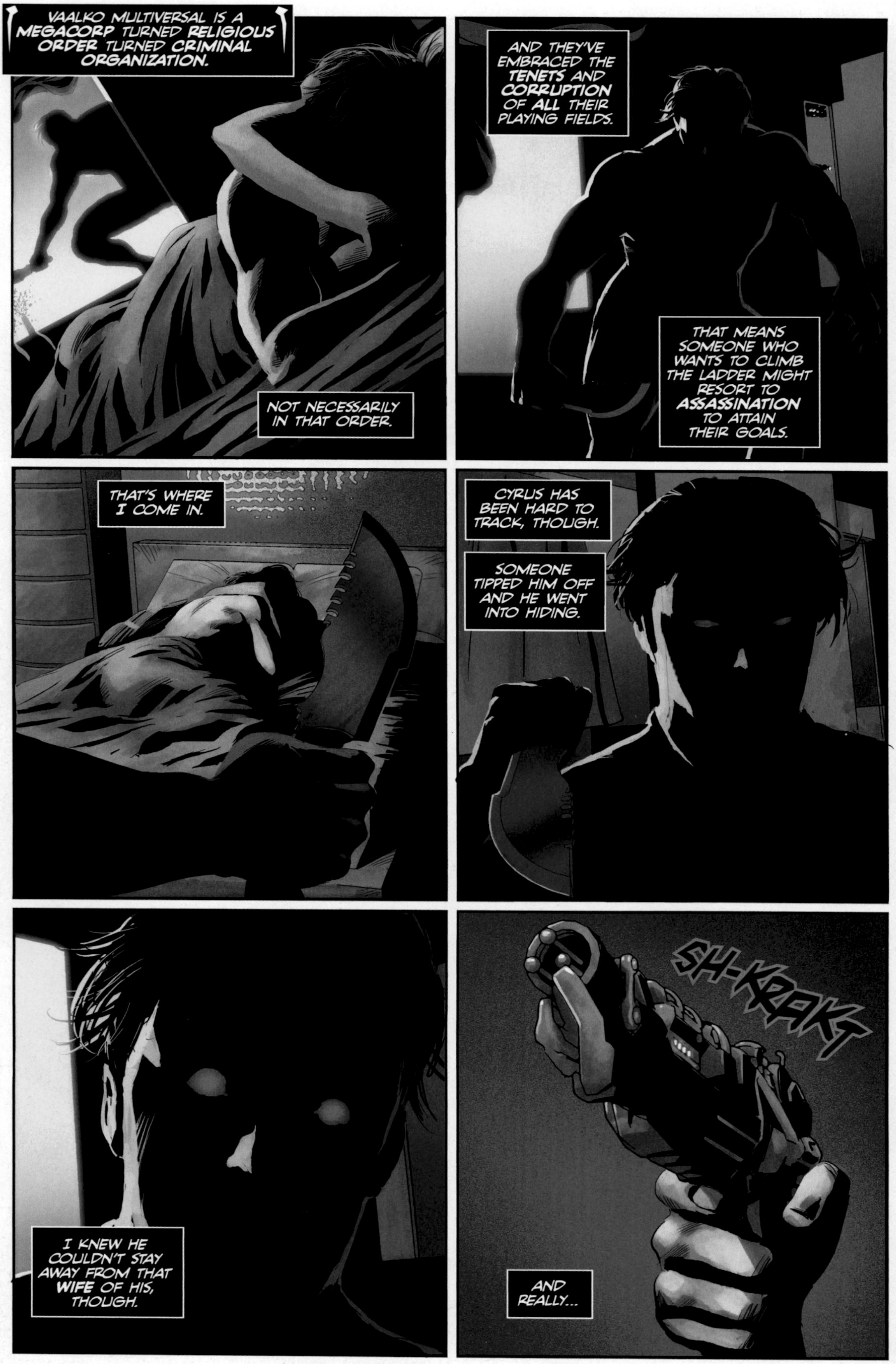
VAALKO MULTIVERSAL IS A MEGACORP TURNED RELIGIOUS ORDER TURNED CRIMINAL ORGANIZATION.
NOT NECESSARILY IN THAT ORDER.
AND THEY'VE EMBRACED THE TENETS AND CORRUPTION OF ALL THEIR PLAYING FIELDS.
THAT MEANS SOMEONE WHO WANTS TO CLIMB THE LADDER MIGHT RESORT TO ASSASSINATION TO ATTAIN THEIR GOALS.
THAT'S WHERE I COME IN.
CYRUS HAS BEEN HARD TO TRACK, THOUGH.
SOMEONE TIPPED HIM OFF AND HE WENT INTO HIDING.
I KNEW HE COULDN'T STAY AWAY FROM THAT WIFE OF HIS, THOUGH.
SH-KRAKT
AND REALLY...

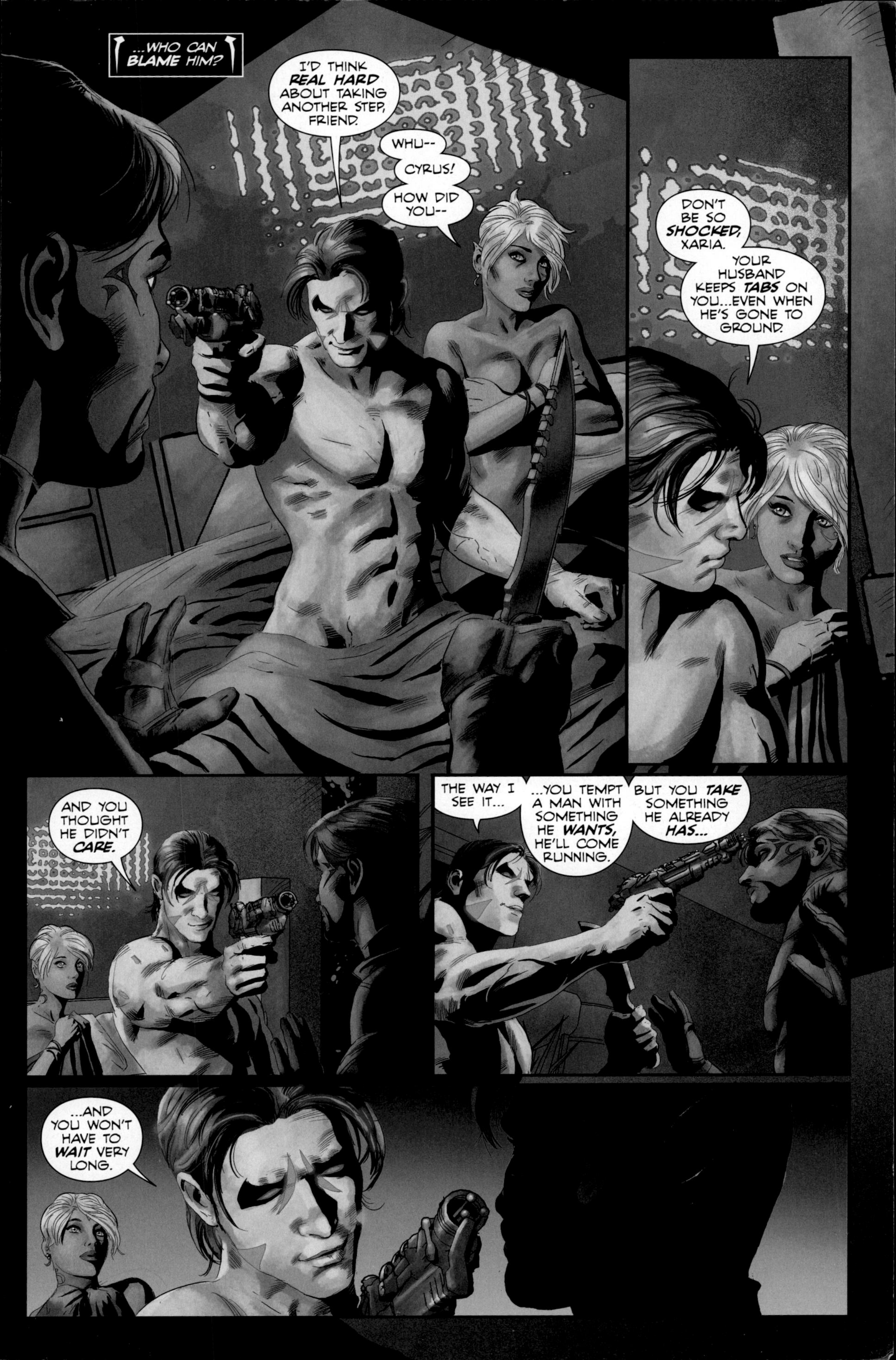
...WHO CAN BLAME HIM?
I'D THINK REAL HARD ABOUT TAKING ANOTHER STEP, FRIEND.
WHU--
CYRUS!
HOW DID YOU--
DON'T BE SO SHOCKED, XARIA.
YOUR HUSBAND KEEPS TABS ON YOU...EVEN WHEN HE'S GONE TO GROUND.
AND YOU THOUGHT HE DIDN'T CARE.
THE WAY I SEE IT...
...YOU TEMPT A MAN WITH SOMETHING HE WANTS, HE'LL COME RUNNING.
BUT YOU TAKE SOMETHING HE ALREADY HAS...
...AND YOU WON'T HAVE TO WAIT VERY LONG.

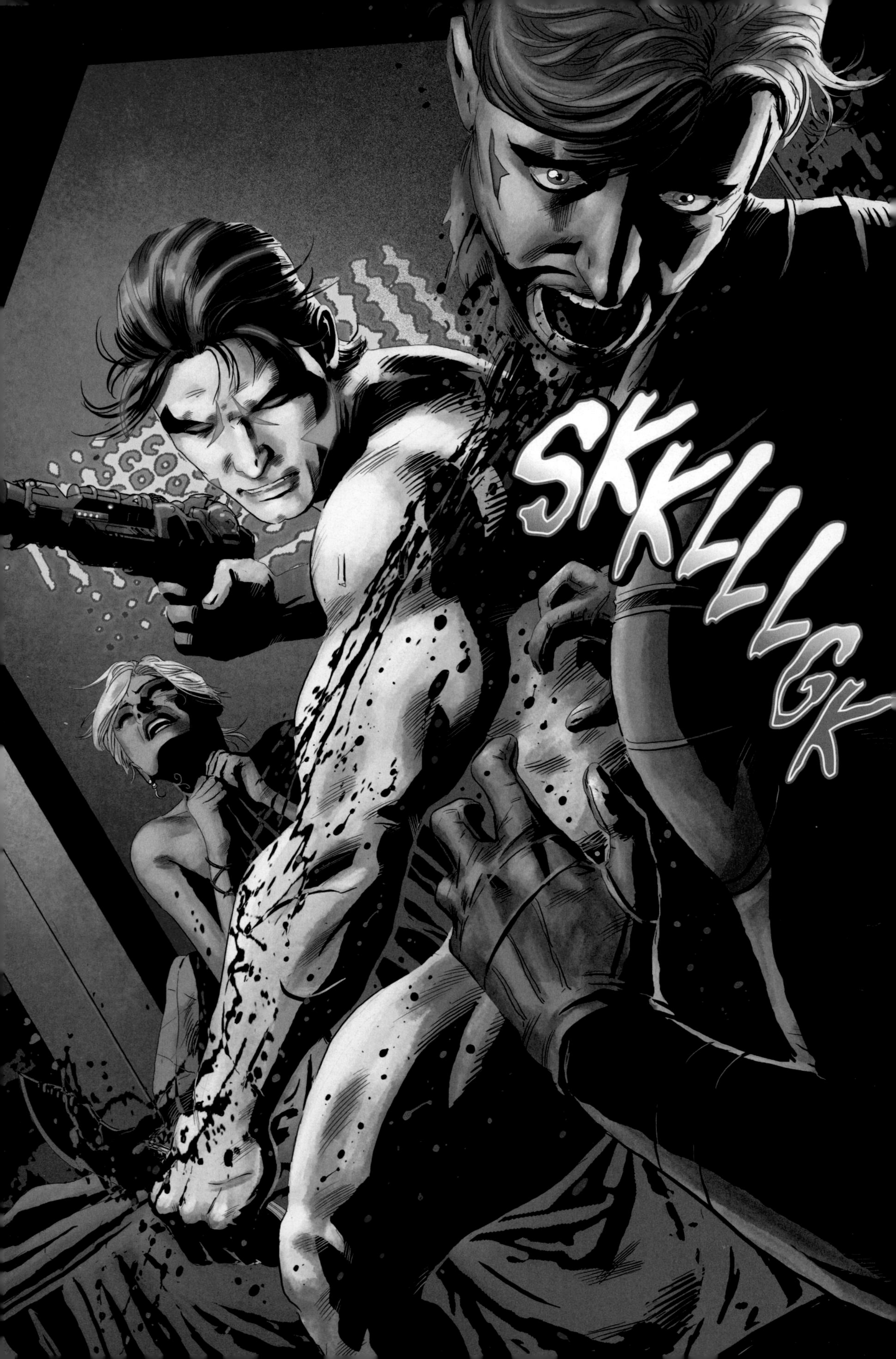
SKLLLGK

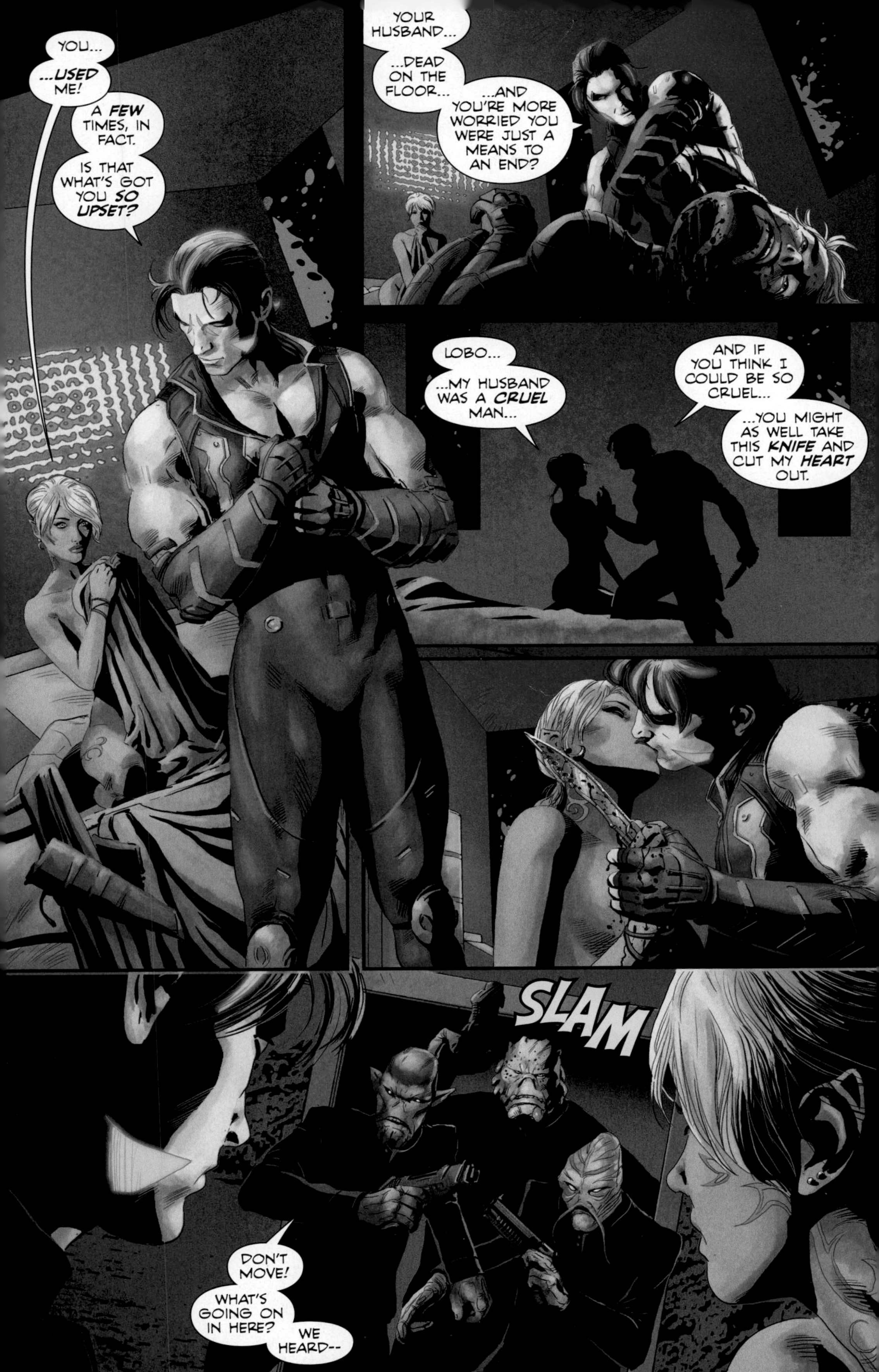
YOU...
...USED ME!
A FEW TIMES, IN FACT.
IS THAT WHAT'S GOT YOU SO UPSET?
YOUR HUSBAND...
...DEAD ON THE FLOOR...
...AND YOU'RE MORE WORRIED YOU WERE JUST A MEANS TO AN END?
LOBO...
...MY HUSBAND WAS A CRUEL MAN...
AND IF YOU THINK I COULD BE SO CRUEL...
...YOU MIGHT AS WELL TAKE THIS KNIFE AND CUT MY HEART OUT.
SLAM
DON'T MOVE!
WHAT'S GOING ON IN HERE?
WE HEARD--

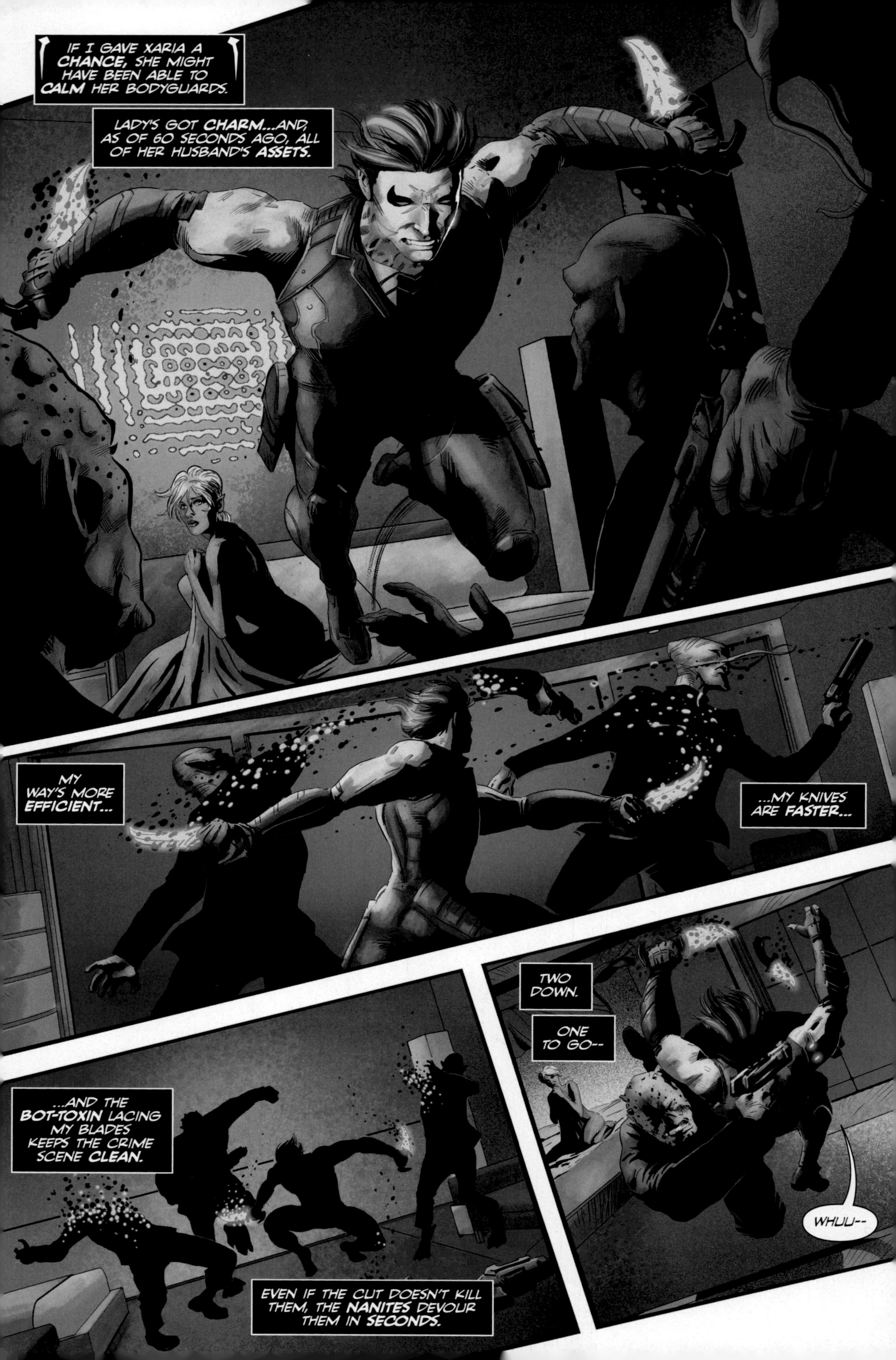

IF I GAVE XARIA A CHANCE, SHE MIGHT HAVE BEEN ABLE TO CALM HER BODYGUARDS.
LADY'S GOT CHARM...AND, AS OF 60 SECONDS AGO, ALL OF HER HUSBAND'S ASSETS.
MY WAY'S MORE EFFICIENT...
...MY KNIVES ARE FASTER...
...AND THE BOT-TOXIN LACING MY BLADES KEEPS THE CRIME SCENE CLEAN.
EVEN IF THE CUT DOESN'T KILL THEM, THE NANITES DEVOUR THEM IN SECONDS.
TWO DOWN.
ONE TO GO--
WHUU--

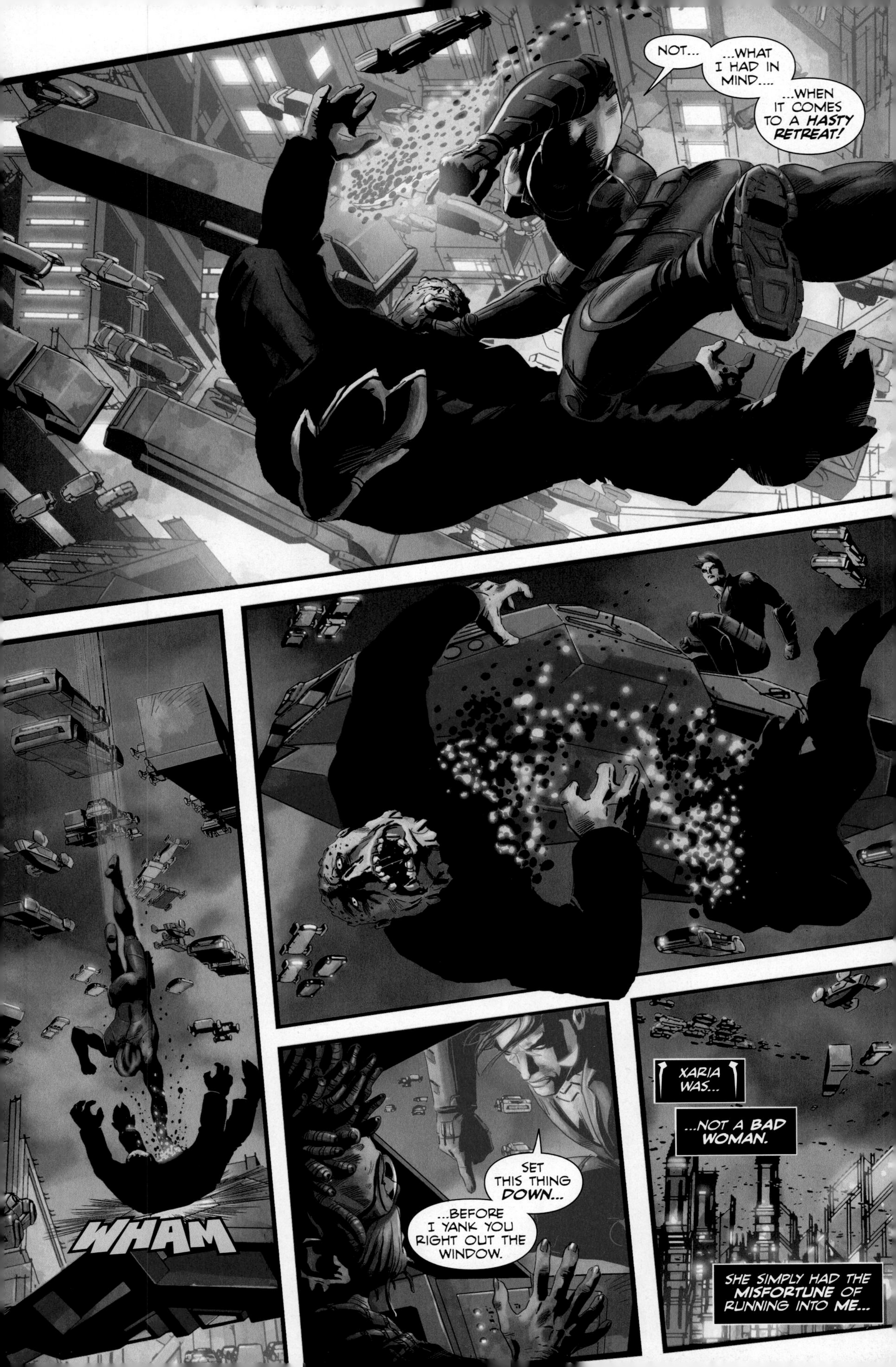

NOT...
...WHAT I HAD IN MIND....
...WHEN IT COMES TO A HASTY RETREAT!
WHAM
SET THIS THING DOWN...
...BEFORE I YANK YOU RIGHT OUT THE WINDOW.
XARIA WAS...
...NOT A BAD WOMAN.
SHE SIMPLY HAD THE MISFORTUNE OF RUNNING INTO ME...

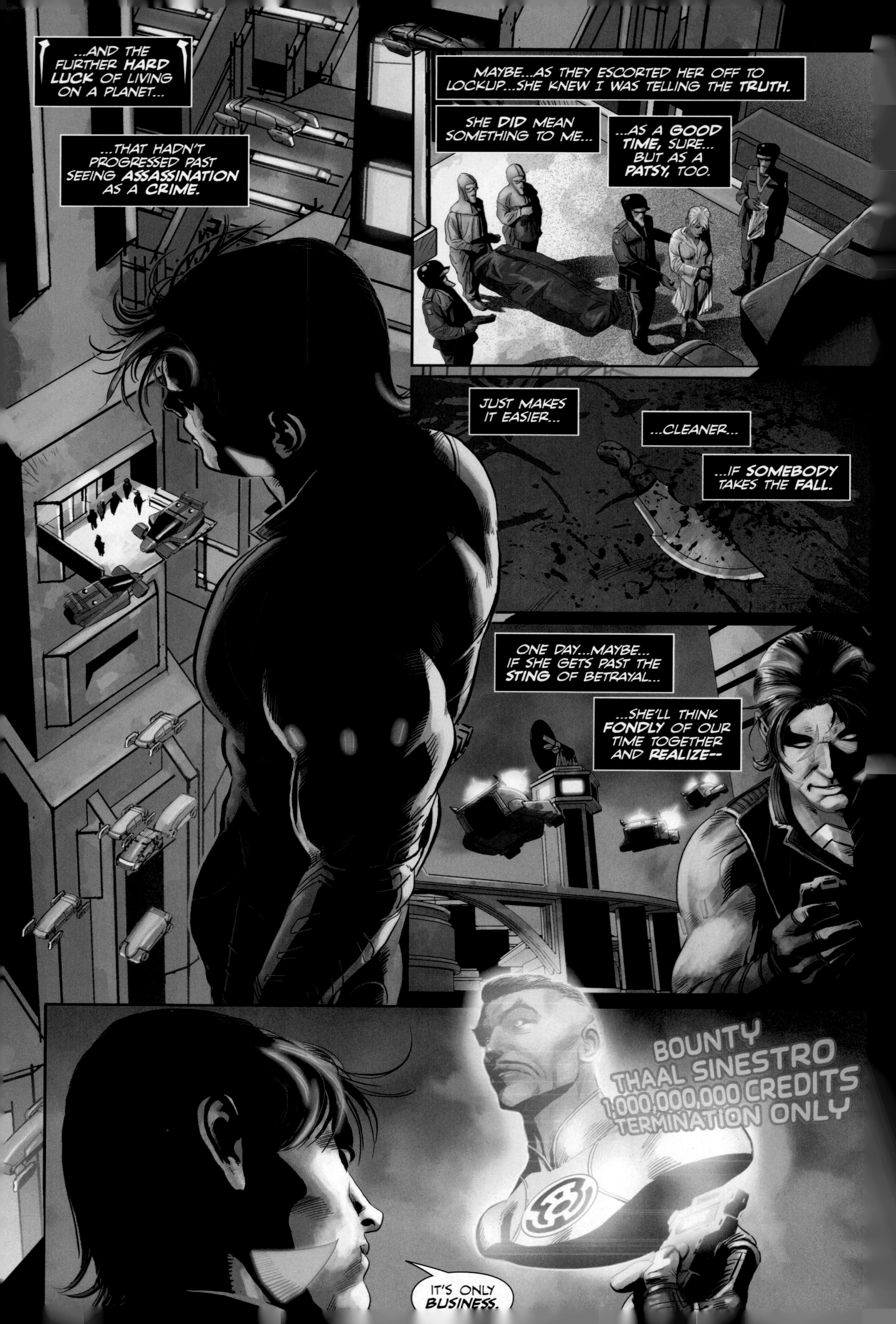
...AND THE FURTHER HARD LUCK OF LIVING ON A PLANET...
...THAT HADN'T PROGRESSED PAST SEEING ASSASSINATION AS A CRIME.
MAYBE...AS THEY ESCORTED HER OFF TO LOCKUP...SHE KNEW I WAS TELLING THE TRUTH.
SHE DID MEAN SOMETHING TO ME...
...AS A GOOD TIME, SURE... BUT AS A PATSY, TOO.
JUST MAKES IT EASIER...
...CLEANER...
...IF SOMEBODY TAKES THE FALL.
ONE DAY...MAYBE... IF SHE GETS PAST THE STING OF BETRAYAL...
...SHE'LL THINK FONDLY OF OUR TIME TOGETHER AND REALIZE--
BOUNTY
THAAL SINESTRO
1,000,000,000 CREDITS
TERMINATION ONLY
IT'S ONLY BUSINESS.

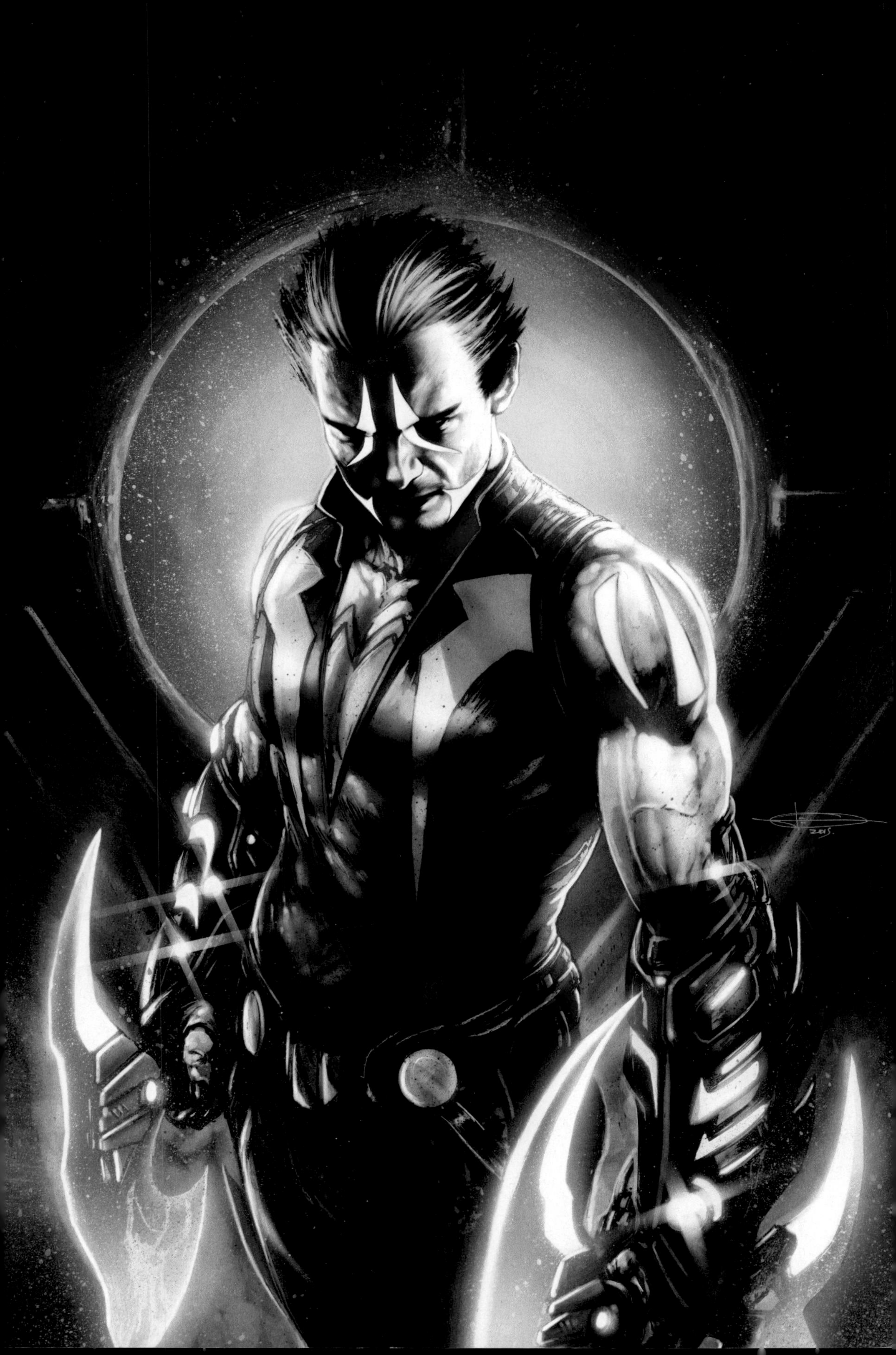

CULLEN BUNN writer CLIFF RICHARDS artist MIKE ATIYEH colorist TRAVIS LANHAM letterer cover art by LEONARDO MANCO

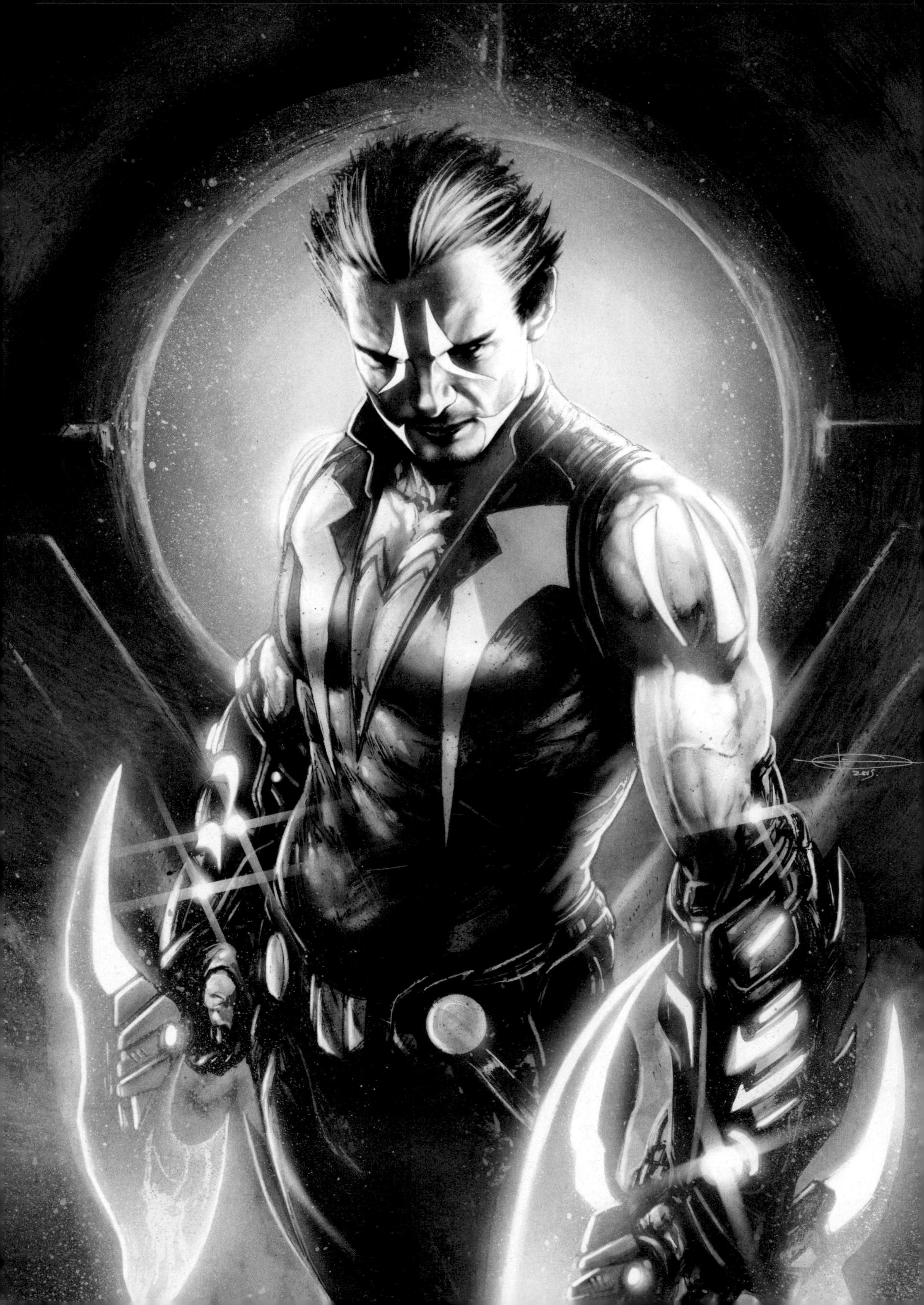

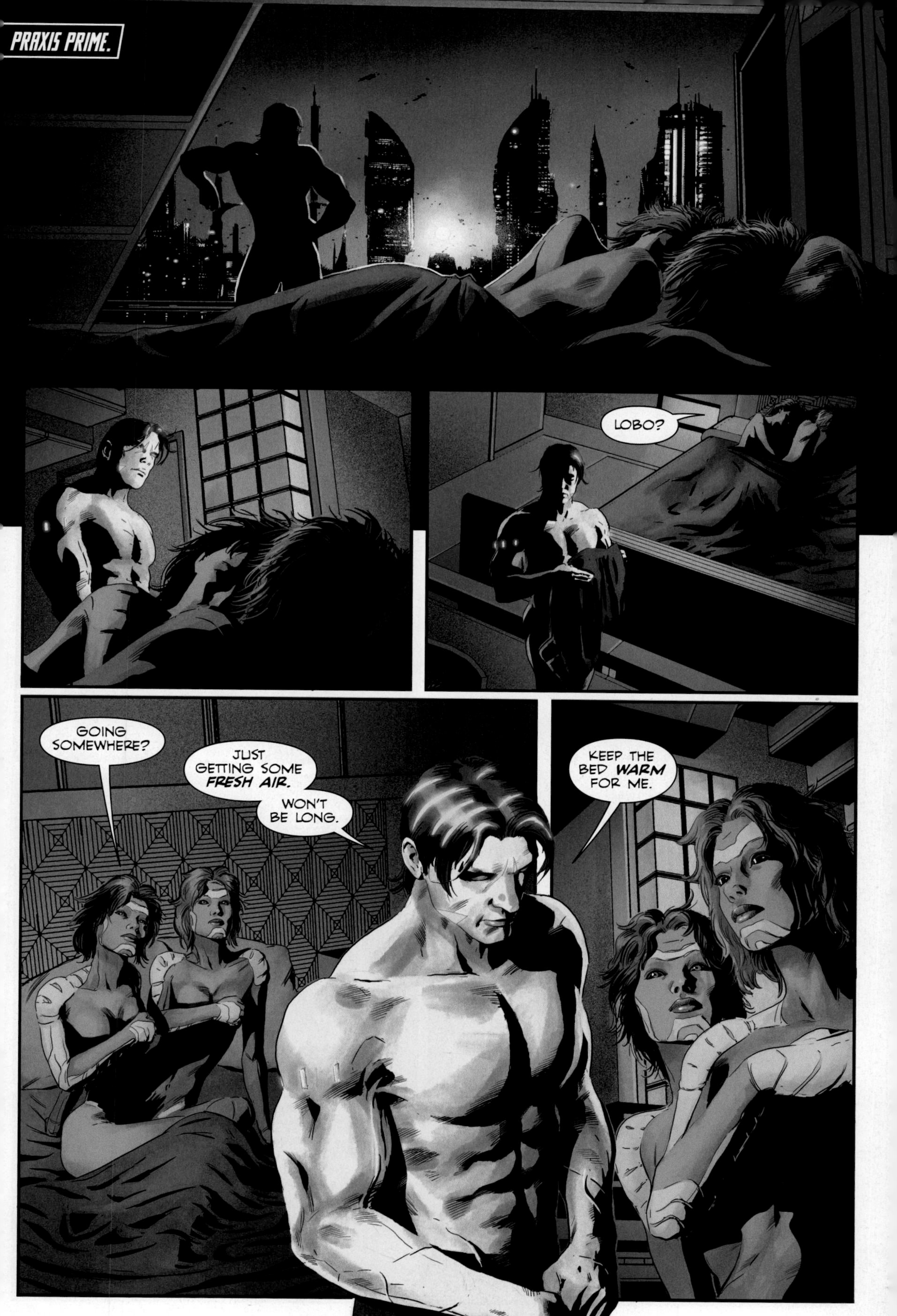
PRAXIS PRIME.
LOBO?
GOING SOMEWHERE?
JUST GETTING SOME FRESH AIR.
WON'T BE LONG.
KEEP THE BED WARM FOR ME.

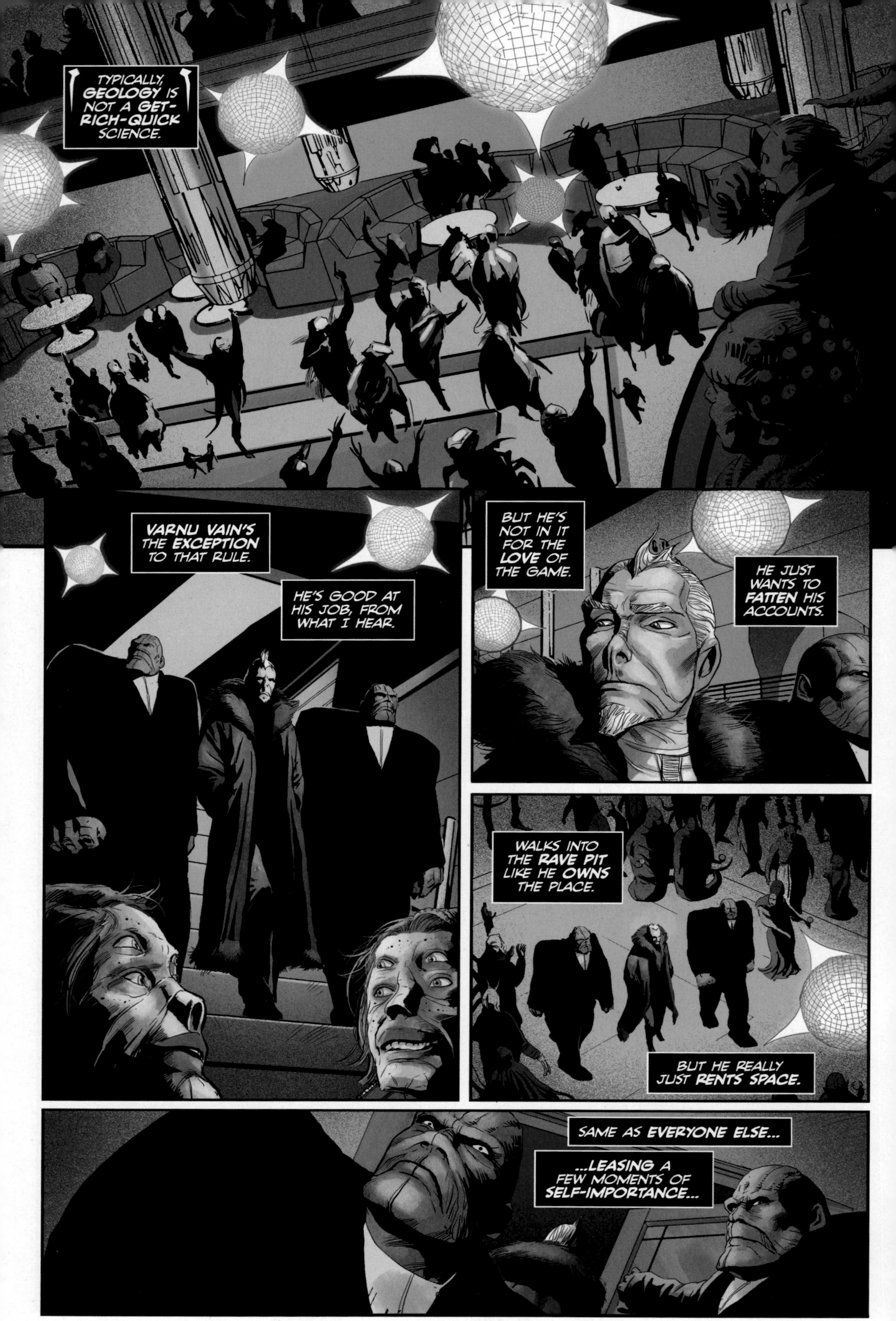
TYPICALLY, GEOLOGY IS NOT A GET-RICH-QUICK SCIENCE.
VARNU VAIN'S THE EXCEPTION TO THAT RULE.
HE'S GOOD AT HIS JOB, FROM WHAT I HEAR.
BUT HE'S NOT IN IT FOR THE LOVE OF THE GAME.
HE JUST WANTS TO FATTEN HIS ACCOUNTS.
WALKS INTO THE RAVE PIT LIKE HE OWNS THE PLACE.
BUT HE REALLY JUST RENTS SPACE.
SAME AS EVERYONE ELSE...
...LEASING A FEW MOMENTS OF SELF-IMPORTANCE...

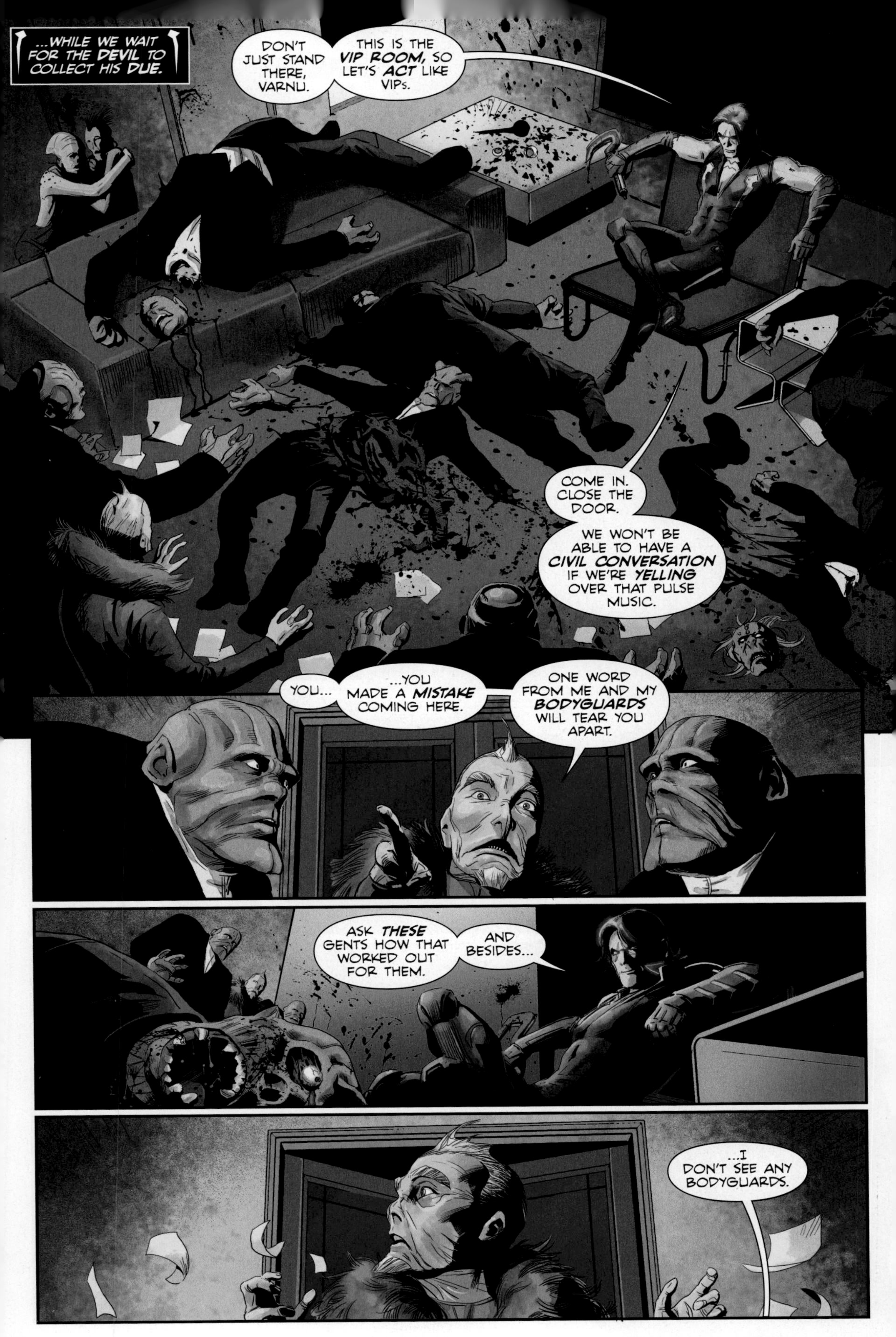
...WHILE WE WAIT FOR THE DEVIL TO COLLECT HIS DUE.
DON'T JUST STAND THERE, VARNU.
THIS IS THE VIP ROOM, SO LET'S ACT LIKE VIPs.
COME IN. CLOSE THE DOOR.
WE WON'T BE ABLE TO HAVE A CIVIL CONVERSATION IF WE'RE YELLING OVER THAT PULSE MUSIC.
YOU...
...YOU MADE A MISTAKE COMING HERE.
ONE WORD FROM ME AND MY BODYGUARDS WILL TEAR YOU APART.
ASK THESE GENTS HOW THAT WORKED OUT FOR THEM.
AND BESIDES...
...I DON'T SEE ANY BODYGUARDS.

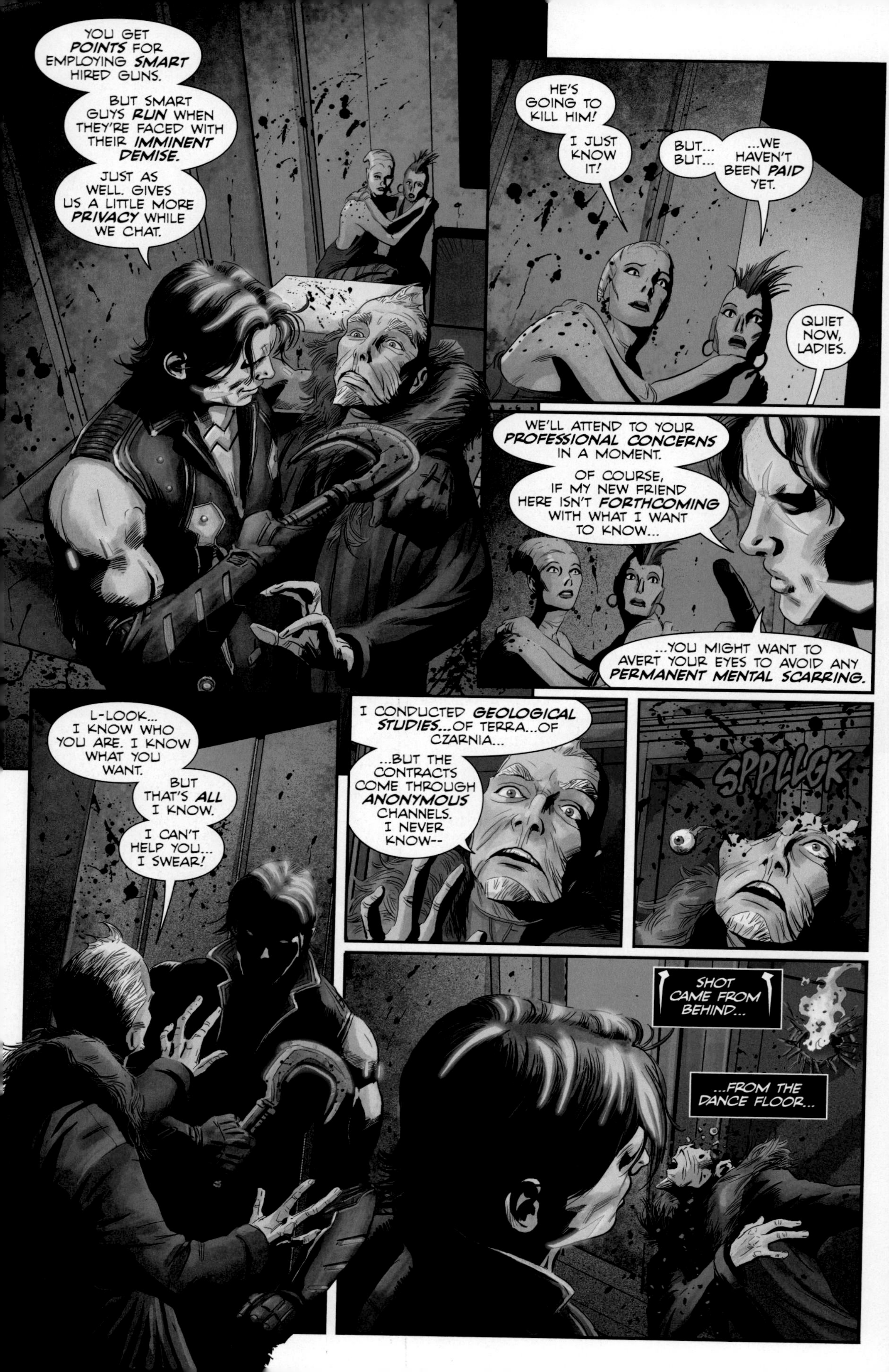
YOU GET POINTS FOR EMPLOYING SMART HIRED GUNS.
BUT SMART GUYS RUN WHEN THEY'RE FACED WITH THEIR IMMINENT DEMISE.
JUST AS WELL. GIVES US A LITTLE MORE PRIVACY WHILE WE CHAT.
HE'S GOING TO KILL HIM!
I JUST KNOW IT!
BUT... BUT...
...WE HAVEN'T BEEN PAID YET.
QUIET NOW, LADIES.
WE'LL ATTEND TO YOUR PROFESSIONAL CONCERNS IN A MOMENT.
OF COURSE, IF MY NEW FRIEND HERE ISN'T FORTHCOMING WITH WHAT I WANT TO KNOW...
...YOU MIGHT WANT TO AVERT YOUR EYES TO AVOID ANY PERMANENT MENTAL SCARRING.
L-LOOK... I KNOW WHO YOU ARE. I KNOW WHAT YOU WANT.
BUT THAT'S ALL I KNOW.
I CAN'T HELP YOU... I SWEAR!
I CONDUCTED GEOLOGICAL STUDIES... OF TERRA... OF CZARNIA...
...BUT THE CONTRACTS COME THROUGH ANONYMOUS CHANNELS. I NEVER KNOW--
SPPLLGK
SHOT CAME FROM BEHIND...
...FROM THE DANCE FLOOR...

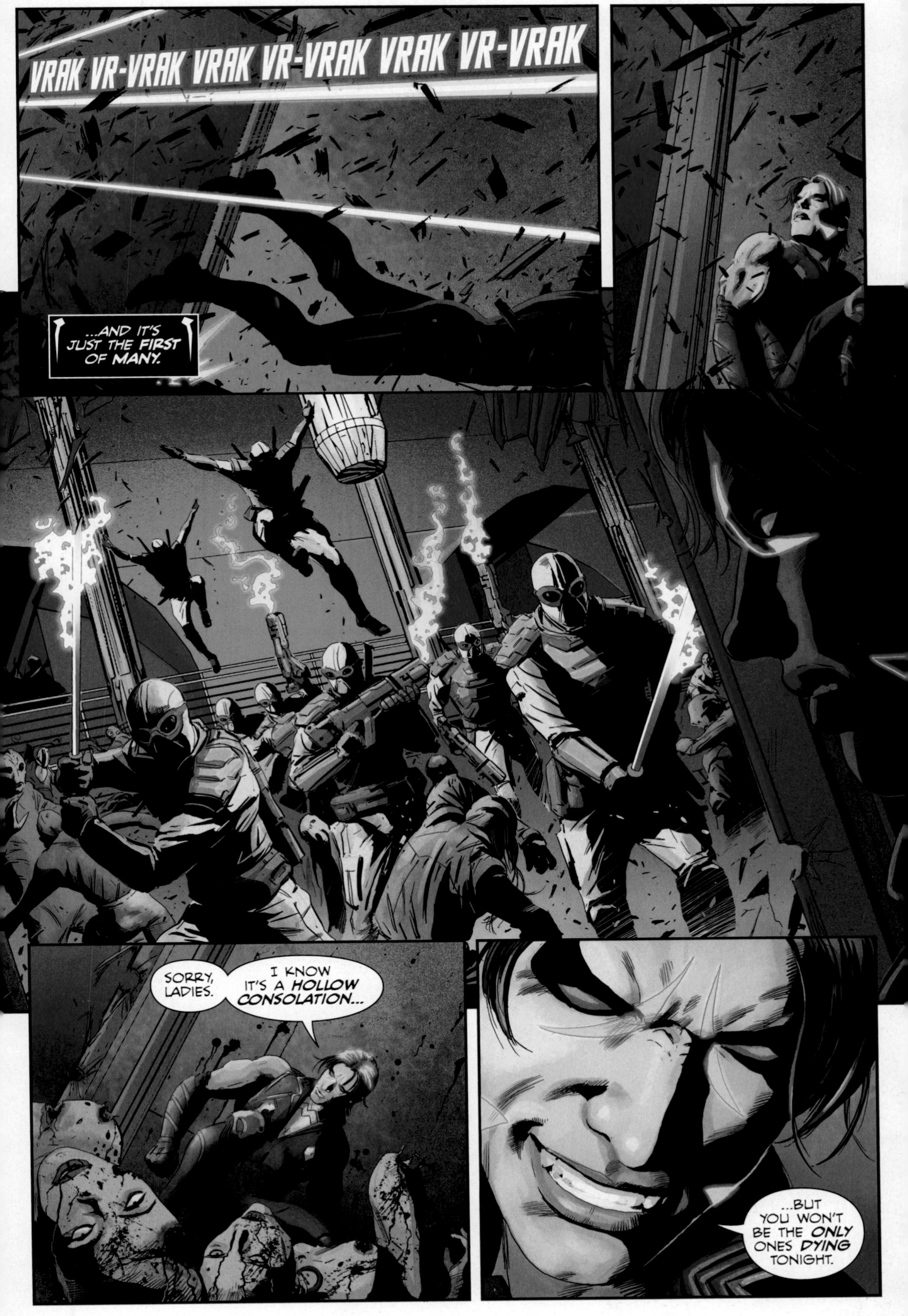
VRAK VR-VRAK VRAK VR-VRAK VRAK VR-VRAK
...AND IT'S JUST THE FIRST OF MANY.
SORRY, LADIES.
I KNOW IT'S A HOLLOW CONSOLATION...
...BUT YOU WON'T BE THE ONLY ONES DYING TONIGHT.

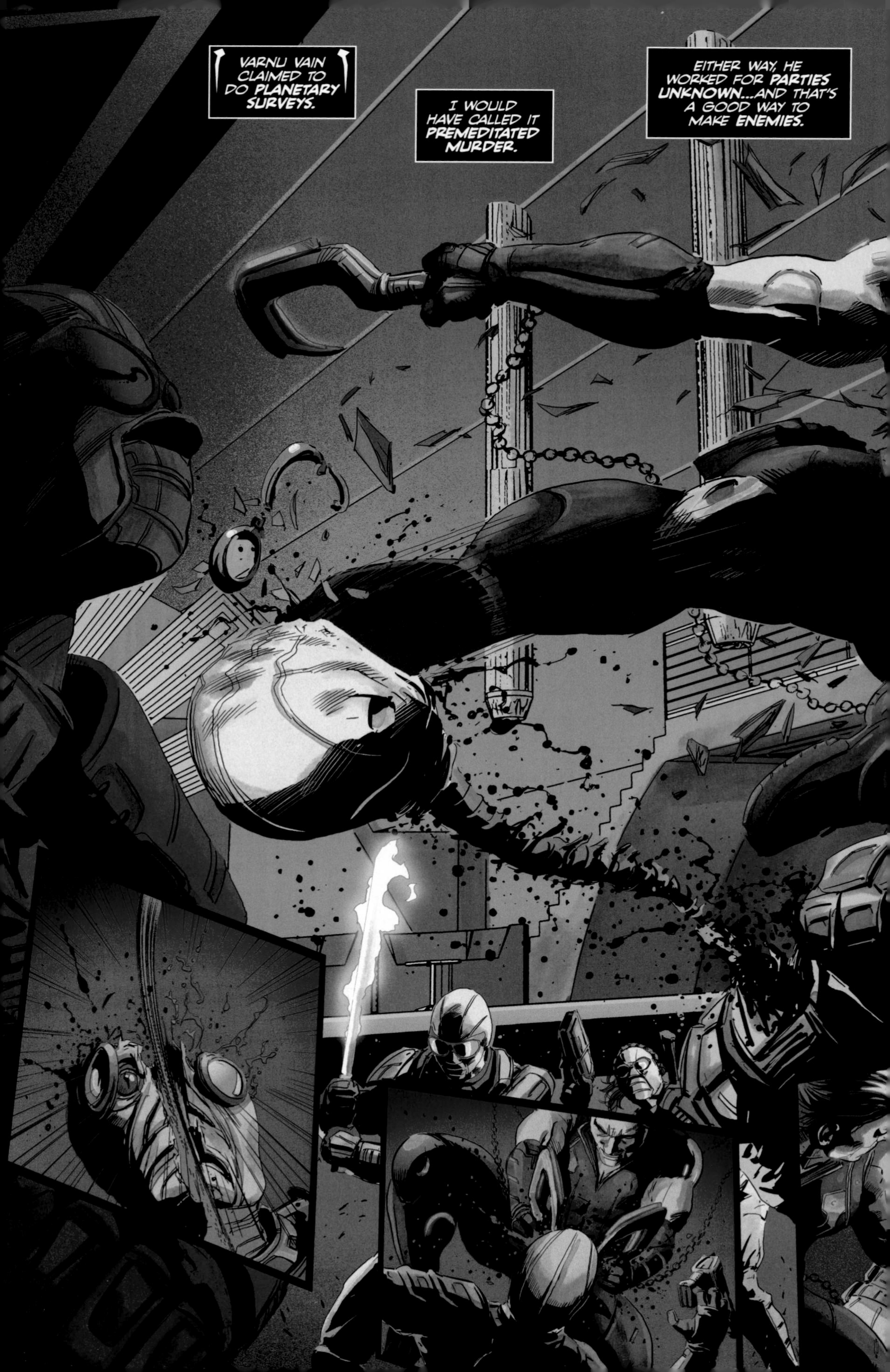
VARNU VAIN CLAIMED TO DO PLANETARY SURVEYS.
I WOULD HAVE CALLED IT PREMEDITATED MURDER.
EITHER WAY, HE WORKED FOR PARTIES UNKNOWN...AND THAT'S A GOOD WAY TO MAKE ENEMIES.

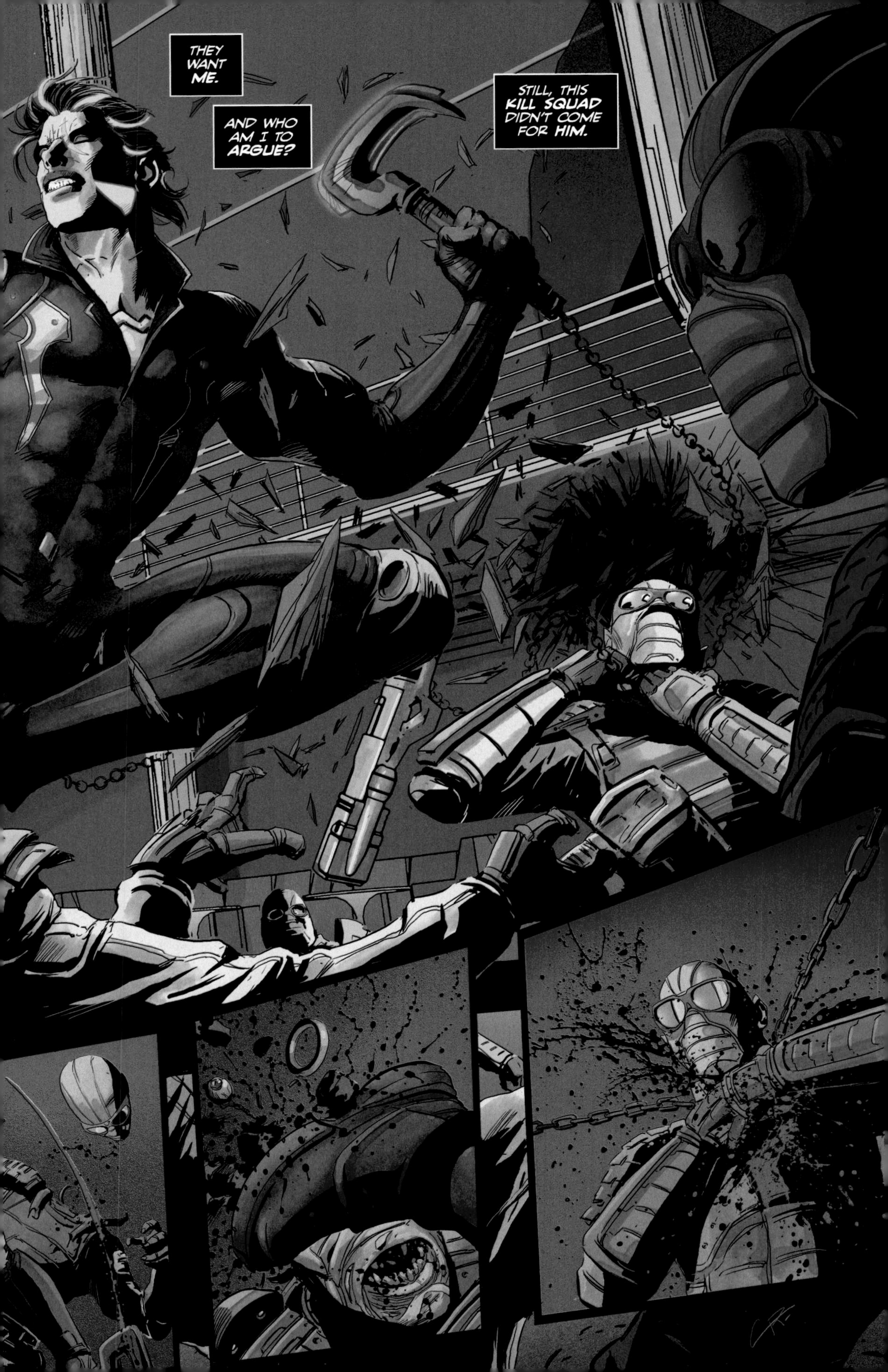
THEY WANT ME.
AND WHO AM I TO ARGUE?
STILL, THIS KILL SQUAD DIDN'T COME FOR HIM.

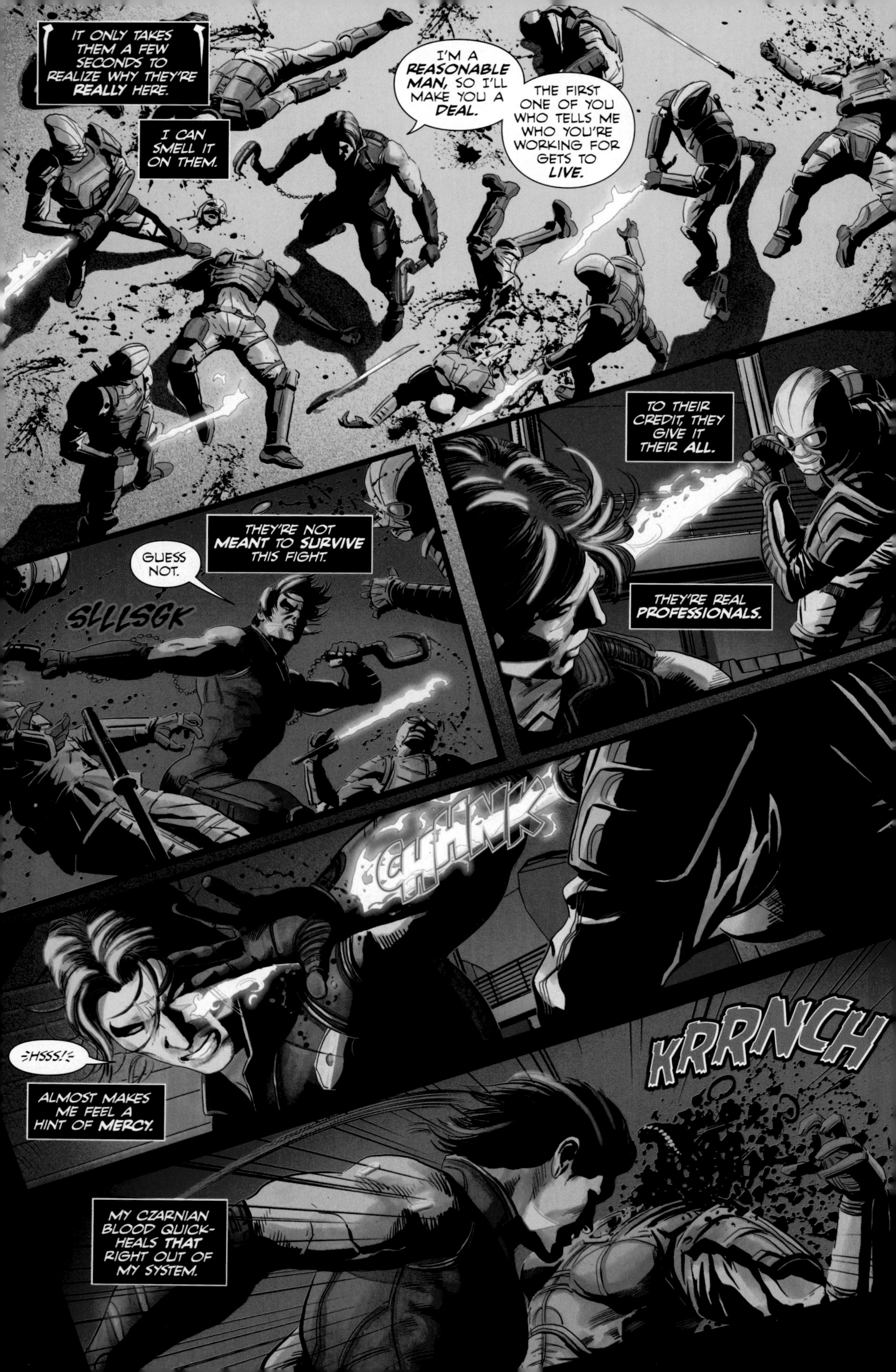
IT ONLY TAKES THEM A FEW SECONDS TO REALIZE WHY THEY'RE REALLY HERE.
I CAN SMELL IT ON THEM.
I'M A REASONABLE MAN, SO I'LL MAKE YOU A DEAL.
THE FIRST ONE OF YOU WHO TELLS ME WHO YOU'RE WORKING FOR GETS TO LIVE.
THEY'RE NOT MEANT TO SURVIVE THIS FIGHT.
GUESS NOT.
SLLLSGK
TO THEIR CREDIT, THEY GIVE IT THEIR ALL.
THEY'RE REAL PROFESSIONALS.
CHHNK
HSSS!
ALMOST MAKES ME FEEL A HINT OF MERCY.
KRRNCH
MY CZARNIAN BLOOD QUICK-HEALS THAT RIGHT OUT OF MY SYSTEM.

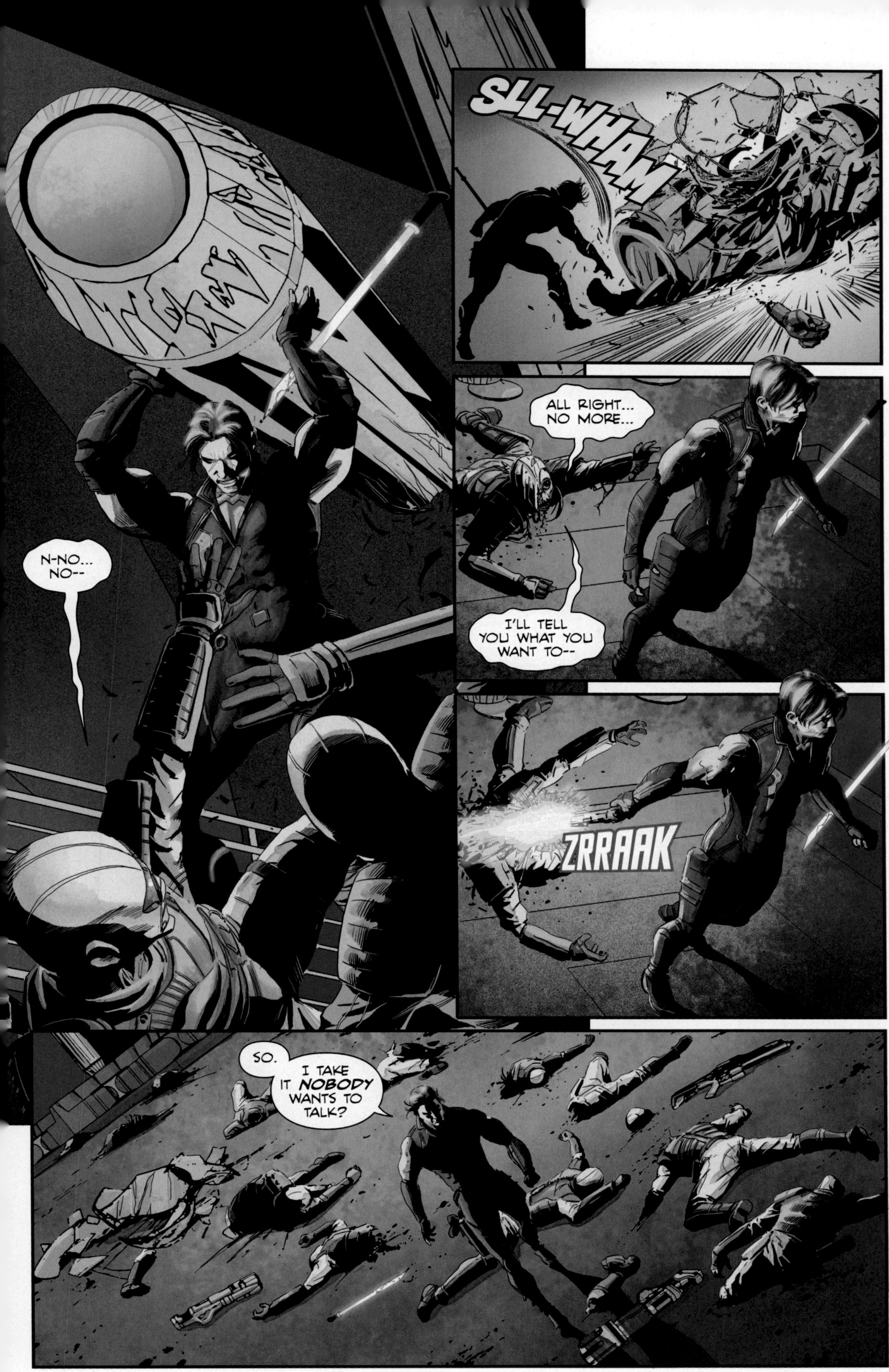
N-NO... NO--
SLL-WHAM
ALL RIGHT... NO MORE...
I'LL TELL YOU WHAT YOU WANT TO--
ZRRAAK
SO.
I TAKE IT NOBODY WANTS TO TALK?

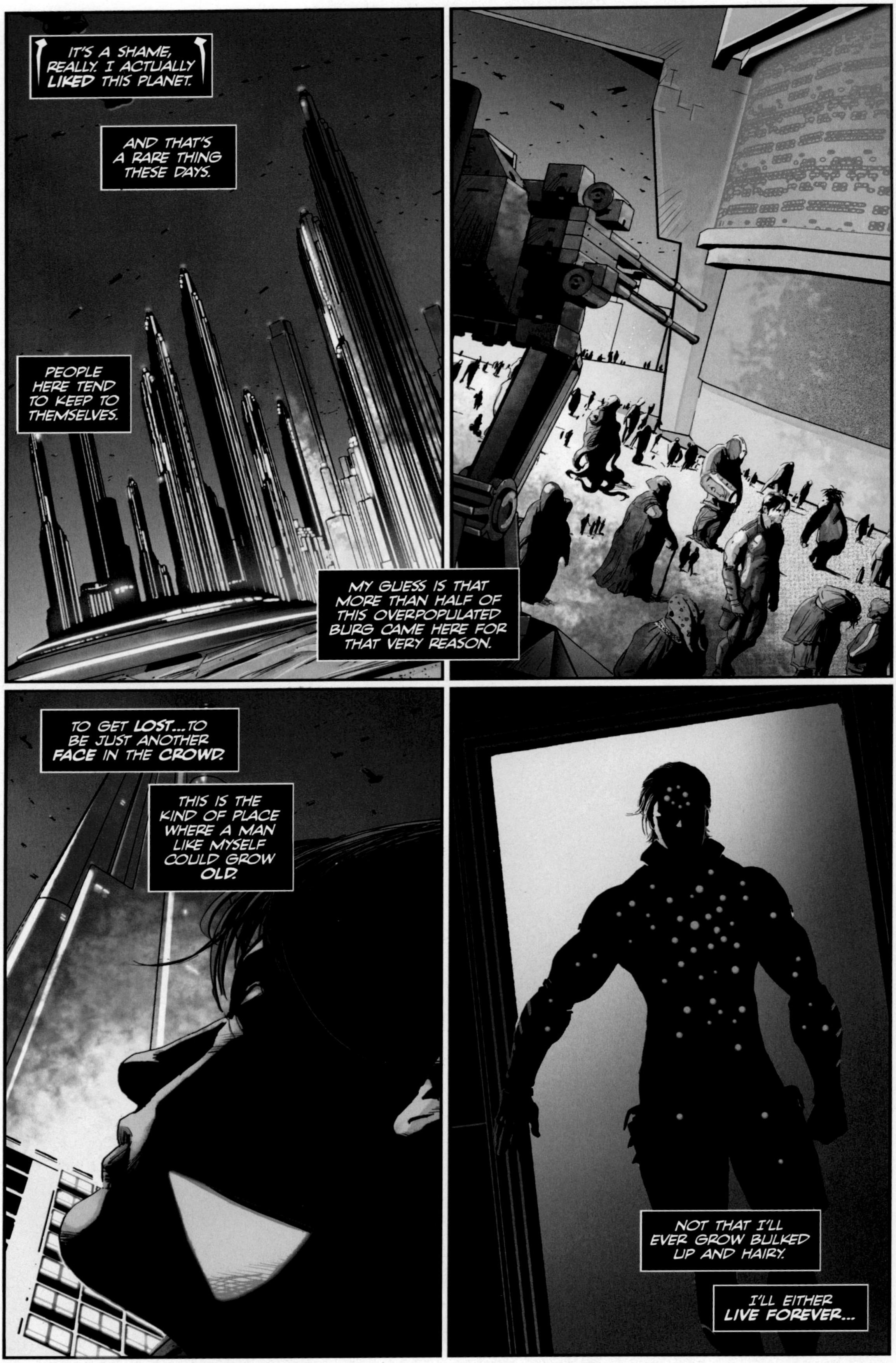
IT'S A SHAME, REALLY. I ACTUALLY LIKED THIS PLANET.
AND THAT'S A RARE THING THESE DAYS.
PEOPLE HERE TEND TO KEEP TO THEMSELVES.
MY GUESS IS THAT MORE THAN HALF OF THIS OVERPOPULATED BURG CAME HERE FOR THAT VERY REASON.
TO GET LOST...TO BE JUST ANOTHER FACE IN THE CROWD.
THIS IS THE KIND OF PLACE WHERE A MAN LIKE MYSELF COULD GROW OLD.
NOT THAT I'LL EVER GROW BULKED UP AND HAIRY.
I'LL EITHER LIVE FOREVER...

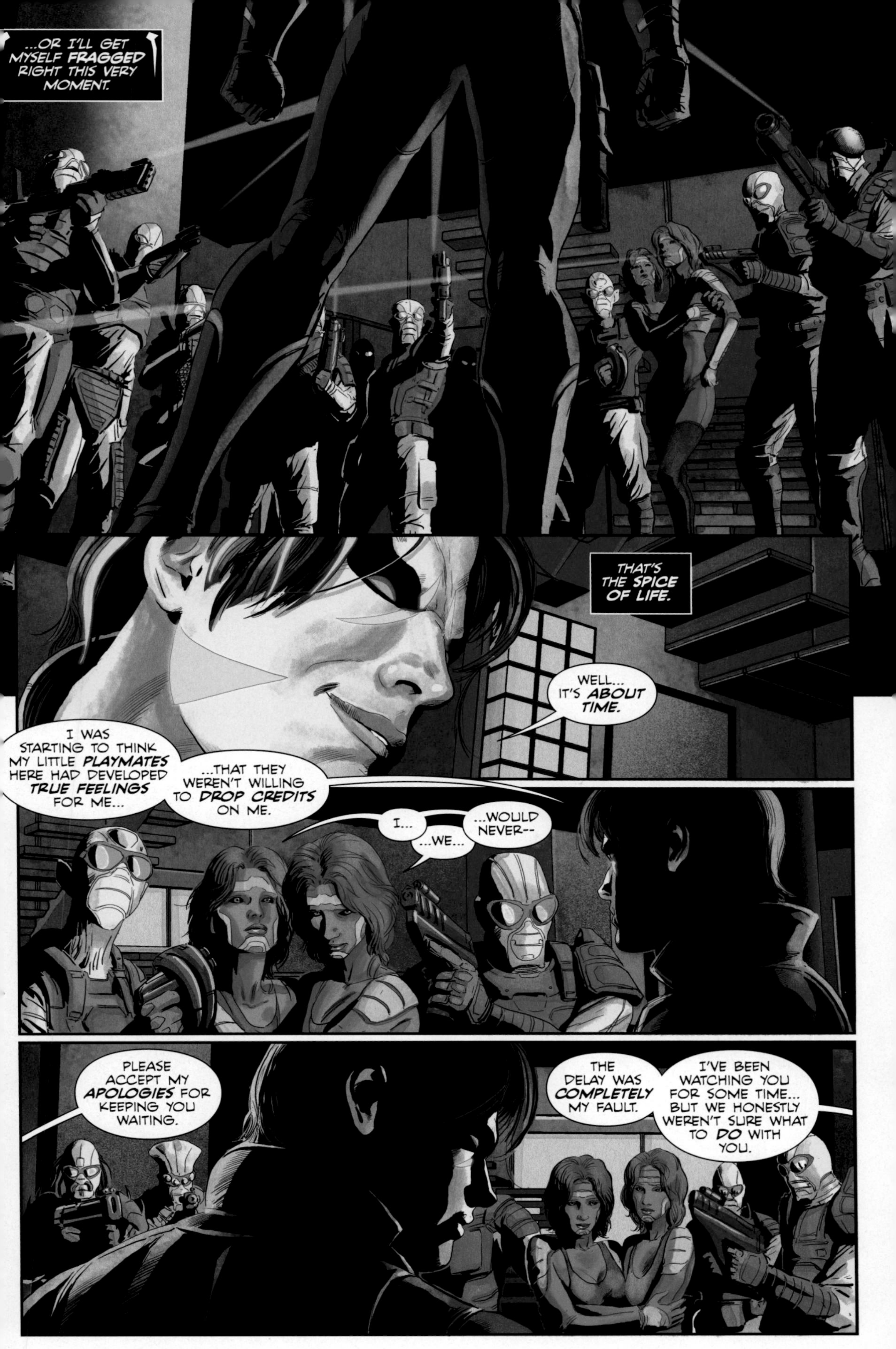
...OR I'LL GET MYSELF FRAGGED RIGHT THIS VERY MOMENT.
THAT'S THE SPICE OF LIFE.
WELL... IT'S ABOUT TIME.
I WAS STARTING TO THINK MY LITTLE PLAYMATES HERE HAD DEVELOPED TRUE FEELINGS FOR ME...
...THAT THEY WEREN'T WILLING TO DROP CREDITS ON ME.
I...
...WE...
...WOULD NEVER--
PLEASE ACCEPT MY APOLOGIES FOR KEEPING YOU WAITING.
THE DELAY WAS COMPLETELY MY FAULT.
I'VE BEEN WATCHING YOU FOR SOME TIME... BUT WE HONESTLY WEREN'T SURE WHAT TO DO WITH YOU.

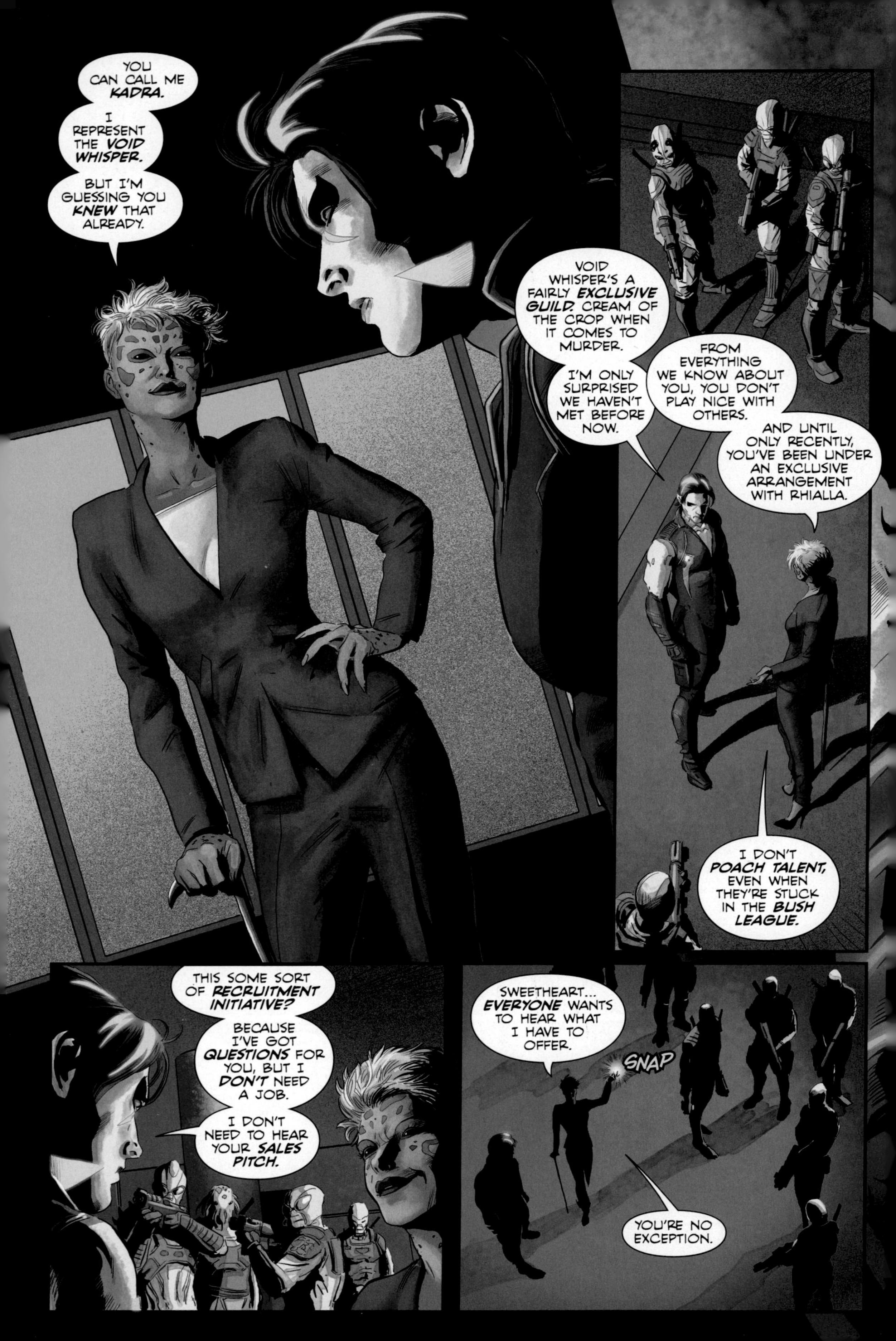
YOU CAN CALL ME KADRA.
I REPRESENT THE VOID WHISPER.
BUT I'M GUESSING YOU KNEW THAT ALREADY.
VOID WHISPER'S A FAIRLY EXCLUSIVE GUILD. CREAM OF THE CROP WHEN IT COMES TO MURDER.
I'M ONLY SURPRISED WE HAVEN'T MET BEFORE NOW.
FROM EVERYTHING WE KNOW ABOUT YOU, YOU DON'T PLAY NICE WITH OTHERS.
AND UNTIL ONLY RECENTLY, YOU'VE BEEN UNDER AN EXCLUSIVE ARRANGEMENT WITH RHIALLA.
I DON'T POACH TALENT, EVEN WHEN THEY'RE STUCK IN THE BUSH LEAGUE.
THIS SOME SORT OF RECRUITMENT INITIATIVE?
BECAUSE I'VE GOT QUESTIONS FOR YOU, BUT I DON'T NEED A JOB.
I DON'T NEED TO HEAR YOUR SALES PITCH.
SWEETHEART... EVERYONE WANTS TO HEAR WHAT I HAVE TO OFFER.
SNAP
YOU'RE NO EXCEPTION.

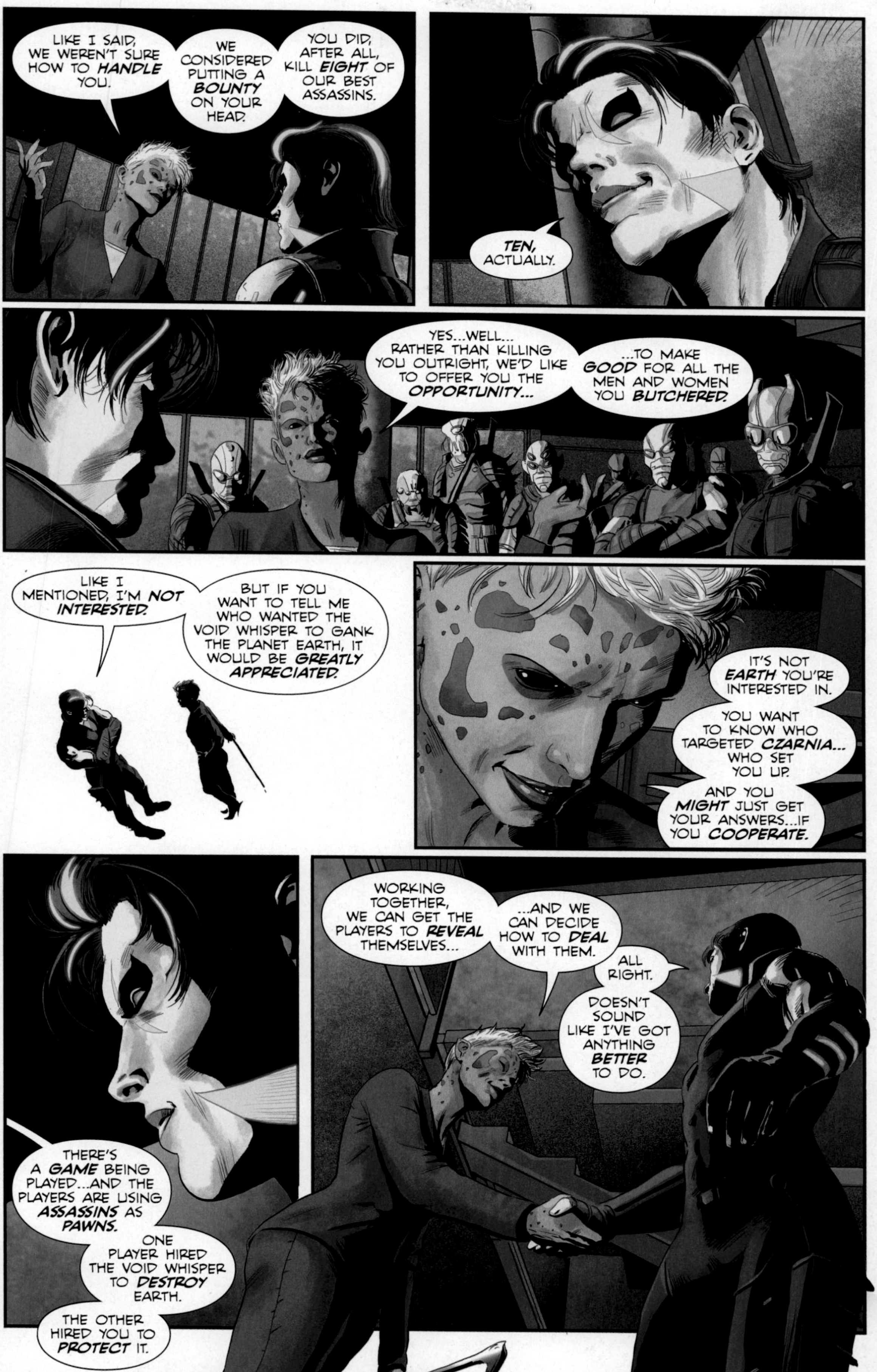
LIKE I SAID, WE WEREN'T SURE HOW TO HANDLE YOU.
WE CONSIDERED PUTTING A BOUNTY ON YOUR HEAD.
YOU DID, AFTER ALL, KILL EIGHT OF OUR BEST ASSASSINS.
TEN, ACTUALLY.
YES...WELL... RATHER THAN KILLING YOU OUTRIGHT, WE'D LIKE TO OFFER YOU THE OPPORTUNITY...
...TO MAKE GOOD FOR ALL THE MEN AND WOMEN YOU BUTCHERED.
LIKE I MENTIONED, I'M NOT INTERESTED.
BUT IF YOU WANT TO TELL ME WHO WANTED THE VOID WHISPER TO GANK THE PLANET EARTH, IT WOULD BE GREATLY APPRECIATED.
IT'S NOT EARTH YOU'RE INTERESTED IN.
YOU WANT TO KNOW WHO TARGETED CZARNIA... WHO SET YOU UP.
AND YOU MIGHT JUST GET YOUR ANSWERS...IF YOU COOPERATE.
THERE'S A GAME BEING PLAYED...AND THE PLAYERS ARE USING ASSASSINS AS PAWNS.
ONE PLAYER HIRED THE VOID WHISPER TO DESTROY EARTH.
THE OTHER HIRED YOU TO PROTECT IT.
WORKING TOGETHER, WE CAN GET THE PLAYERS TO REVEAL THEMSELVES...
...AND WE CAN DECIDE HOW TO DEAL WITH THEM.
ALL RIGHT.
DOESN'T SOUND LIKE I'VE GOT ANYTHING BETTER TO DO.

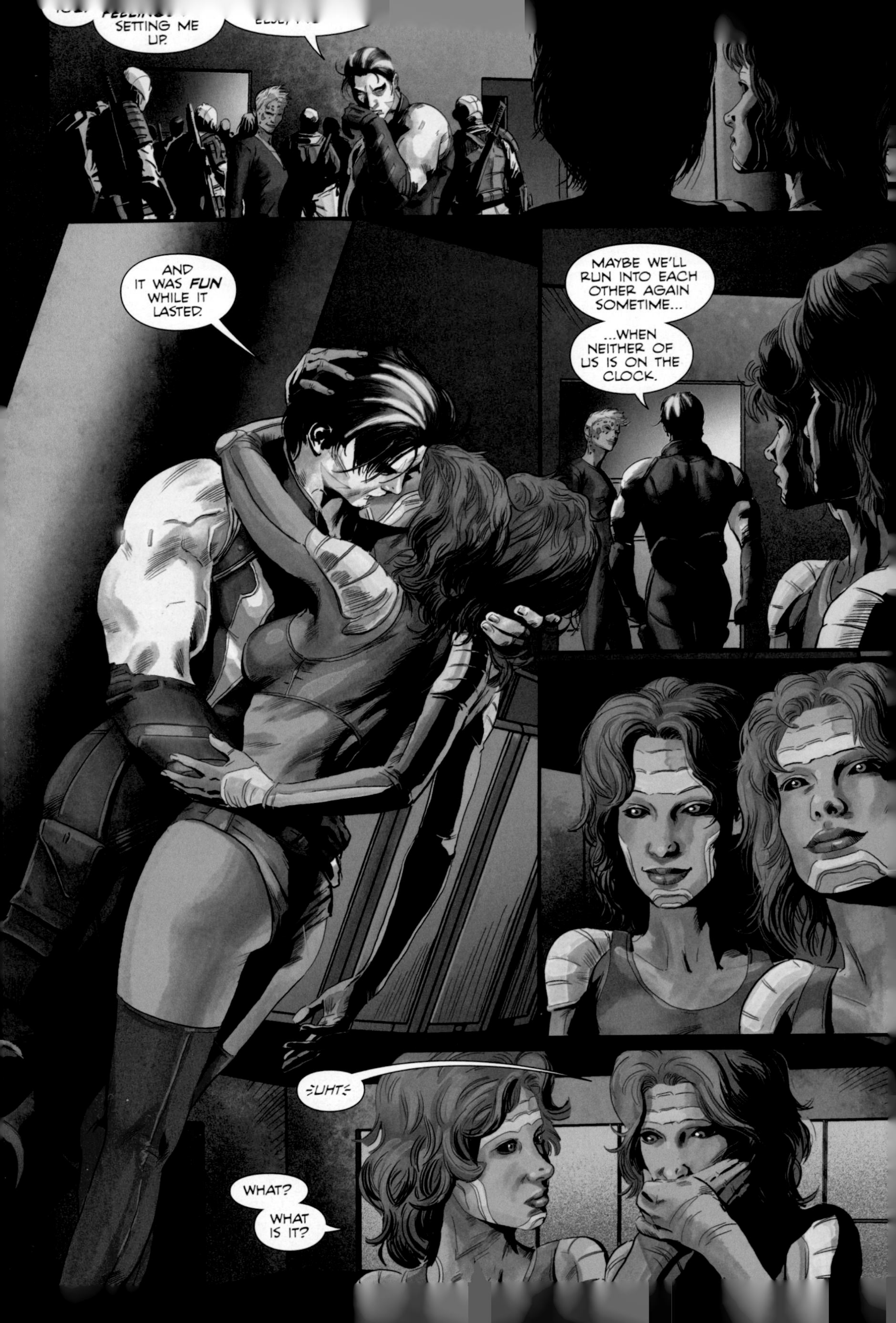
SETTING ME UP.
AND IT WAS FUN WHILE IT LASTED.
MAYBE WE'LL RUN INTO EACH OTHER AGAIN SOMETIME...
...WHEN NEITHER OF US IS ON THE CLOCK.
=UHT=
WHAT?
WHAT IS IT?

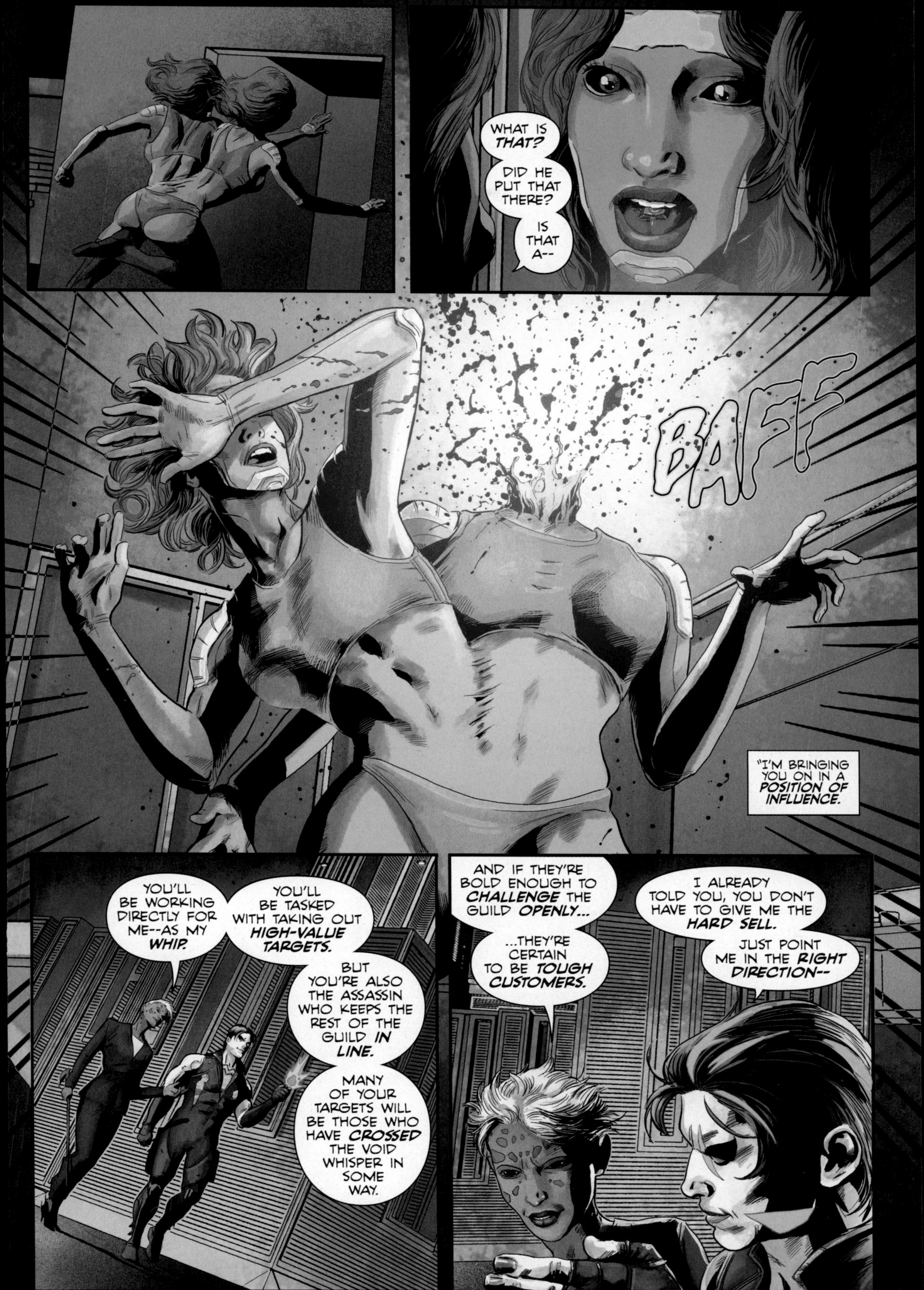

WHAT IS THAT?
DID HE PUT THAT THERE?
IS THAT A--
BAFF
"I'M BRINGING YOU ON IN A POSITION OF INFLUENCE.
YOU'LL BE WORKING DIRECTLY FOR ME--AS MY WHIP.
YOU'LL BE TASKED WITH TAKING OUT HIGH-VALUE TARGETS.
BUT YOU'RE ALSO THE ASSASSIN WHO KEEPS THE REST OF THE GUILD IN LINE.
MANY OF YOUR TARGETS WILL BE THOSE WHO HAVE CROSSED THE VOID WHISPER IN SOME WAY.
AND IF THEY'RE BOLD ENOUGH TO CHALLENGE THE GUILD OPENLY...
...THEY'RE CERTAIN TO BE TOUGH CUSTOMERS.
I ALREADY TOLD YOU, YOU DON'T HAVE TO GIVE ME THE HARD SELL.
JUST POINT ME IN THE RIGHT DIRECTION--

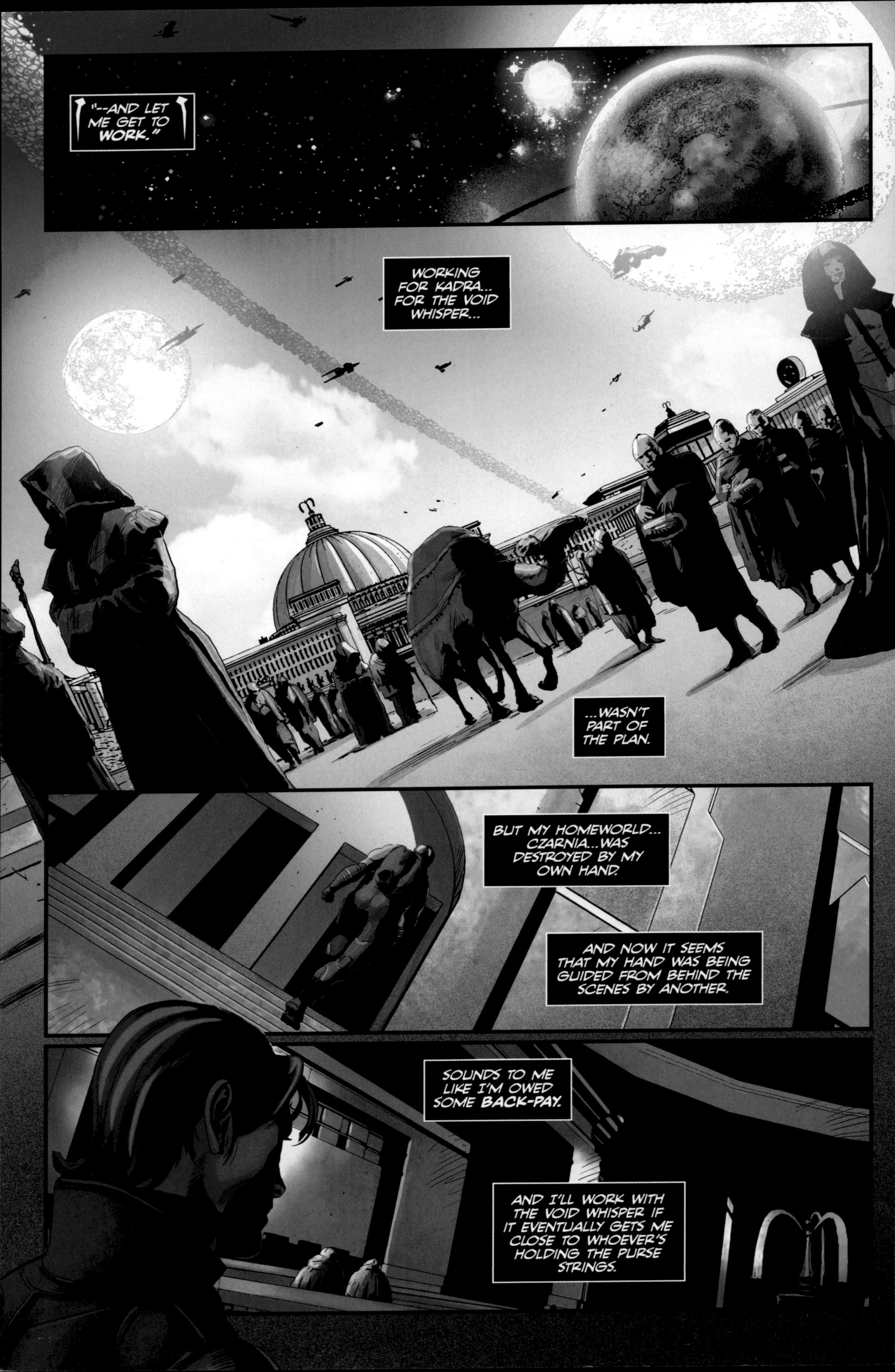
"--AND LET ME GET TO WORK."
WORKING FOR KADRA... FOR THE VOID WHISPER...
...WASN'T PART OF THE PLAN.
BUT MY HOMEWORLD... CZARNIA...WAS DESTROYED BY MY OWN HAND.
AND NOW IT SEEMS THAT MY HAND WAS BEING GUIDED FROM BEHIND THE SCENES BY ANOTHER.
SOUNDS TO ME LIKE I'M OWED SOME BACK-PAY.
AND I'LL WORK WITH THE VOID WHISPER IF IT EVENTUALLY GETS ME CLOSE TO WHOEVER'S HOLDING THE PURSE STRINGS.

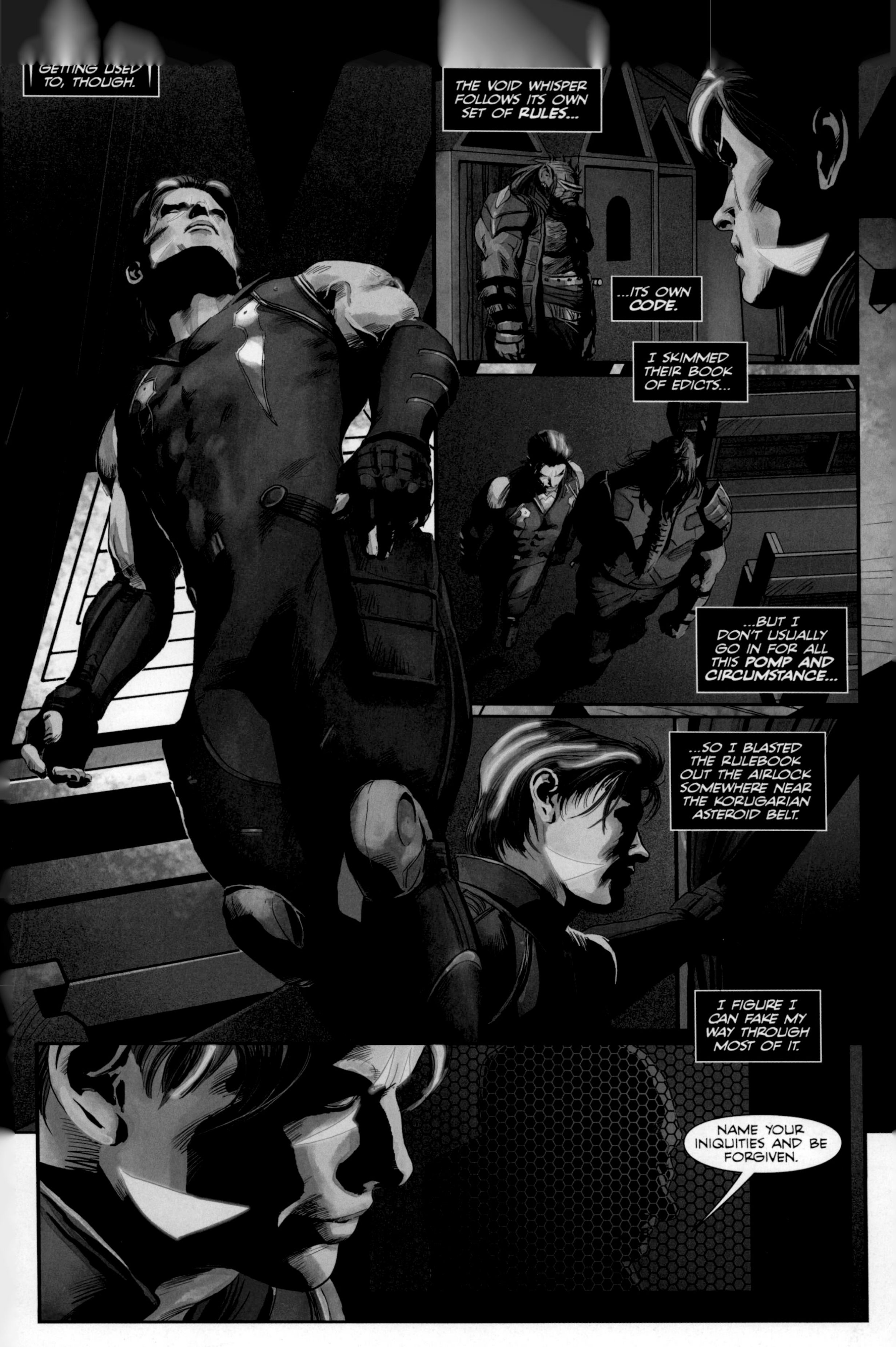
GETTING USED TO, THOUGH.
THE VOID WHISPER FOLLOWS ITS OWN SET OF RULES...
...ITS OWN CODE.
I SKIMMED THEIR BOOK OF EDICTS...
...BUT I DON'T USUALLY GO IN FOR ALL THIS POMP AND CIRCUMSTANCE...
...SO I BLASTED THE RULEBOOK OUT THE AIRLOCK SOMEWHERE NEAR THE KORUGARIAN ASTEROID BELT.
I FIGURE I CAN FAKE MY WAY THROUGH MOST OF IT.
NAME YOUR INIQUITIES AND BE FORGIVEN.

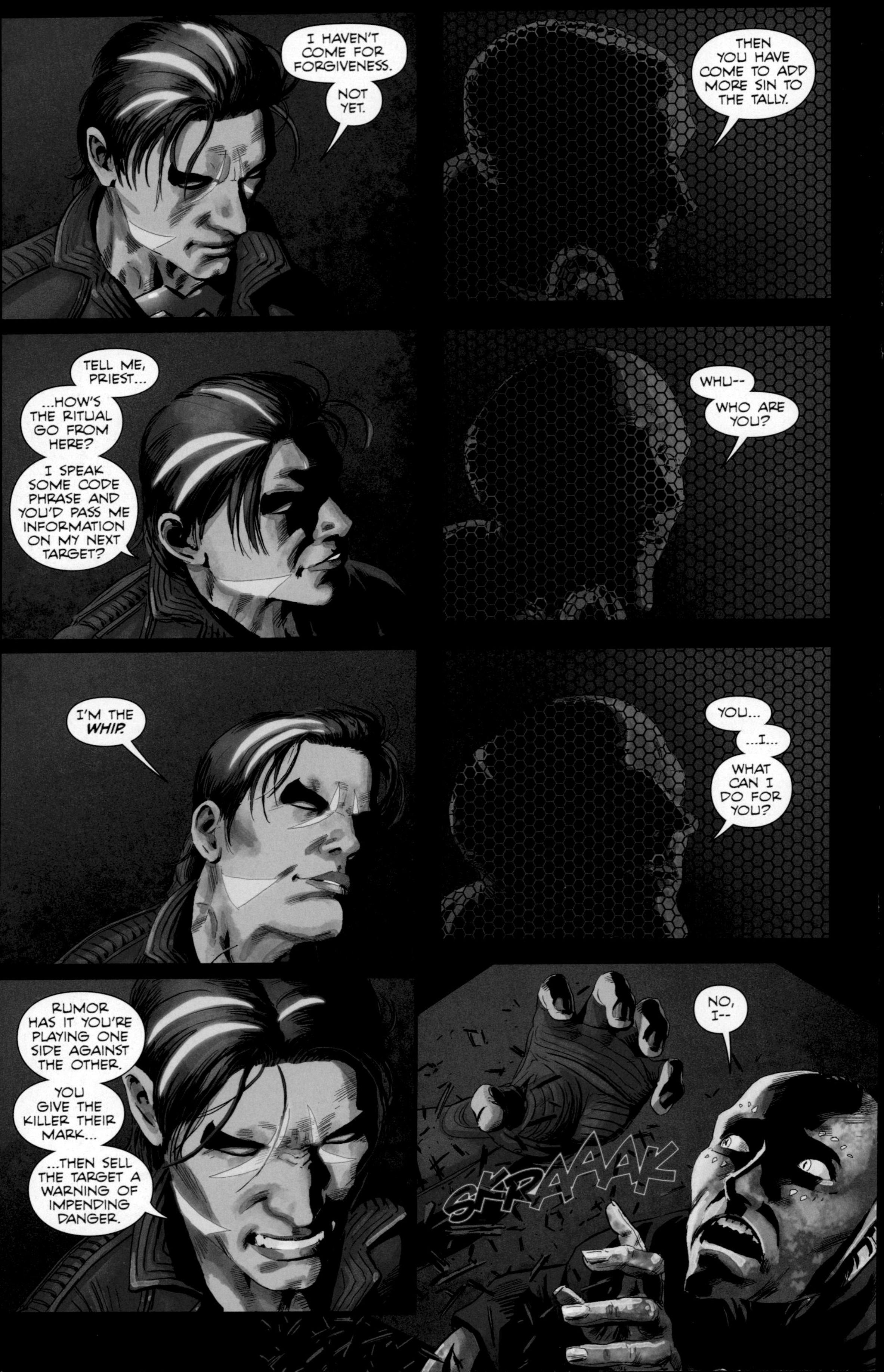
I HAVEN'T COME FOR FORGIVENESS.
NOT YET.
THEN YOU HAVE COME TO ADD MORE SIN TO THE TALLY.
TELL ME, PRIEST...
...HOW'S THE RITUAL GO FROM HERE?
I SPEAK SOME CODE PHRASE AND YOU'D PASS ME INFORMATION ON MY NEXT TARGET?
WHU--
WHO ARE YOU?
I'M THE *WHIP.*
YOU...
...I...
WHAT CAN I DO FOR YOU?
RUMOR HAS IT YOU'RE PLAYING ONE SIDE AGAINST THE OTHER.
YOU GIVE THE KILLER THEIR MARK...
...THEN SELL THE TARGET A WARNING OF IMPENDING DANGER.
NO, I--
SKRAAAK

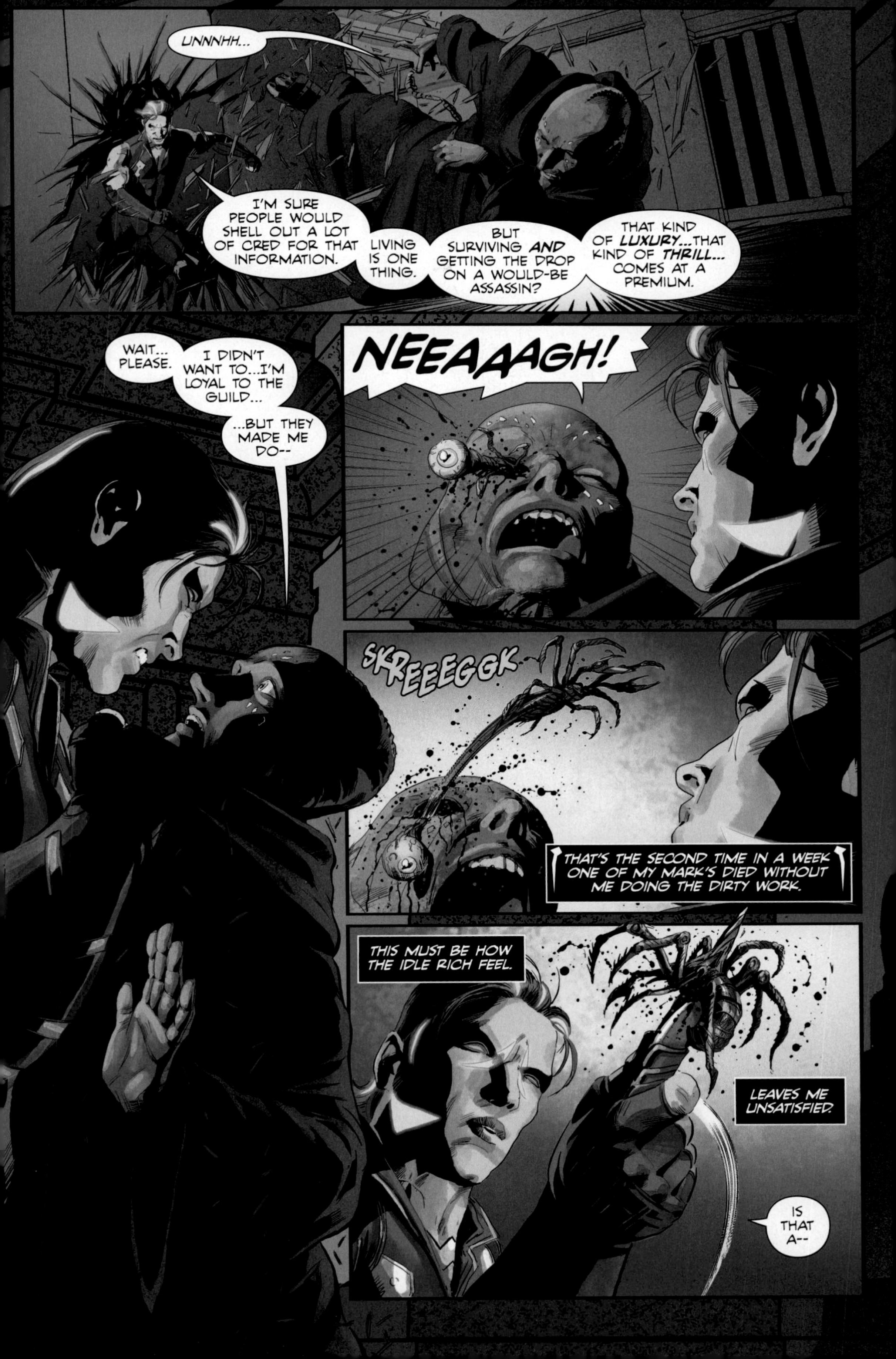

UNNNHH...
I'M SURE PEOPLE WOULD SHELL OUT A LOT OF CRED FOR THAT INFORMATION.
LIVING IS ONE THING.
BUT SURVIVING AND GETTING THE DROP ON A WOULD-BE ASSASSIN?
THAT KIND OF LUXURY...THAT KIND OF THRILL... COMES AT A PREMIUM.
WAIT... PLEASE.
I DIDN'T WANT TO...I'M LOYAL TO THE GUILD...
...BUT THEY MADE ME DO--
NEEAAAGH!
SKREEEEGGK
THAT'S THE SECOND TIME IN A WEEK ONE OF MY MARK'S DIED WITHOUT ME DOING THE DIRTY WORK.
THIS MUST BE HOW THE IDLE RICH FEEL.
LEAVES ME UNSATISFIED.
IS THAT A--

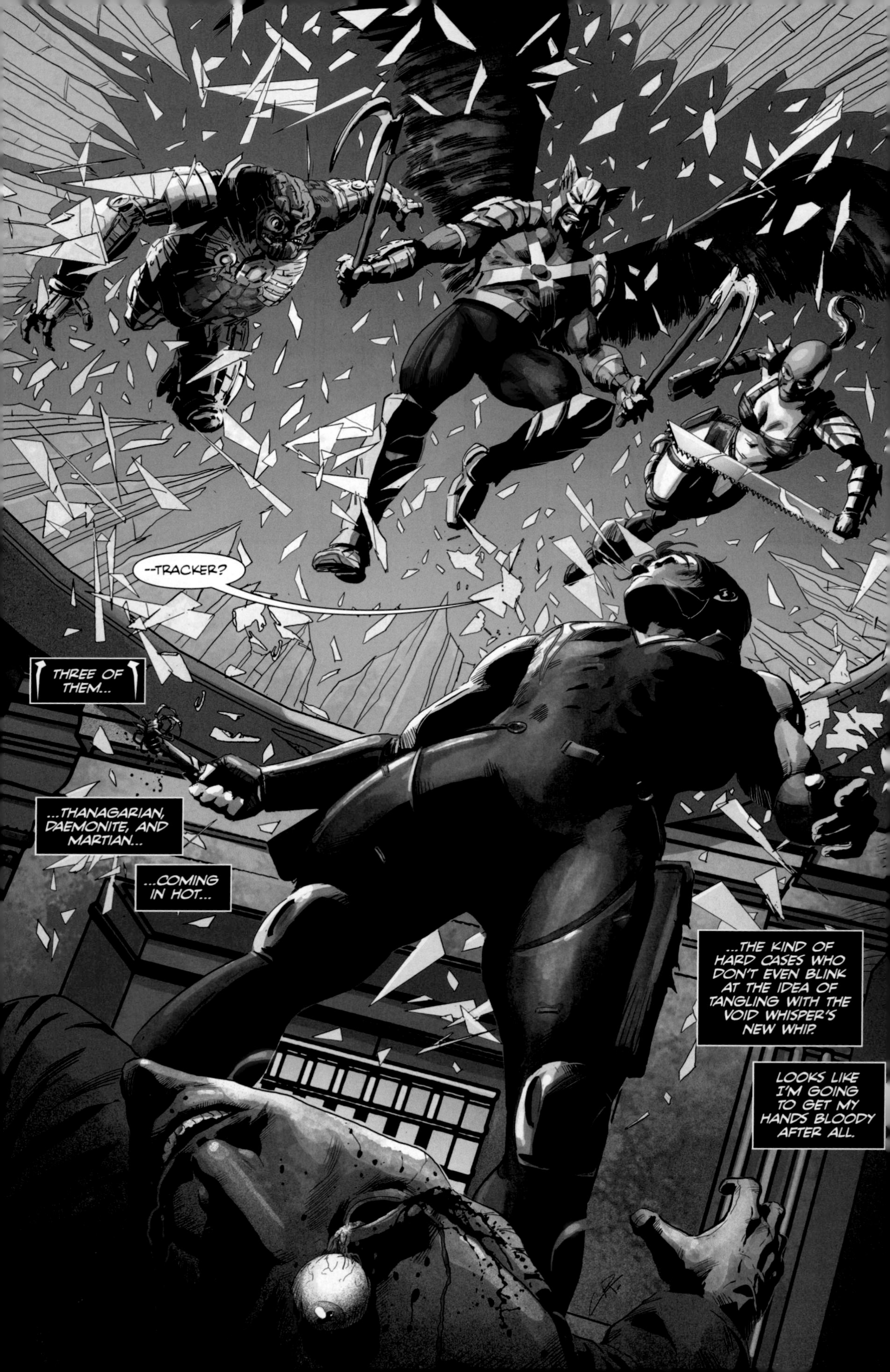
--TRACKER?
THREE OF THEM...
...THANAGARIAN, DAEMONITE, AND MARTIAN...
...COMING IN HOT...
...THE KIND OF HARD CASES WHO DON'T EVEN BLINK AT THE IDEA OF TANGLING WITH THE VOID WHISPER'S NEW WHIP.
LOOKS LIKE I'M GOING TO GET MY HANDS BLOODY AFTER ALL.

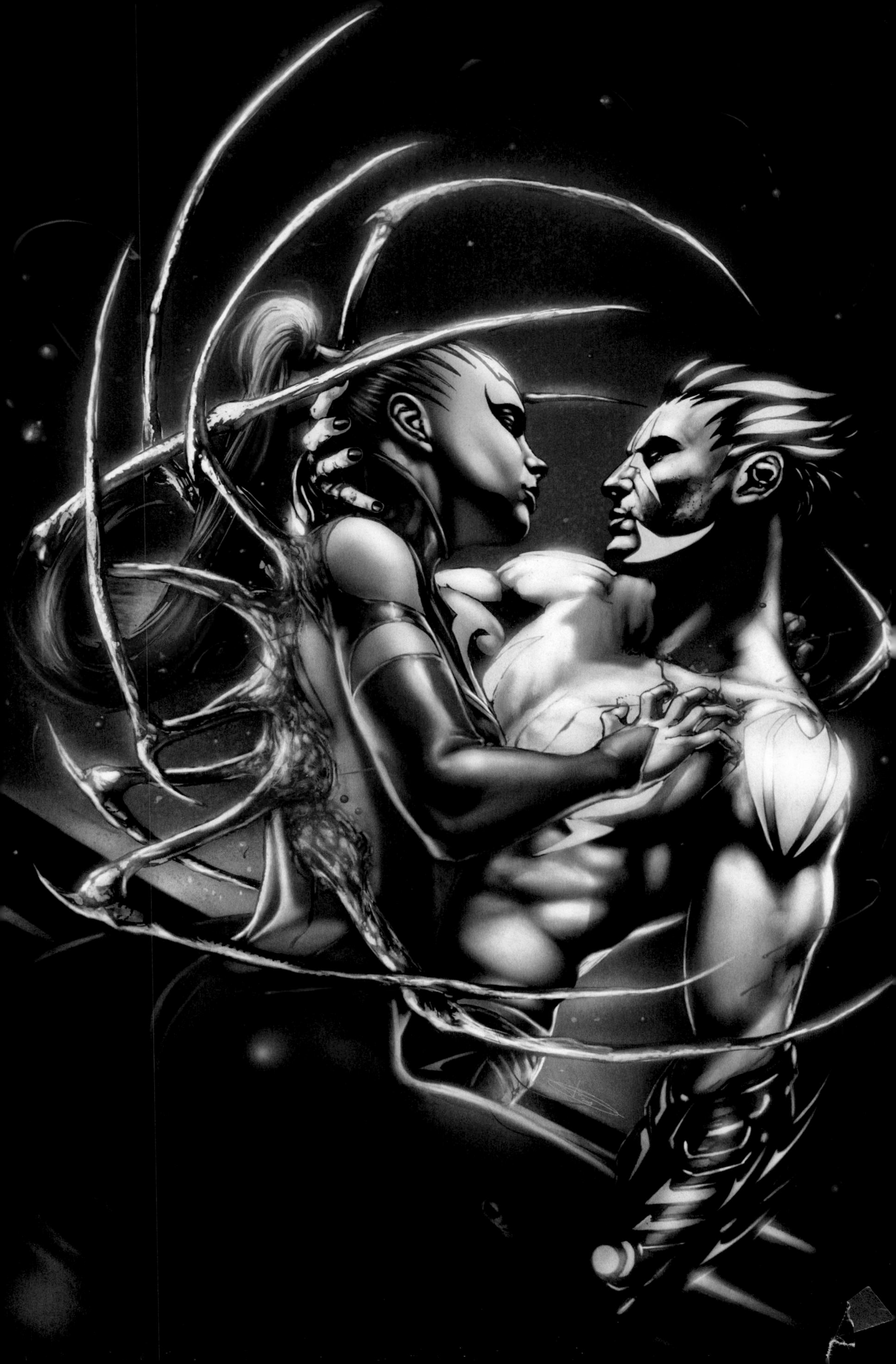

SURROUNDED

CULLEN BUNN writer **CLIFF RICHARDS** artist **BLOND** colorist **TRAVIS LANHAM** letterer cover art by **LEONARDO MANCO**

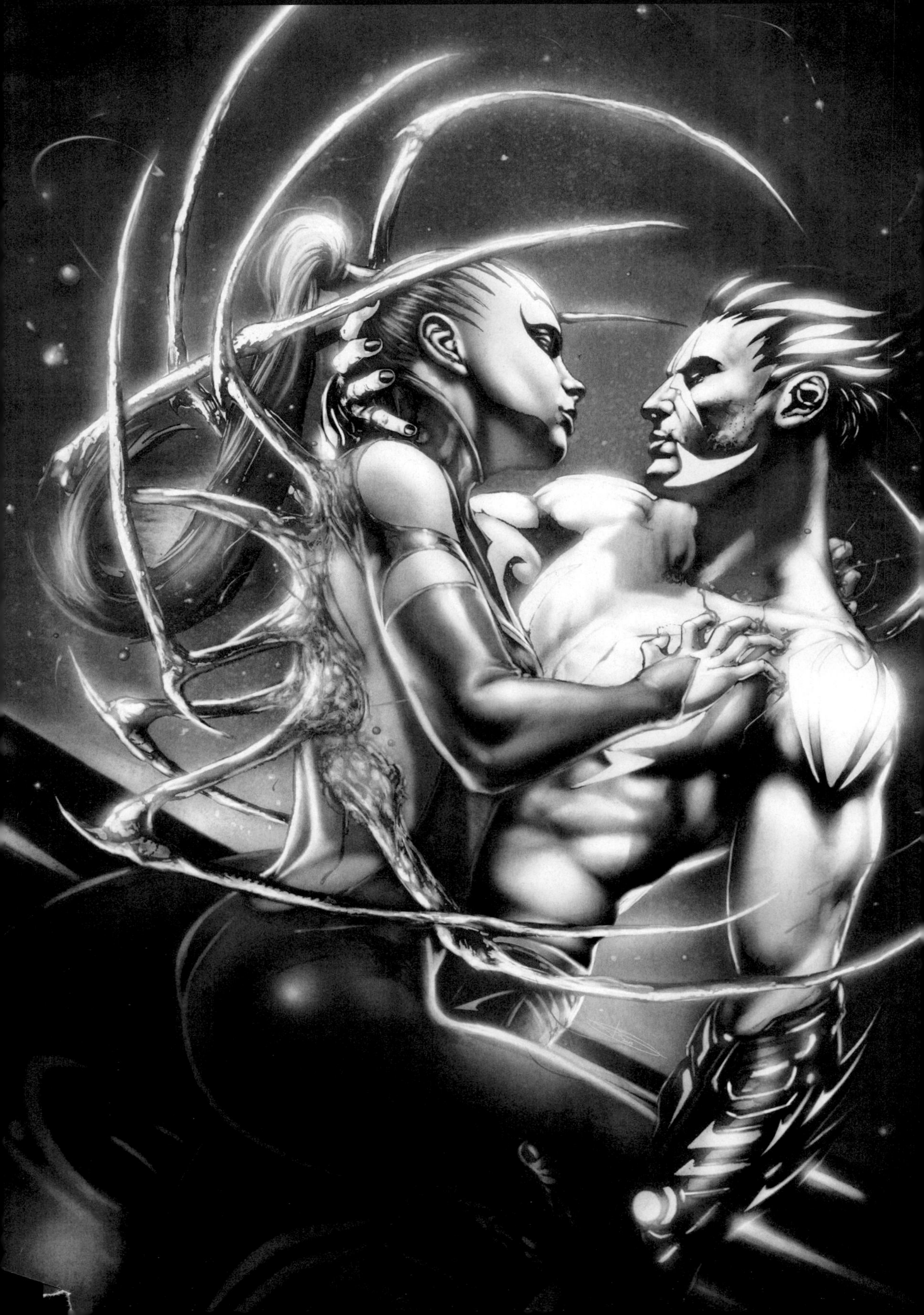

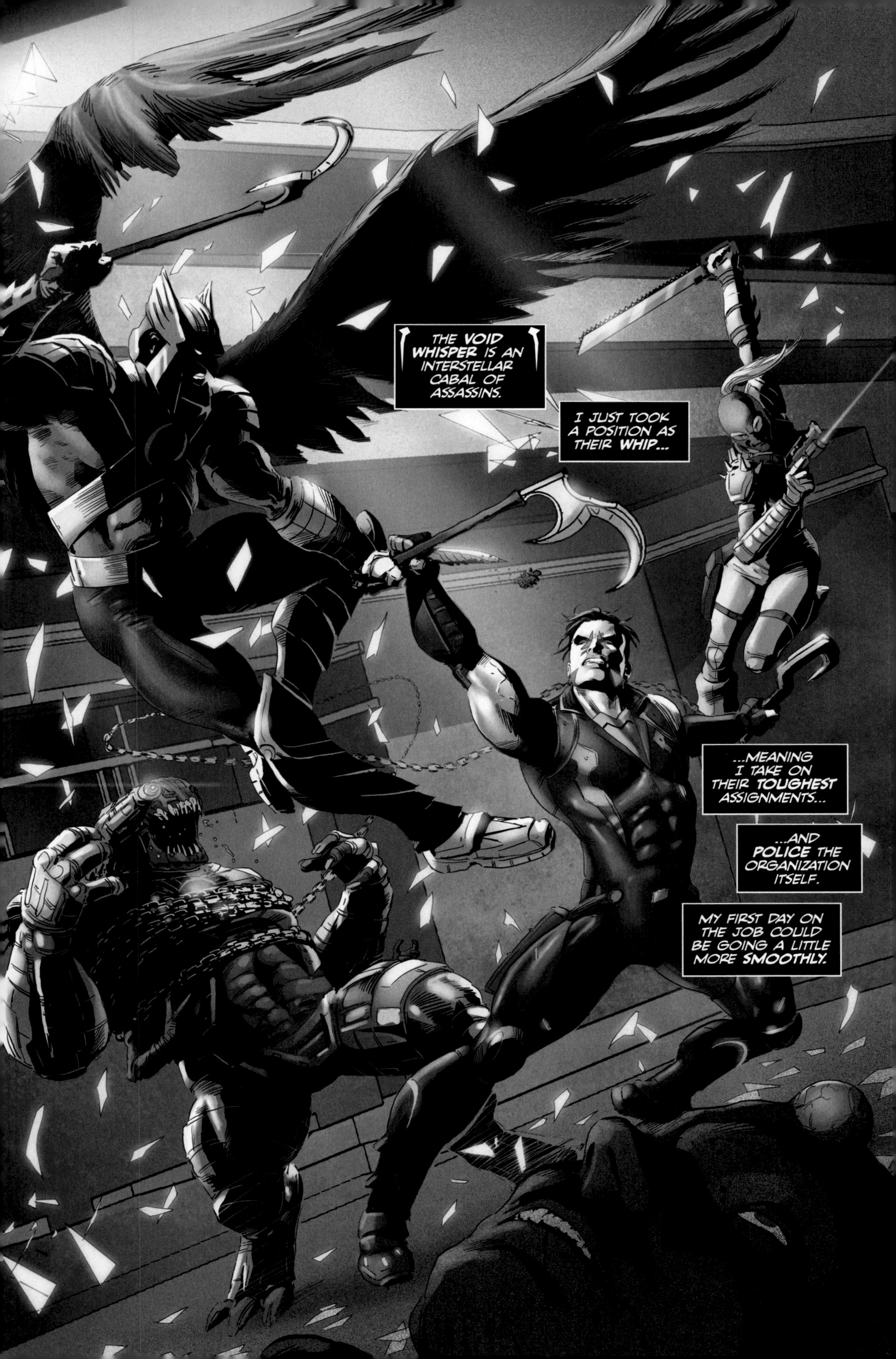
THE VOID WHISPER IS AN INTERSTELLAR CABAL OF ASSASSINS.
I JUST TOOK A POSITION AS THEIR WHIP...
...MEANING I TAKE ON THEIR TOUGHEST ASSIGNMENTS...
...AND POLICE THE ORGANIZATION ITSELF.
MY FIRST DAY ON THE JOB COULD BE GOING A LITTLE MORE SMOOTHLY.

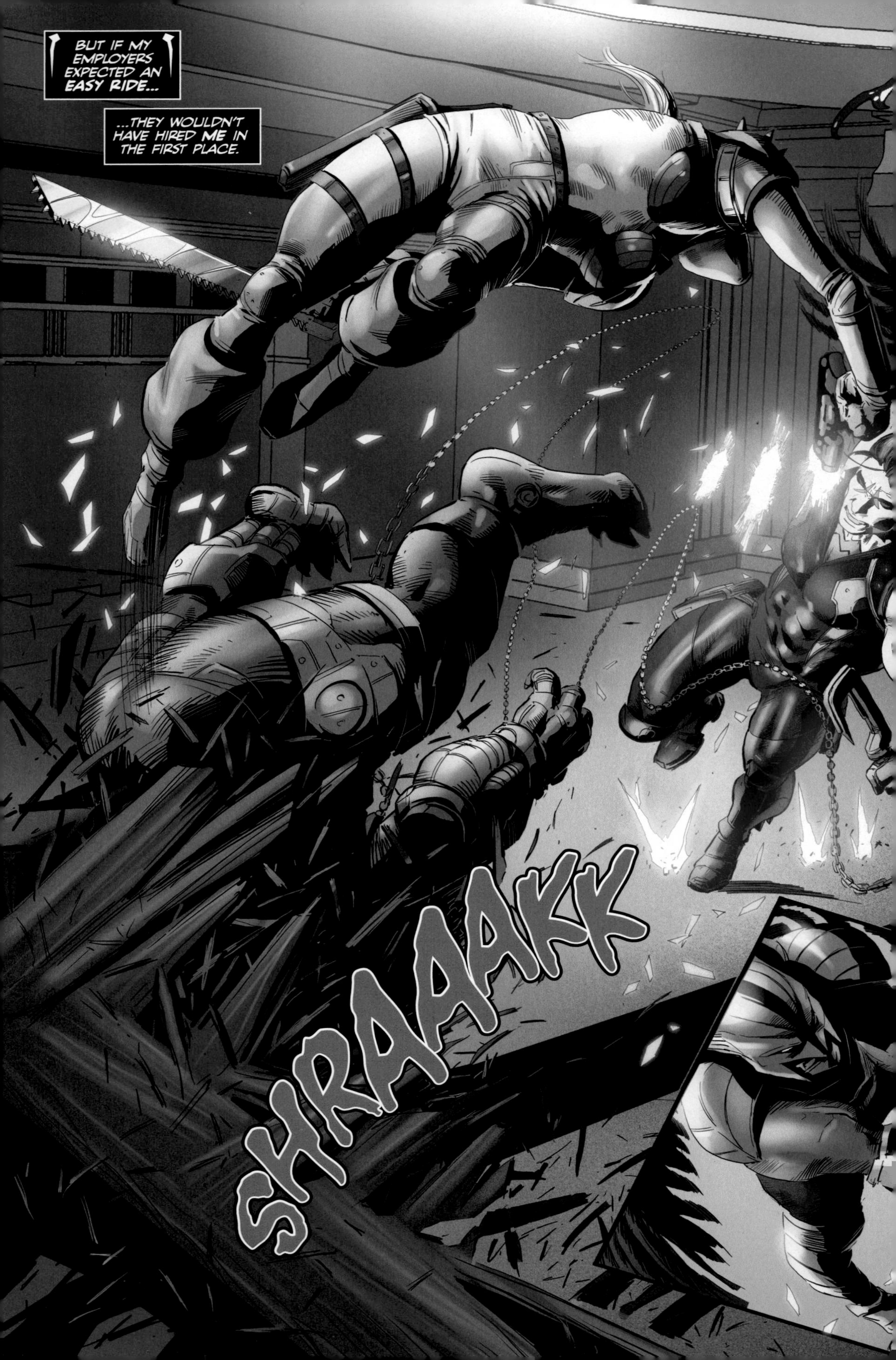
BUT IF MY EMPLOYERS EXPECTED AN EASY RIDE...
...THEY WOULDN'T HAVE HIRED ME IN THE FIRST PLACE.
SHRAAAKK

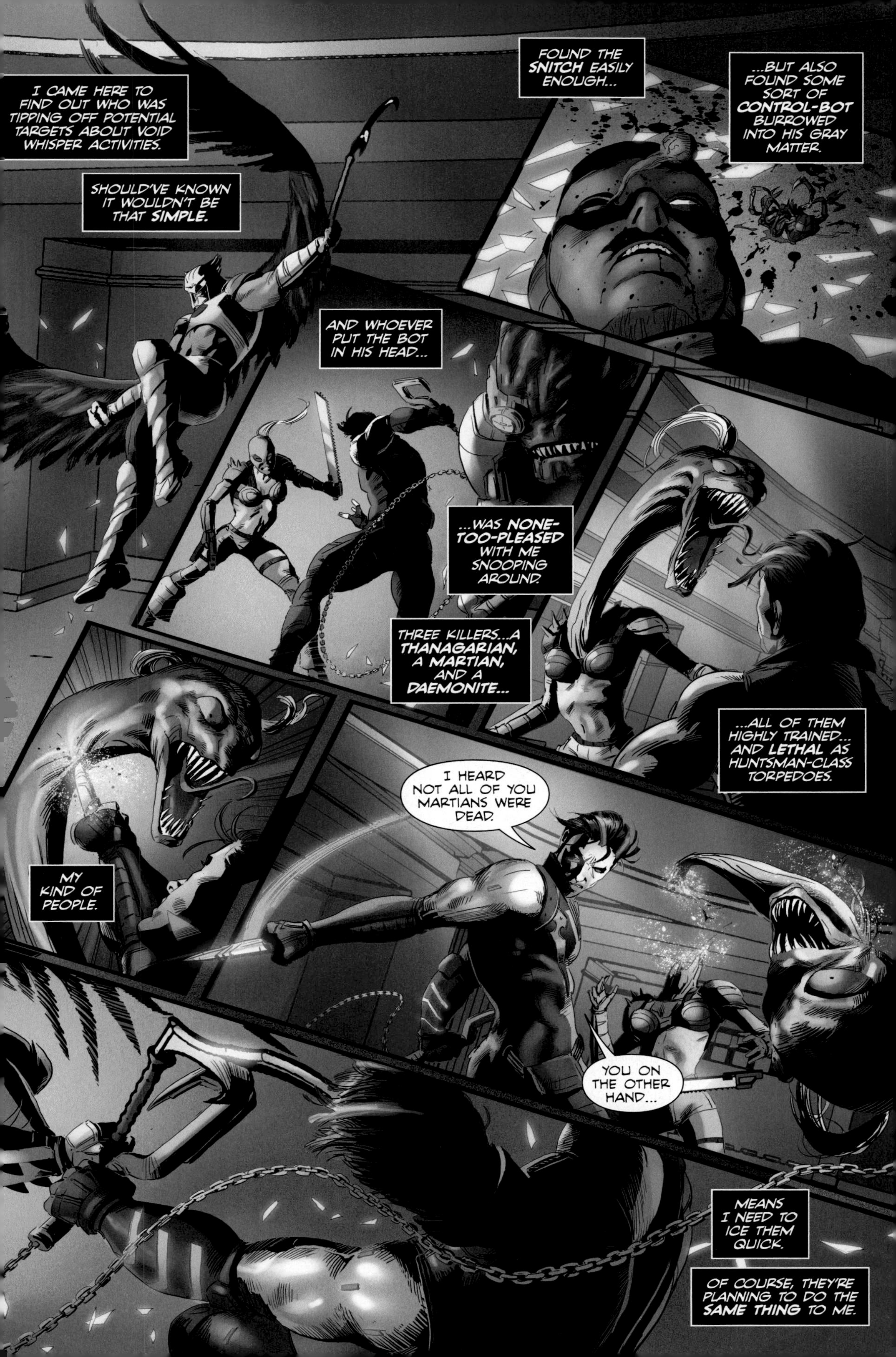
I CAME HERE TO FIND OUT WHO WAS TIPPING OFF POTENTIAL TARGETS ABOUT VOID WHISPER ACTIVITIES.
SHOULD'VE KNOWN IT WOULDN'T BE THAT SIMPLE.
FOUND THE SNITCH EASILY ENOUGH...
...BUT ALSO FOUND SOME SORT OF CONTROL-BOT BURROWED INTO HIS GRAY MATTER.
AND WHOEVER PUT THE BOT IN HIS HEAD...
...WAS NONE-TOO-PLEASED WITH ME SNOOPING AROUND.
THREE KILLERS...A THANAGARIAN, A MARTIAN, AND A DAEMONITE...
...ALL OF THEM HIGHLY TRAINED... AND LETHAL AS HUNTSMAN-CLASS TORPEDOES.
MY KIND OF PEOPLE.
I HEARD NOT ALL OF YOU MARTIANS WERE DEAD.
YOU ON THE OTHER HAND...
MEANS I NEED TO ICE THEM QUICK.
OF COURSE, THEY'RE PLANNING TO DO THE SAME THING TO ME.

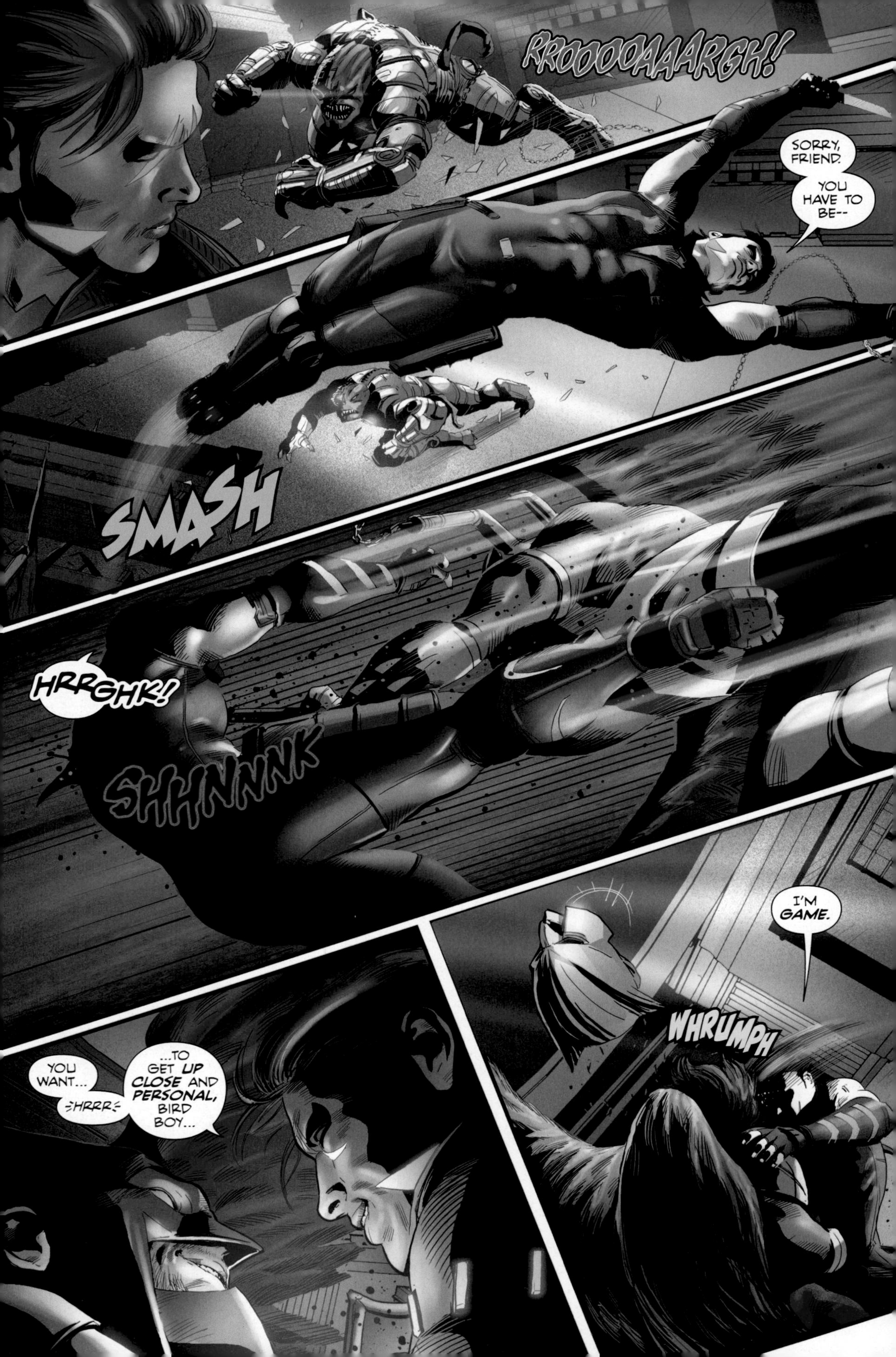
RROOOOAAARGH!
SORRY, FRIEND.
YOU HAVE TO BE--
SMASH
HRRGHK!
SHHNNNK
I'M GAME.
WHRUMPH
YOU WANT...
=HRRR=
...TO GET UP CLOSE AND PERSONAL, BIRD BOY...

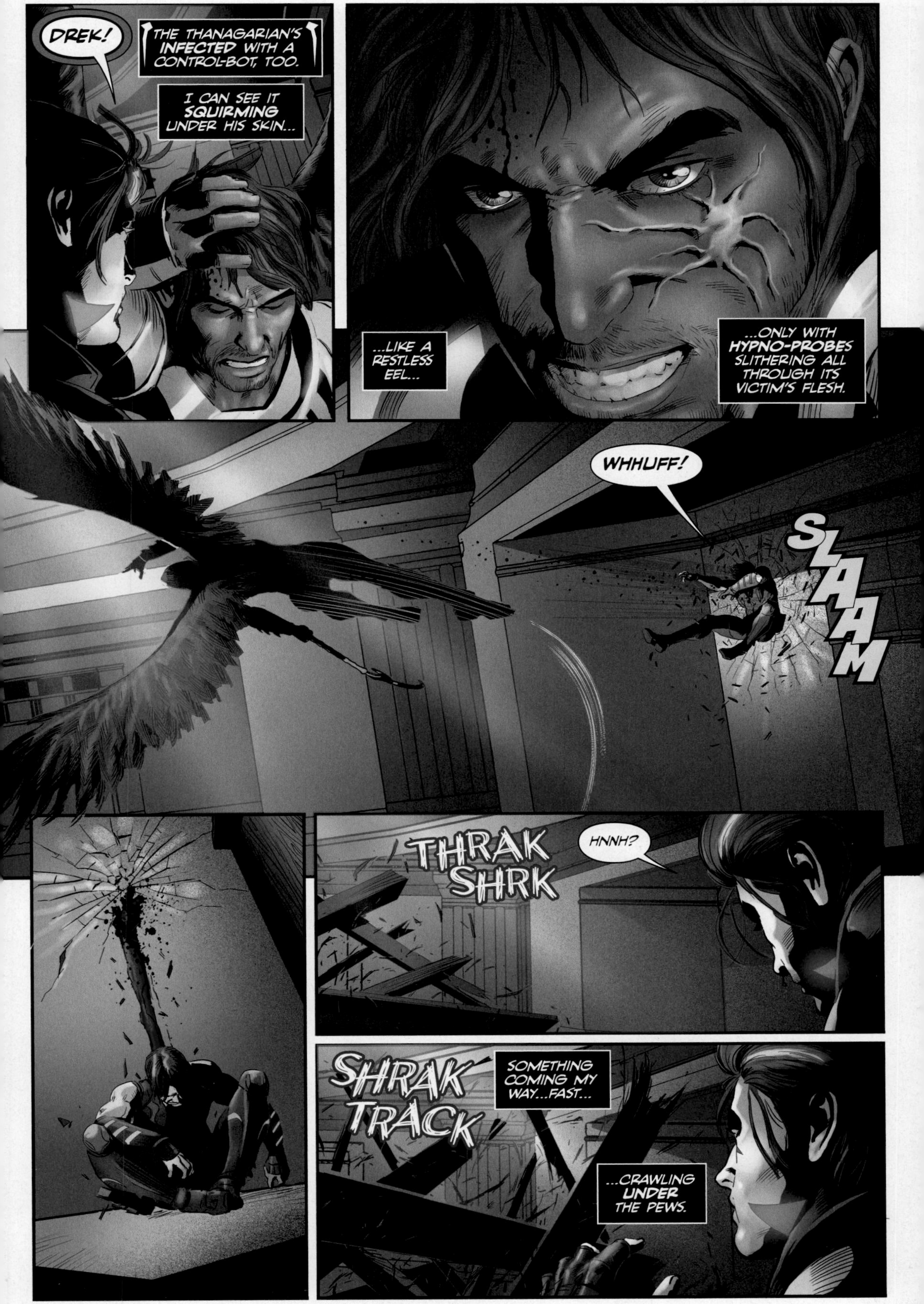

DREK!
THE THANAGARIAN'S INFECTED WITH A CONTROL-BOT, TOO.
I CAN SEE IT SQUIRMING UNDER HIS SKIN...
...LIKE A RESTLESS EEL...
...ONLY WITH HYPNO-PROBES SLITHERING ALL THROUGH ITS VICTIM'S FLESH.
WHHUFF!
SLAAAM
THRAK SHRK
HNNH?
SHRAK TRACK
SOMETHING COMING MY WAY...FAST...
...CRAWLING UNDER THE PEWS.

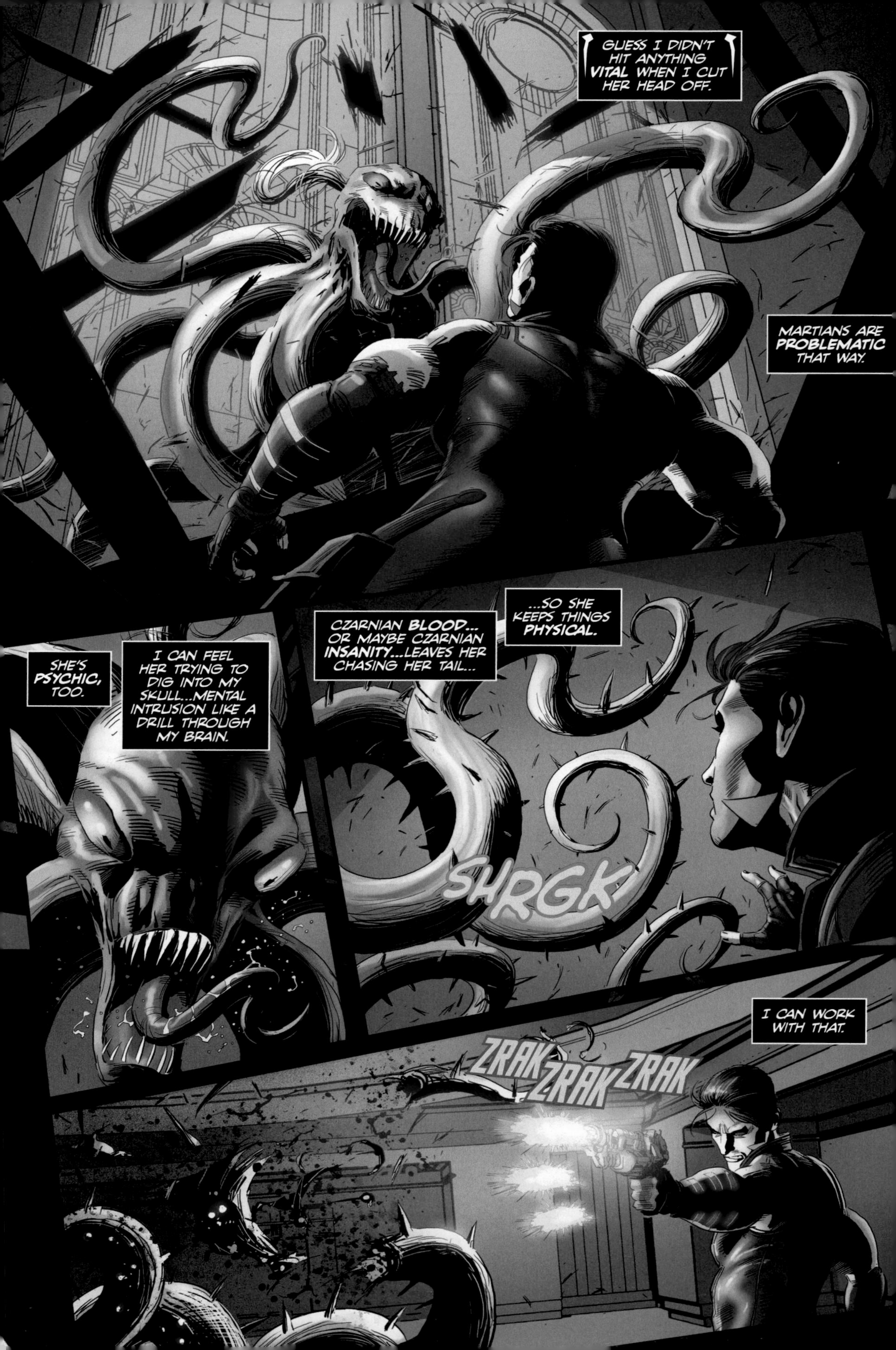
GUESS I DIDN'T HIT ANYTHING VITAL WHEN I CUT HER HEAD OFF.
MARTIANS ARE PROBLEMATIC THAT WAY.
SHE'S PSYCHIC, TOO.
I CAN FEEL HER TRYING TO DIG INTO MY SKULL...MENTAL INTRUSION LIKE A DRILL THROUGH MY BRAIN.
CZARNIAN BLOOD... OR MAYBE CZARNIAN INSANITY...LEAVES HER CHASING HER TAIL...
...SO SHE KEEPS THINGS PHYSICAL.
SHRGK
I CAN WORK WITH THAT.
ZRAK ZRAK ZRAK

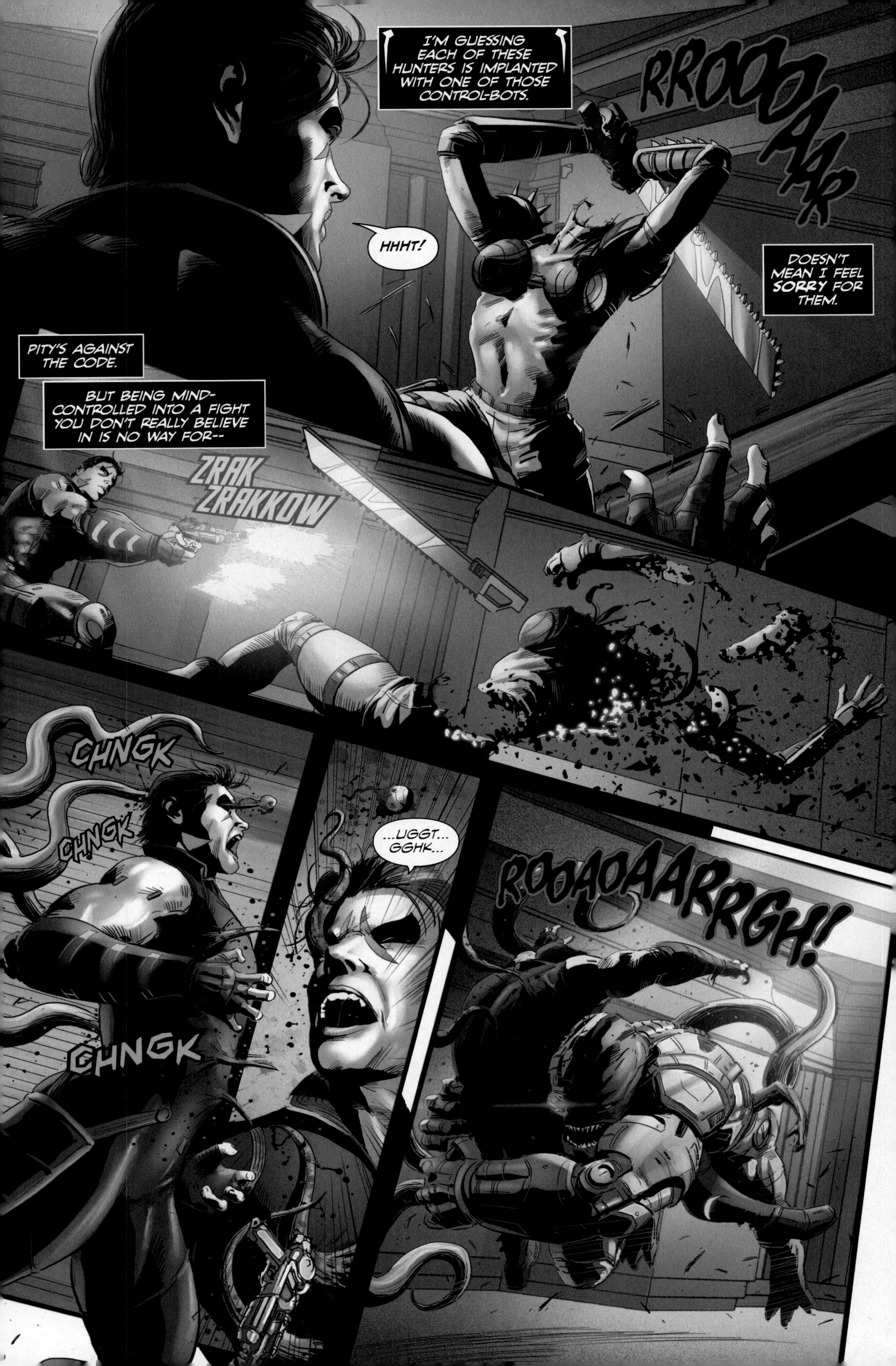

I'M GUESSING EACH OF THESE HUNTERS IS IMPLANTED WITH ONE OF THOSE CONTROL-BOTS.
RROOOAAR
HHHT!
DOESN'T MEAN I FEEL SORRY FOR THEM.
PITY'S AGAINST THE CODE.
BUT BEING MIND-CONTROLLED INTO A FIGHT YOU DON'T REALLY BELIEVE IN IS NO WAY FOR--
ZRAK ZRAKKOW
CHNGK
CHNGK
CHNGK
...UGGT... GGHK...
ROOAOAARRGH!

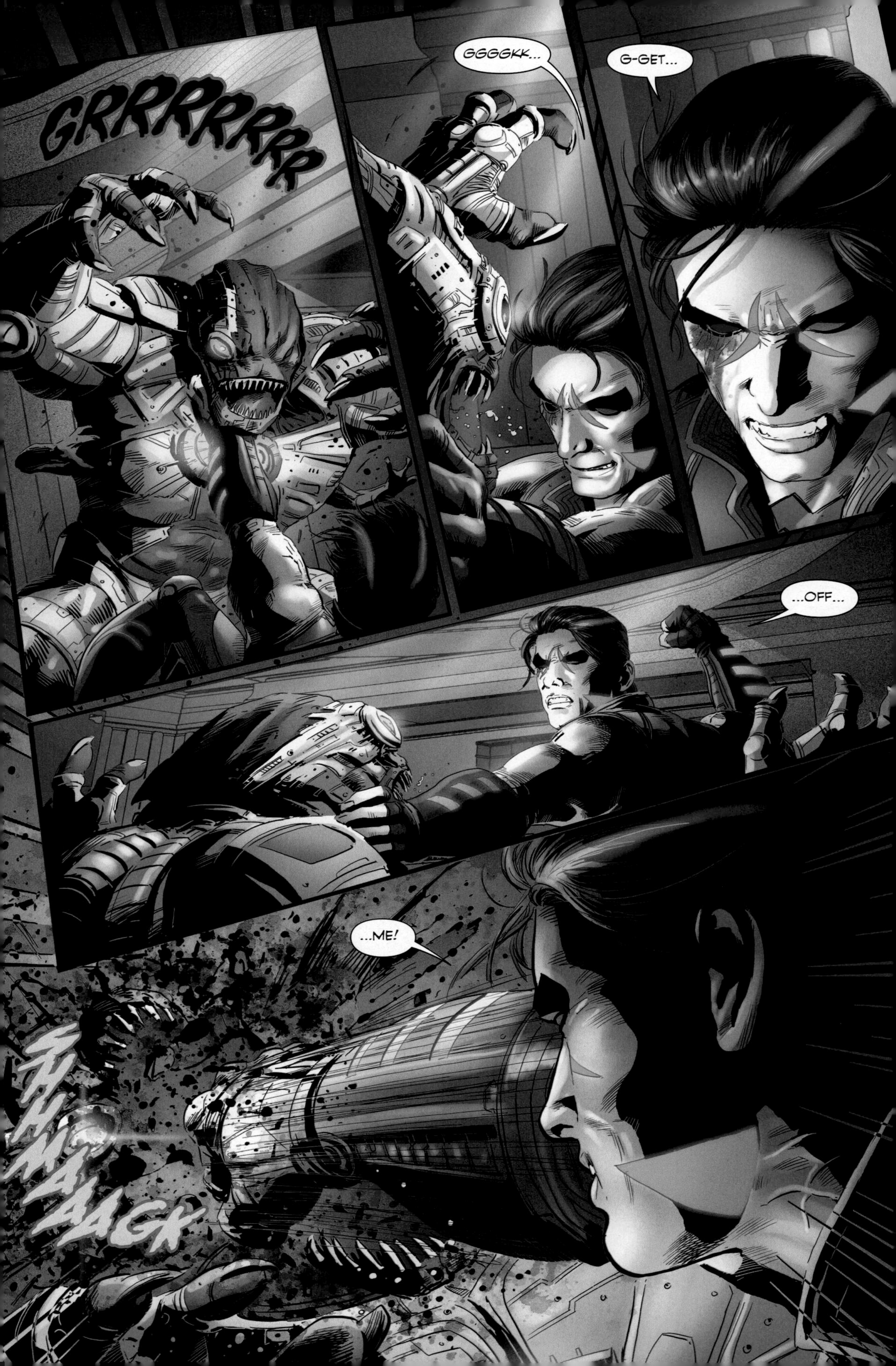
GRRRRRRRR
GGGGKK...
G-GET...
...OFF...
...ME!
WHHHAAAGK

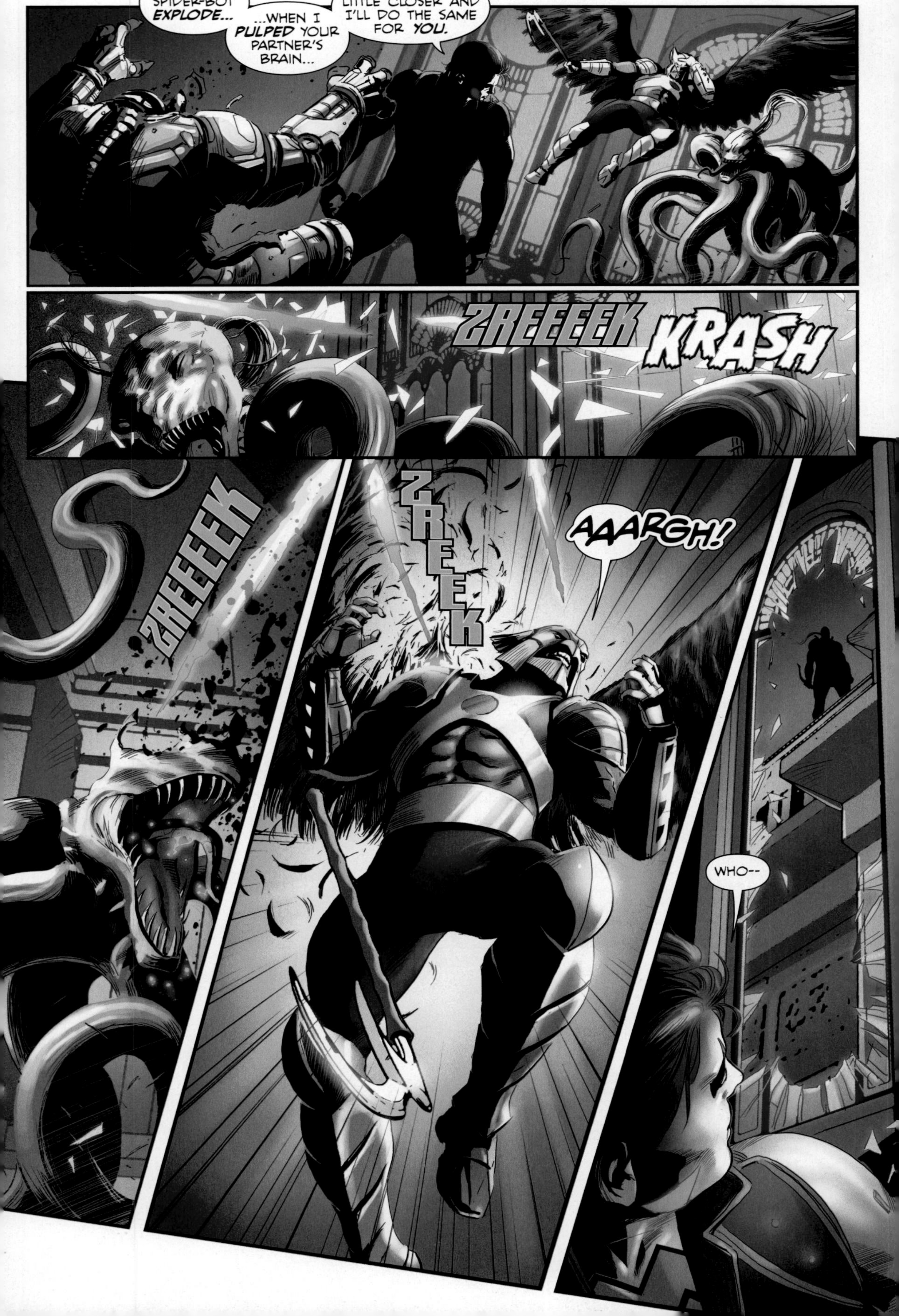
F-FELT THE SPIDER-BOT EXPLODE...
...WHEN I PULPED YOUR PARTNER'S BRAIN...
...COME A LITTLE CLOSER AND I'LL DO THE SAME FOR YOU.
ZREEEEK
KRASH
ZREEEEK
ZREEK
AAARGH!
WHO--

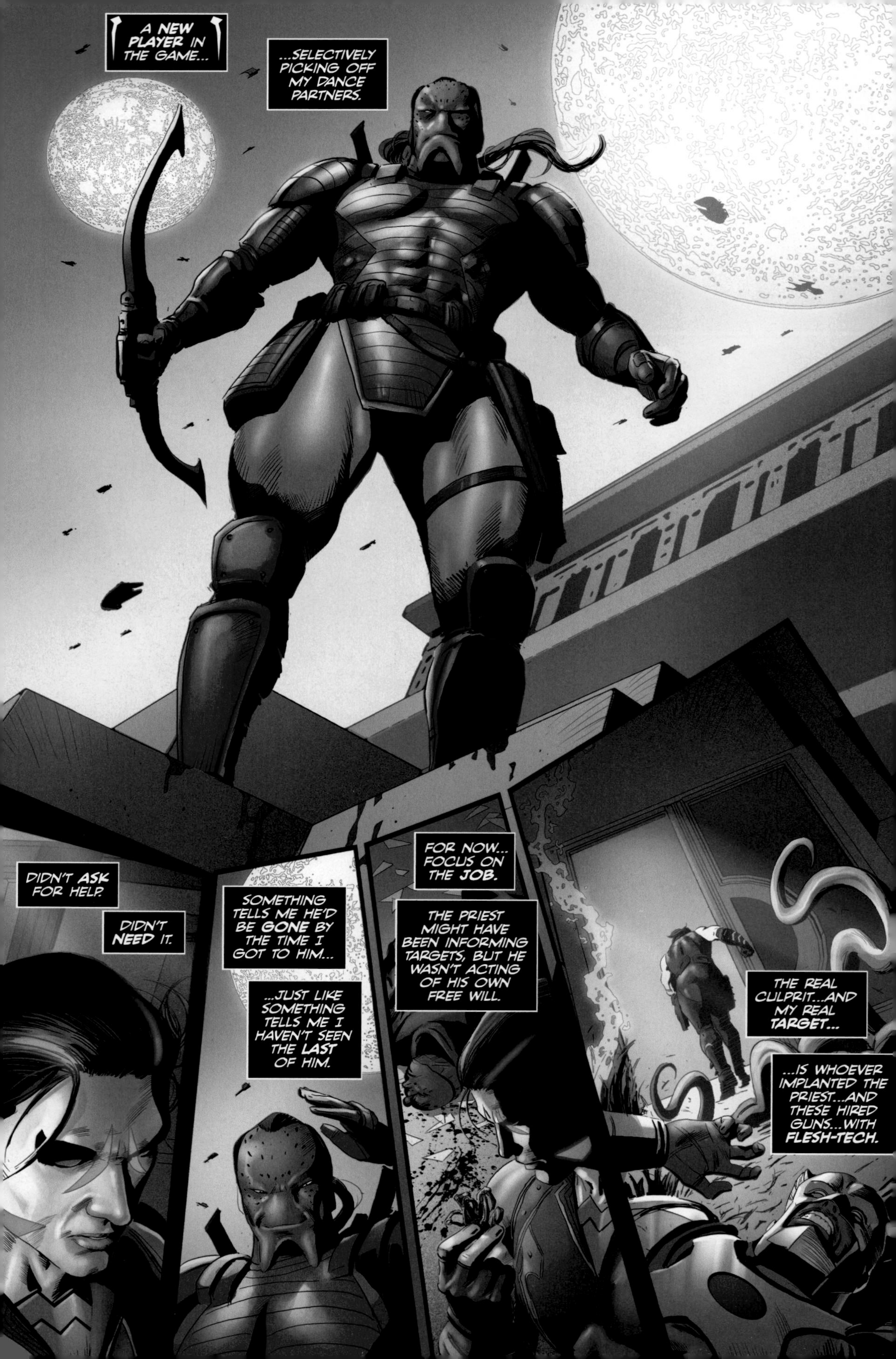
A NEW PLAYER IN THE GAME...
...SELECTIVELY PICKING OFF MY DANCE PARTNERS.
DIDN'T ASK FOR HELP.
DIDN'T NEED IT.
SOMETHING TELLS ME HE'D BE GONE BY THE TIME I GOT TO HIM...
...JUST LIKE SOMETHING TELLS ME I HAVEN'T SEEN THE LAST OF HIM.
FOR NOW... FOCUS ON THE JOB.
THE PRIEST MIGHT HAVE BEEN INFORMING TARGETS, BUT HE WASN'T ACTING OF HIS OWN FREE WILL.
THE REAL CULPRIT...AND MY REAL TARGET...
...IS WHOEVER IMPLANTED THE PRIEST...AND THESE HIRED GUNS...WITH FLESH-TECH.

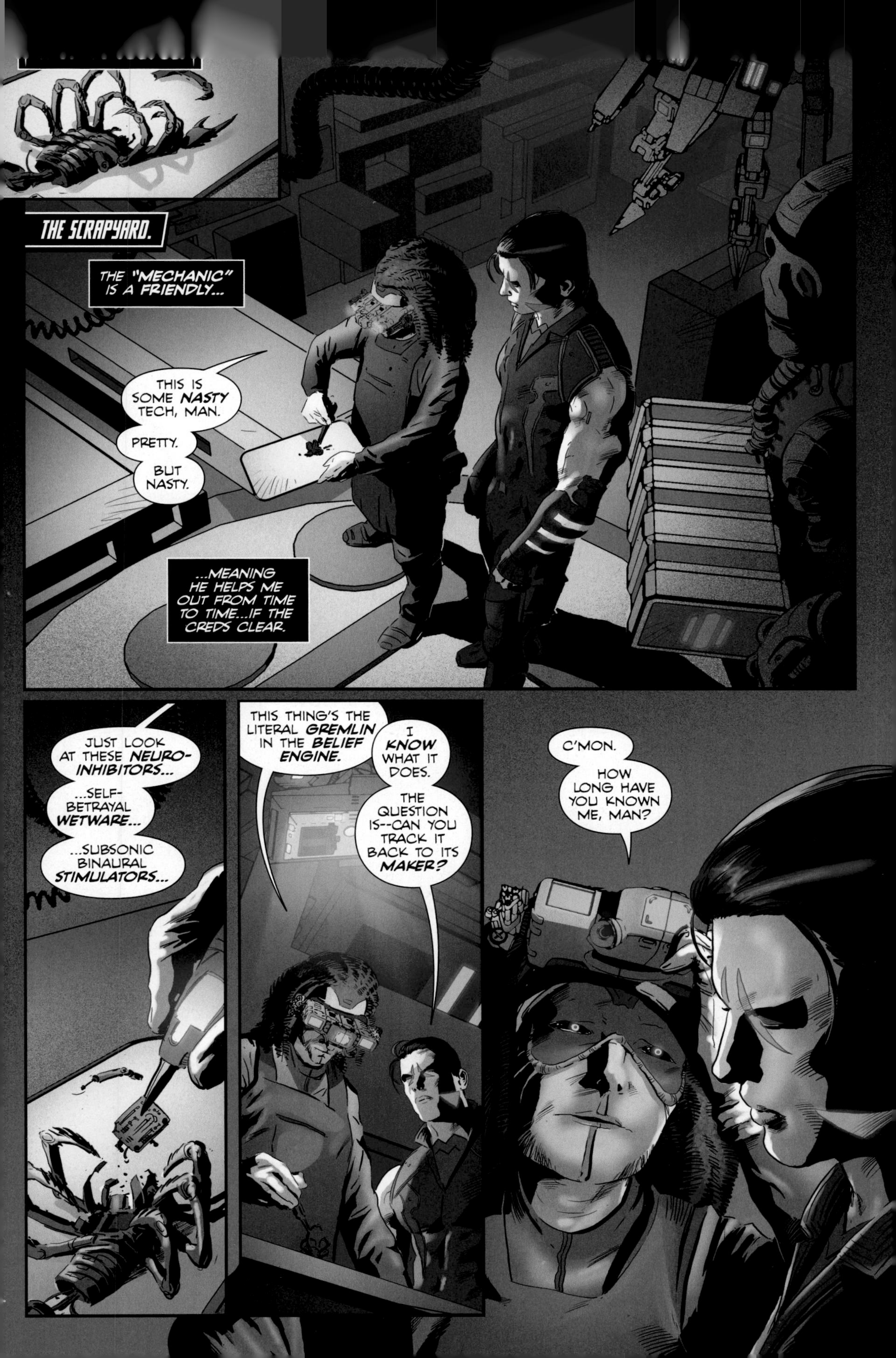

THE SCRAPYARD.
THE "MECHANIC" IS A FRIENDLY...
THIS IS SOME NASTY TECH, MAN.
PRETTY.
BUT NASTY.
...MEANING HE HELPS ME OUT FROM TIME TO TIME...IF THE CREDS CLEAR.
JUST LOOK AT THESE NEURO-INHIBITORS...
...SELF-BETRAYAL WETWARE...
...SUBSONIC BINAURAL STIMULATORS...
THIS THING'S THE LITERAL GREMLIN IN THE BELIEF ENGINE.
I KNOW WHAT IT DOES.
THE QUESTION IS--CAN YOU TRACK IT BACK TO ITS MAKER?
C'MON.
HOW LONG HAVE YOU KNOWN ME, MAN?

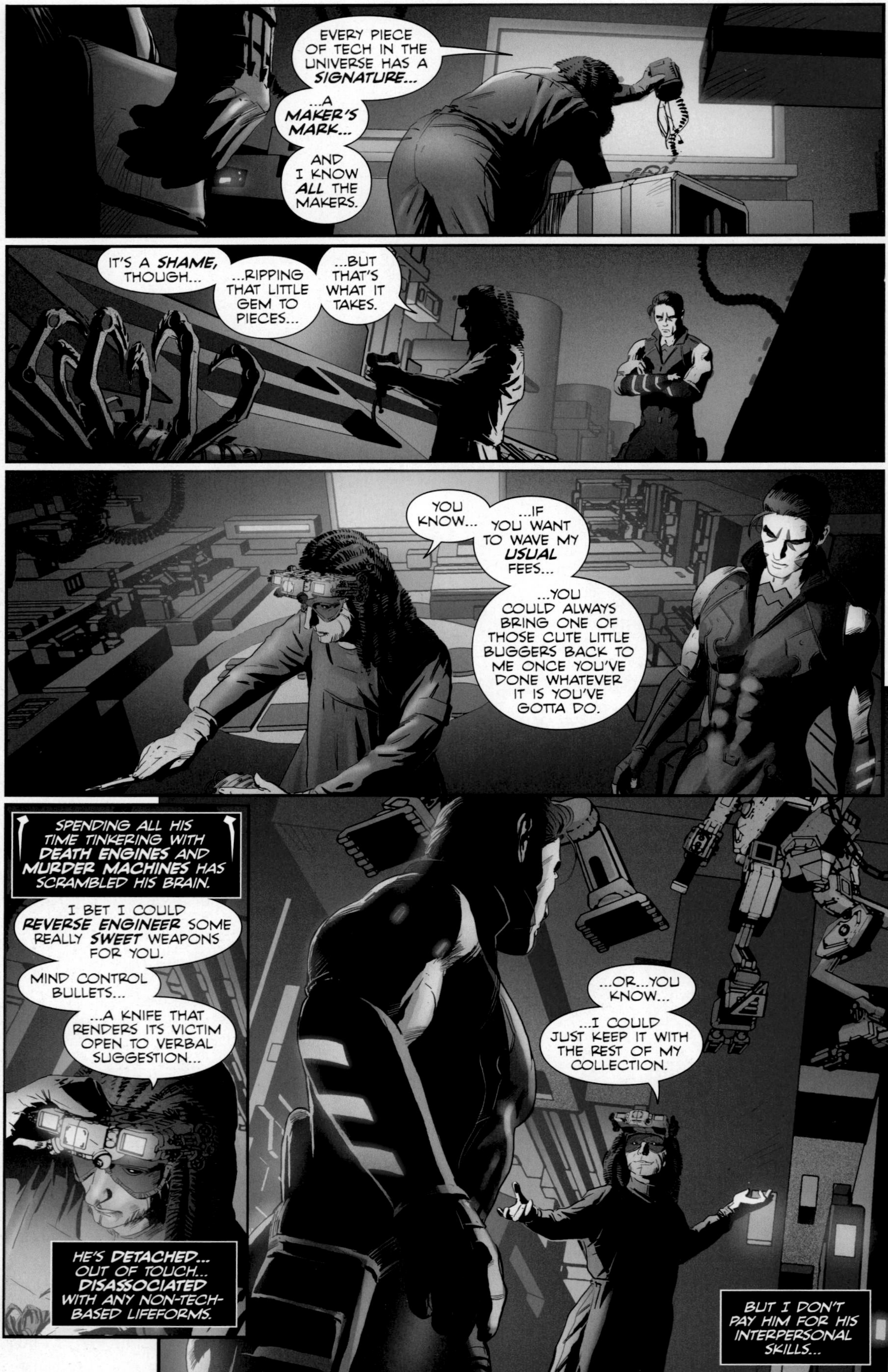
EVERY PIECE OF TECH IN THE UNIVERSE HAS A SIGNATURE...
...A MAKER'S MARK...
AND I KNOW ALL THE MAKERS.
IT'S A SHAME, THOUGH...
...RIPPING THAT LITTLE GEM TO PIECES...
...BUT THAT'S WHAT IT TAKES.
YOU KNOW...
...IF YOU WANT TO WAVE MY USUAL FEES...
...YOU COULD ALWAYS BRING ONE OF THOSE CUTE LITTLE BUGGERS BACK TO ME ONCE YOU'VE DONE WHATEVER IT IS YOU'VE GOTTA DO.
SPENDING ALL HIS TIME TINKERING WITH DEATH ENGINES AND MURDER MACHINES HAS SCRAMBLED HIS BRAIN.
I BET I COULD REVERSE ENGINEER SOME REALLY SWEET WEAPONS FOR YOU.
MIND CONTROL BULLETS...
...A KNIFE THAT RENDERS ITS VICTIM OPEN TO VERBAL SUGGESTION...
...OR...YOU KNOW...
...I COULD JUST KEEP IT WITH THE REST OF MY COLLECTION.
HE'S DETACHED... OUT OF TOUCH... DISASSOCIATED WITH ANY NON-TECH-BASED LIFEFORMS.
BUT I DON'T PAY HIM FOR HIS INTERPERSONAL SKILLS...

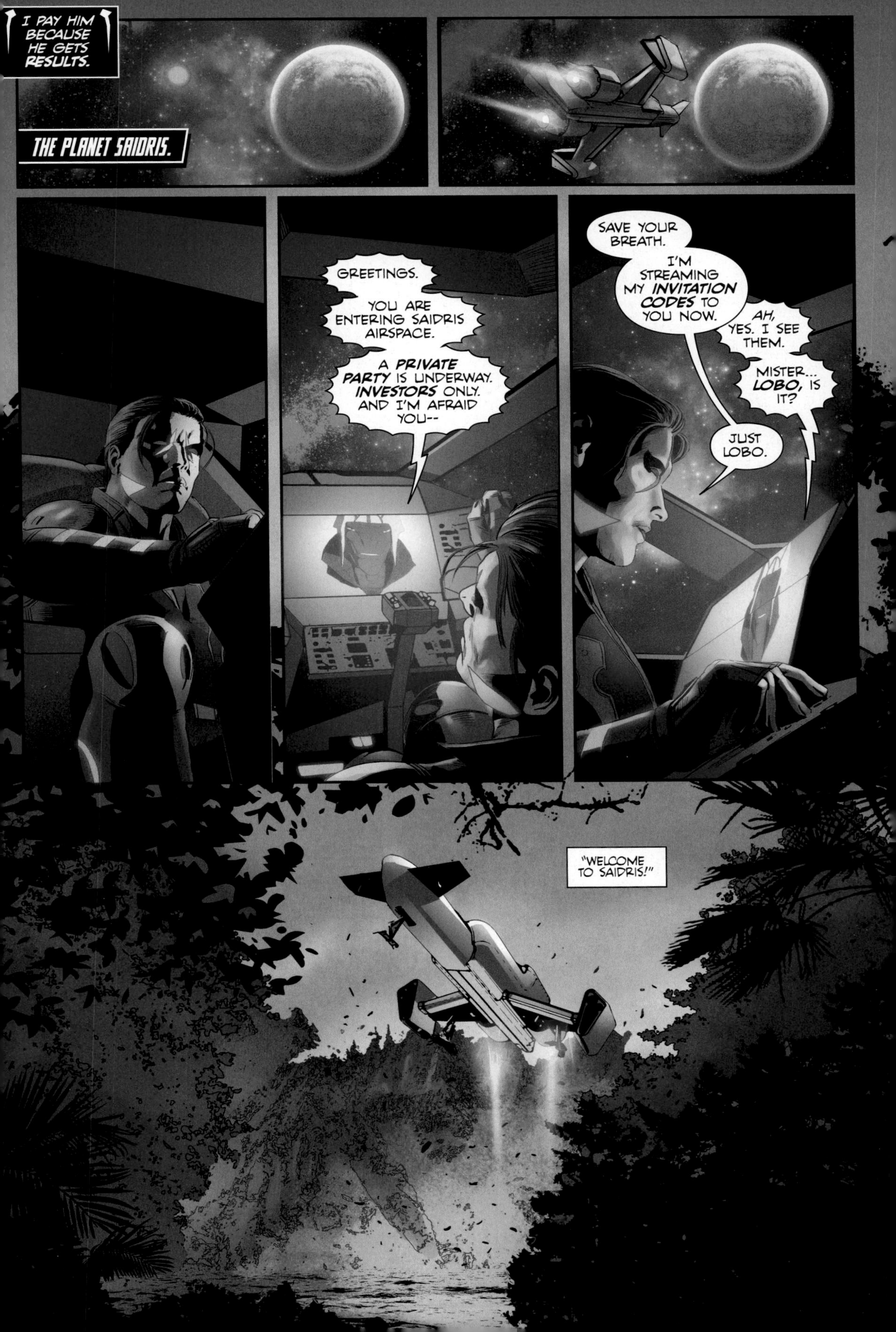
I PAY HIM BECAUSE HE GETS RESULTS.
THE PLANET SAIDRIS.
GREETINGS.
YOU ARE ENTERING SAIDRIS AIRSPACE.
A PRIVATE PARTY IS UNDERWAY. INVESTORS ONLY. AND I'M AFRAID YOU--
SAVE YOUR BREATH.
I'M STREAMING MY INVITATION CODES TO YOU NOW.
AH, YES. I SEE THEM.
MISTER... LOBO, IS IT?
JUST LOBO.
"WELCOME TO SAIDRIS!"

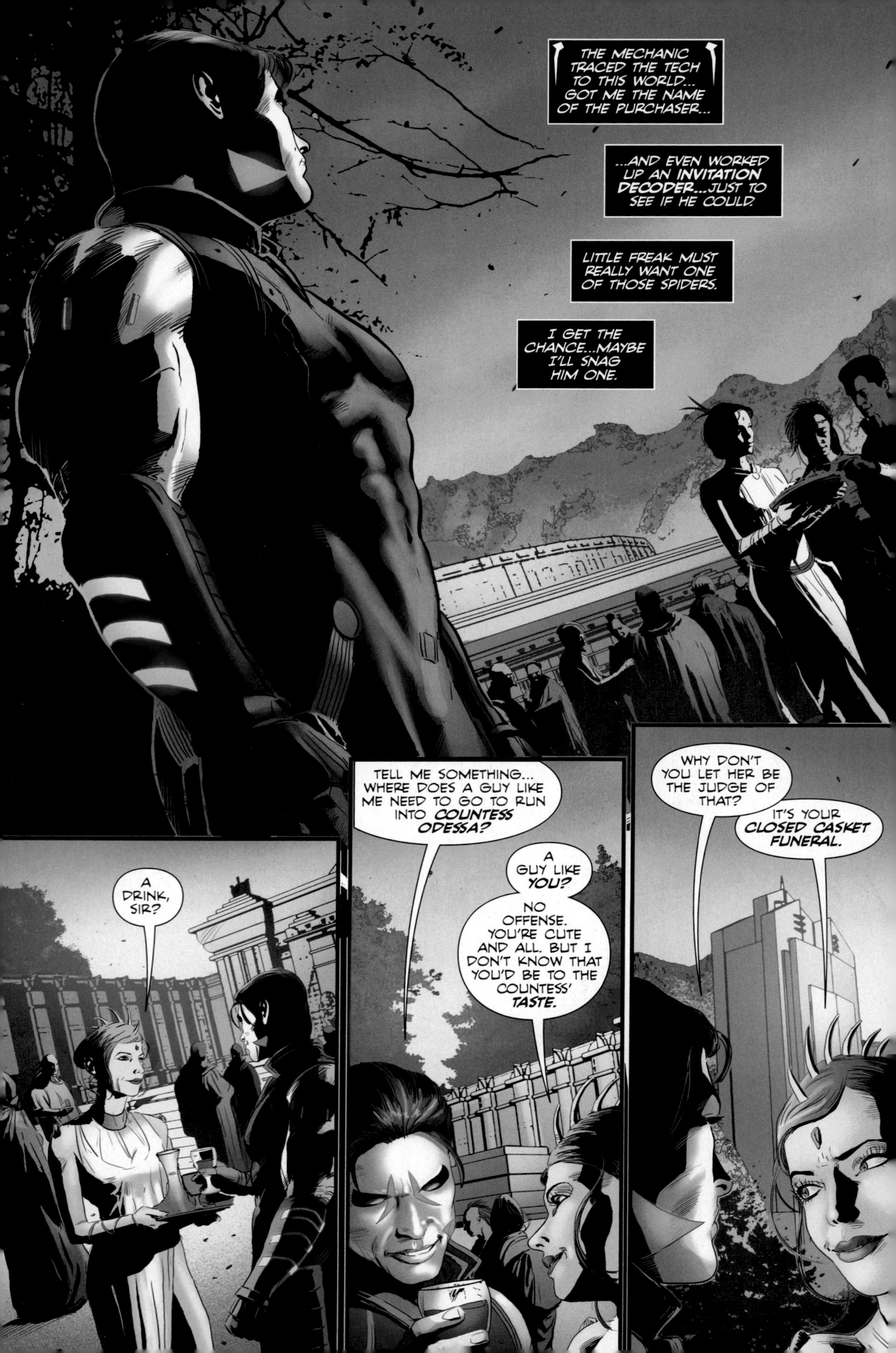
THE MECHANIC TRACED THE TECH TO THIS WORLD... GOT ME THE NAME OF THE PURCHASER...
...AND EVEN WORKED UP AN **INVITATION DECODER...** JUST TO SEE IF HE COULD.
LITTLE FREAK MUST REALLY WANT ONE OF THOSE SPIDERS.
I GET THE CHANCE...MAYBE I'LL SNAG HIM ONE.
A DRINK, SIR?
TELL ME SOMETHING... WHERE DOES A GUY LIKE ME NEED TO GO TO RUN INTO ***COUNTESS ODESSA?***
A GUY LIKE ***YOU?***
NO OFFENSE. YOU'RE CUTE AND ALL. BUT I DON'T KNOW THAT YOU'D BE TO THE COUNTESS' ***TASTE.***
WHY DON'T YOU LET HER BE THE JUDGE OF THAT?
IT'S YOUR ***CLOSED CASKET FUNERAL.***

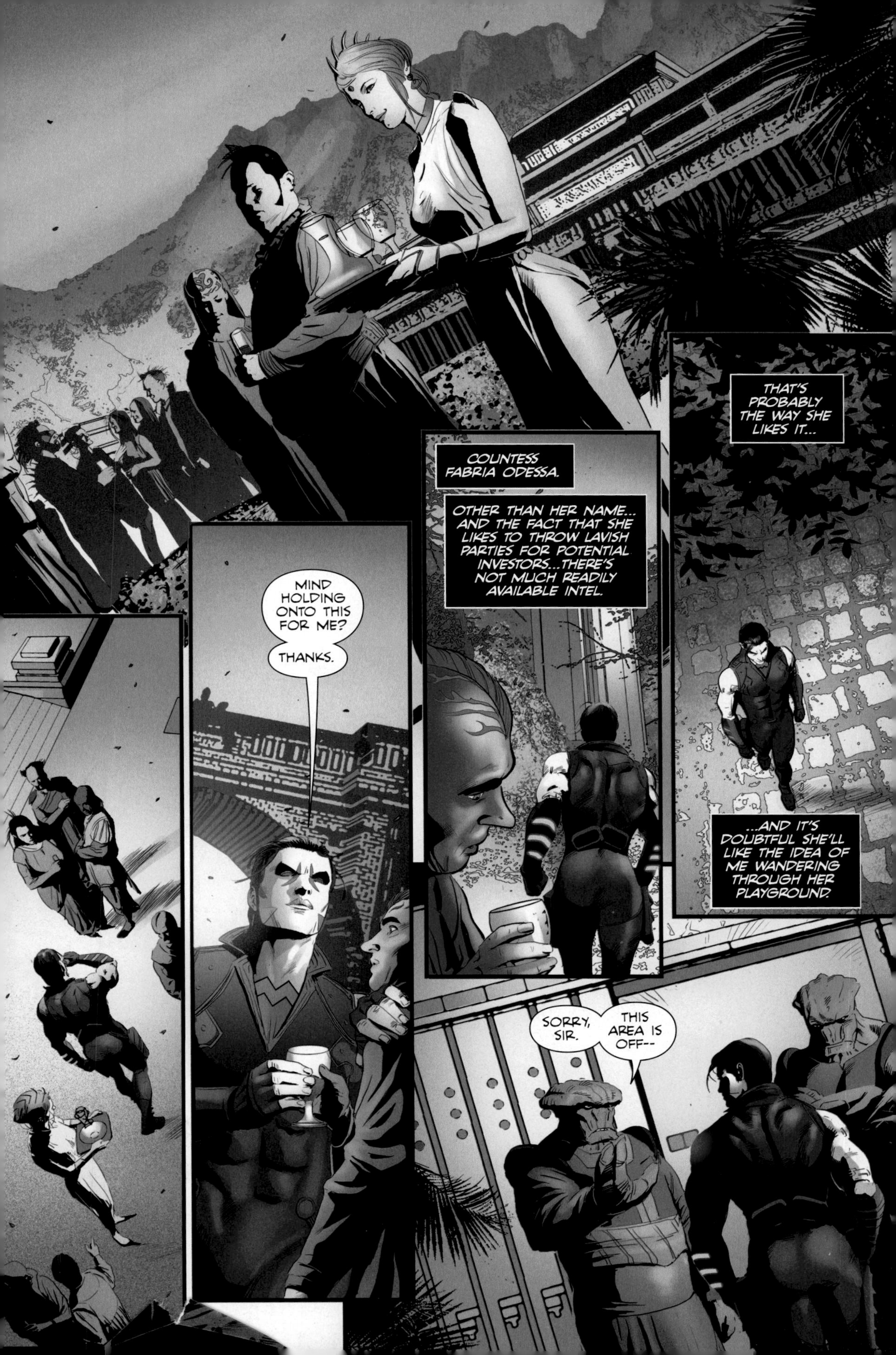
MIND HOLDING ONTO THIS FOR ME?
THANKS.
COUNTESS FABRIA ODESSA.
OTHER THAN HER NAME... AND THE FACT THAT SHE LIKES TO THROW LAVISH PARTIES FOR POTENTIAL INVESTORS...THERE'S NOT MUCH READILY AVAILABLE INTEL.
THAT'S PROBABLY THE WAY SHE LIKES IT...
...AND IT'S DOUBTFUL SHE'LL LIKE THE IDEA OF ME WANDERING THROUGH HER PLAYGROUND.
SORRY, SIR.
THIS AREA IS OFF--

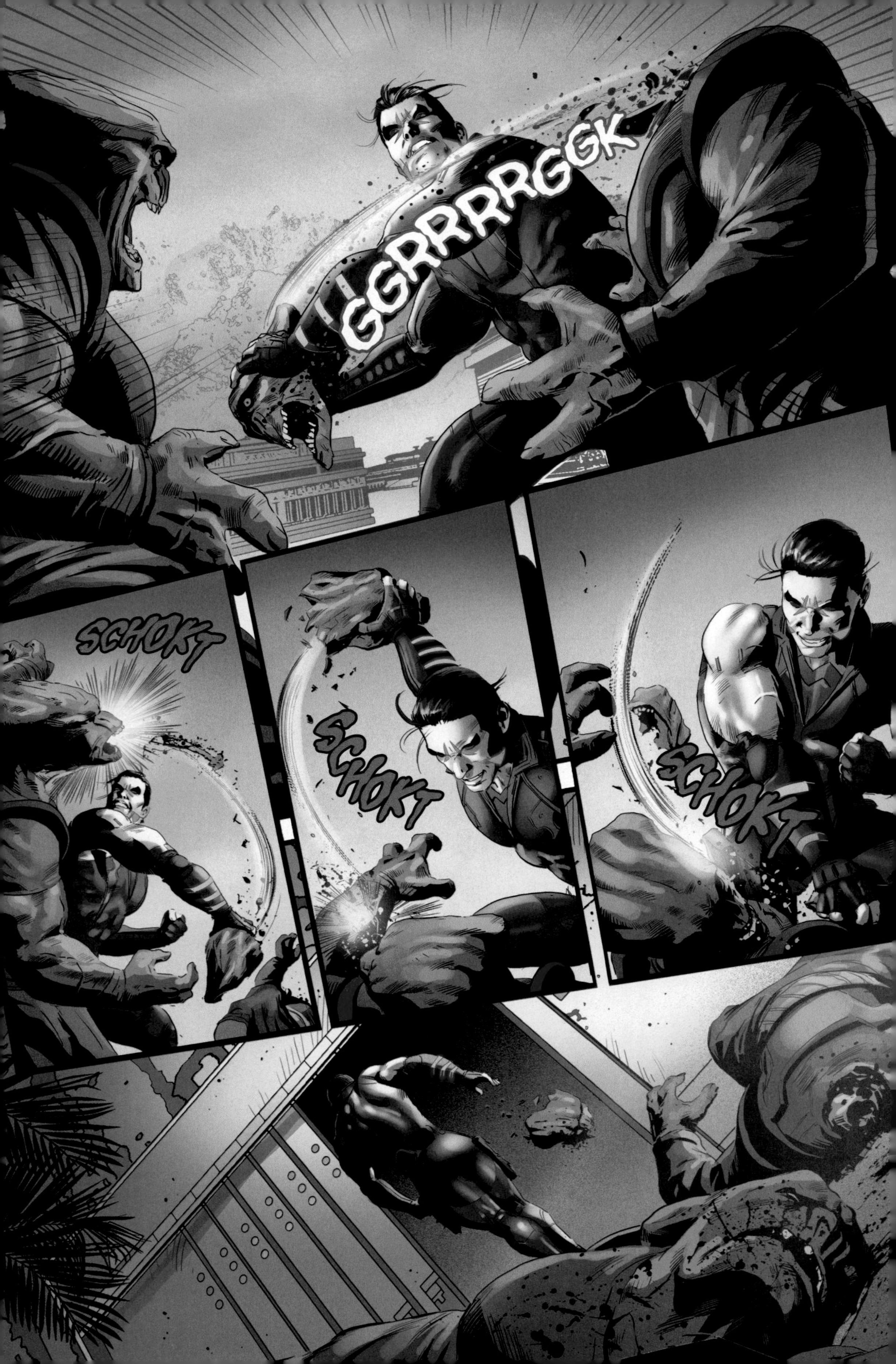
GGRRRRGGK
SCHOKT
SCHOKT
SCHOKT

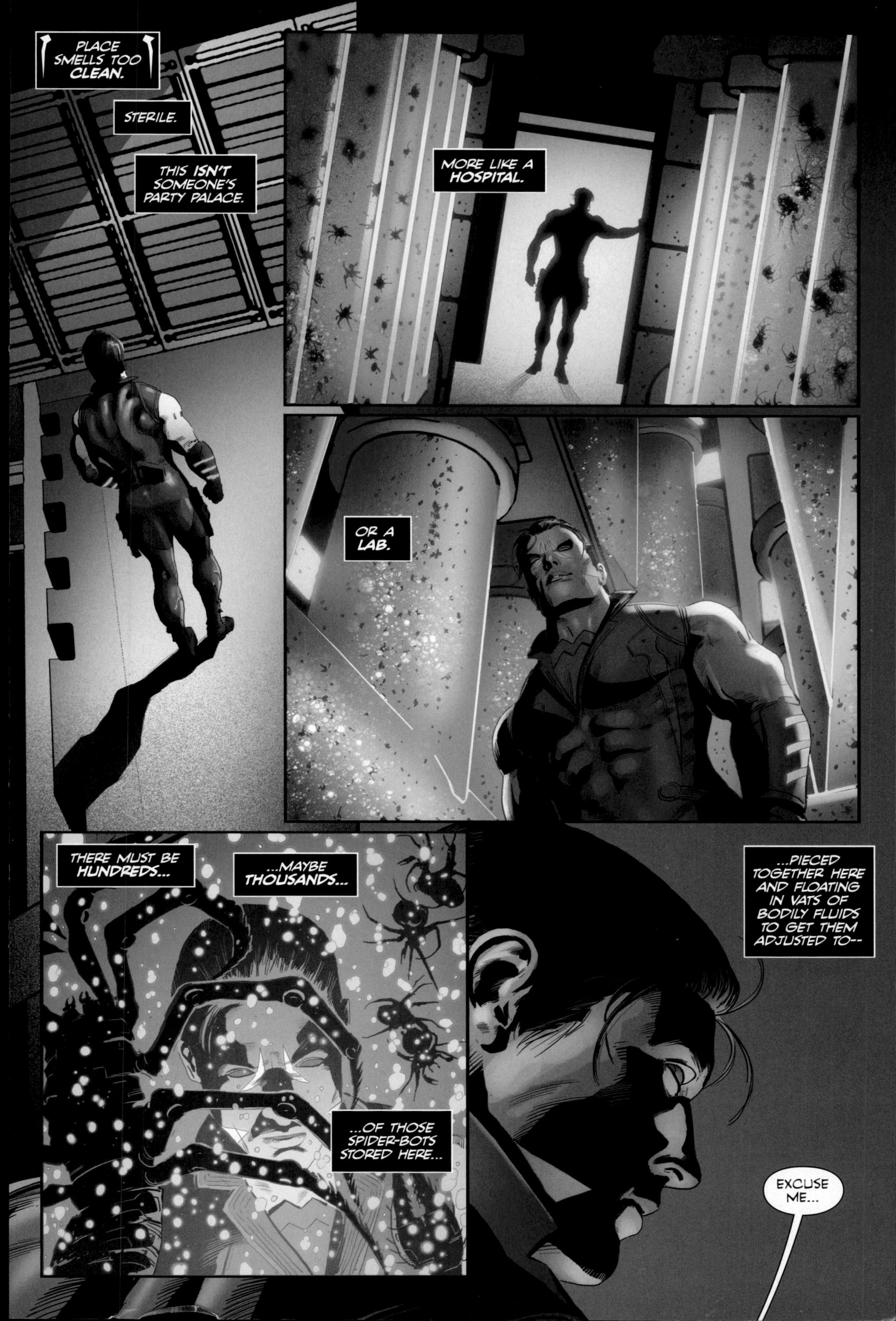
PLACE SMELLS TOO CLEAN.
STERILE.
THIS ISN'T SOMEONE'S PARTY PALACE.
MORE LIKE A HOSPITAL.
OR A LAB.
THERE MUST BE HUNDREDS...
...MAYBE THOUSANDS...
...OF THOSE SPIDER-BOTS STORED HERE...
...PIECED TOGETHER HERE AND FLOATING IN VATS OF BODILY FLUIDS TO GET THEM ADJUSTED TO--
EXCUSE ME...

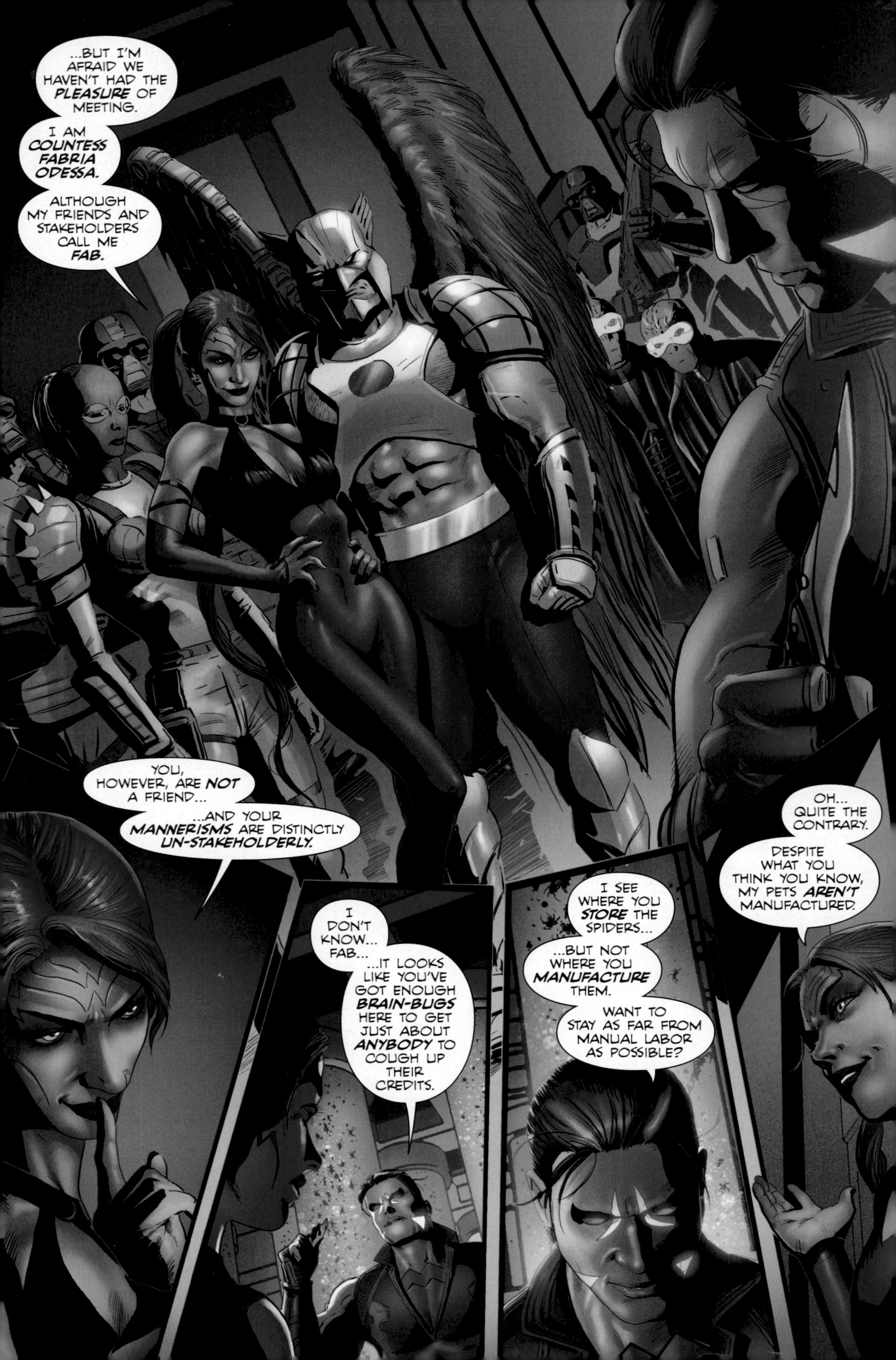

...BUT I'M AFRAID WE HAVEN'T HAD THE PLEASURE OF MEETING.
I AM COUNTESS FABRIA ODESSA.
ALTHOUGH MY FRIENDS AND STAKEHOLDERS CALL ME FAB.
YOU, HOWEVER, ARE NOT A FRIEND...
...AND YOUR MANNERISMS ARE DISTINCTLY UN-STAKEHOLDERLY.
I DON'T KNOW... FAB...
...IT LOOKS LIKE YOU'VE GOT ENOUGH BRAIN-BUGS HERE TO GET JUST ABOUT ANYBODY TO COUGH UP THEIR CREDITS.
I SEE WHERE YOU STORE THE SPIDERS...
...BUT NOT WHERE YOU MANUFACTURE THEM.
WANT TO STAY AS FAR FROM MANUAL LABOR AS POSSIBLE?
OH... QUITE THE CONTRARY.
DESPITE WHAT YOU THINK YOU KNOW, MY PETS AREN'T MANUFACTURED.

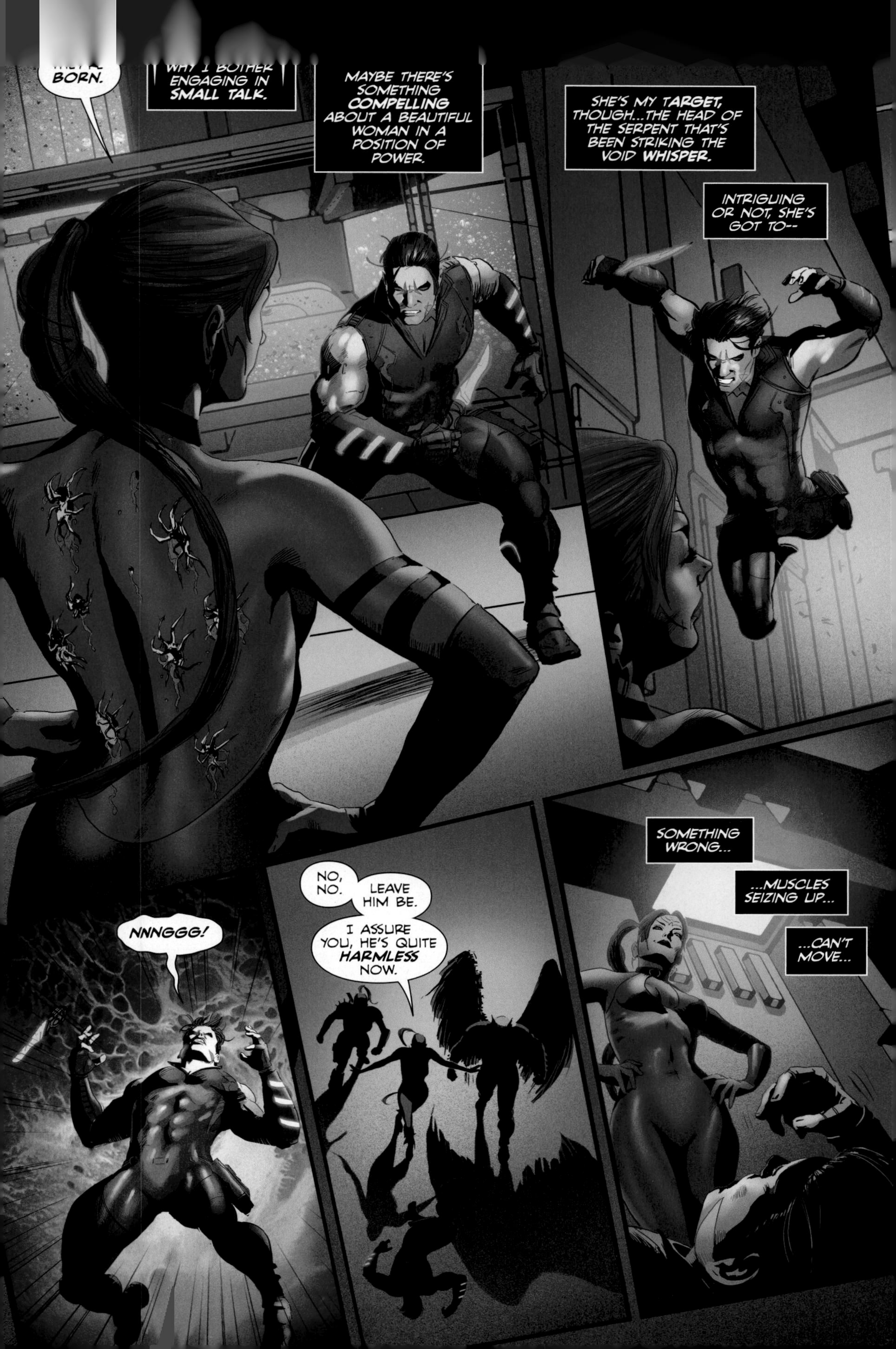
BORN.
WHY I BOTHER ENGAGING IN SMALL TALK.
MAYBE THERE'S SOMETHING COMPELLING ABOUT A BEAUTIFUL WOMAN IN A POSITION OF POWER.
SHE'S MY TARGET, THOUGH...THE HEAD OF THE SERPENT THAT'S BEEN STRIKING THE VOID WHISPER.
INTRIGUING OR NOT, SHE'S GOT TO--
NNNGGG!
NO, NO.
LEAVE HIM BE.
I ASSURE YOU, HE'S QUITE HARMLESS NOW.
SOMETHING WRONG...
...MUSCLES SEIZING UP...
...CAN'T MOVE...

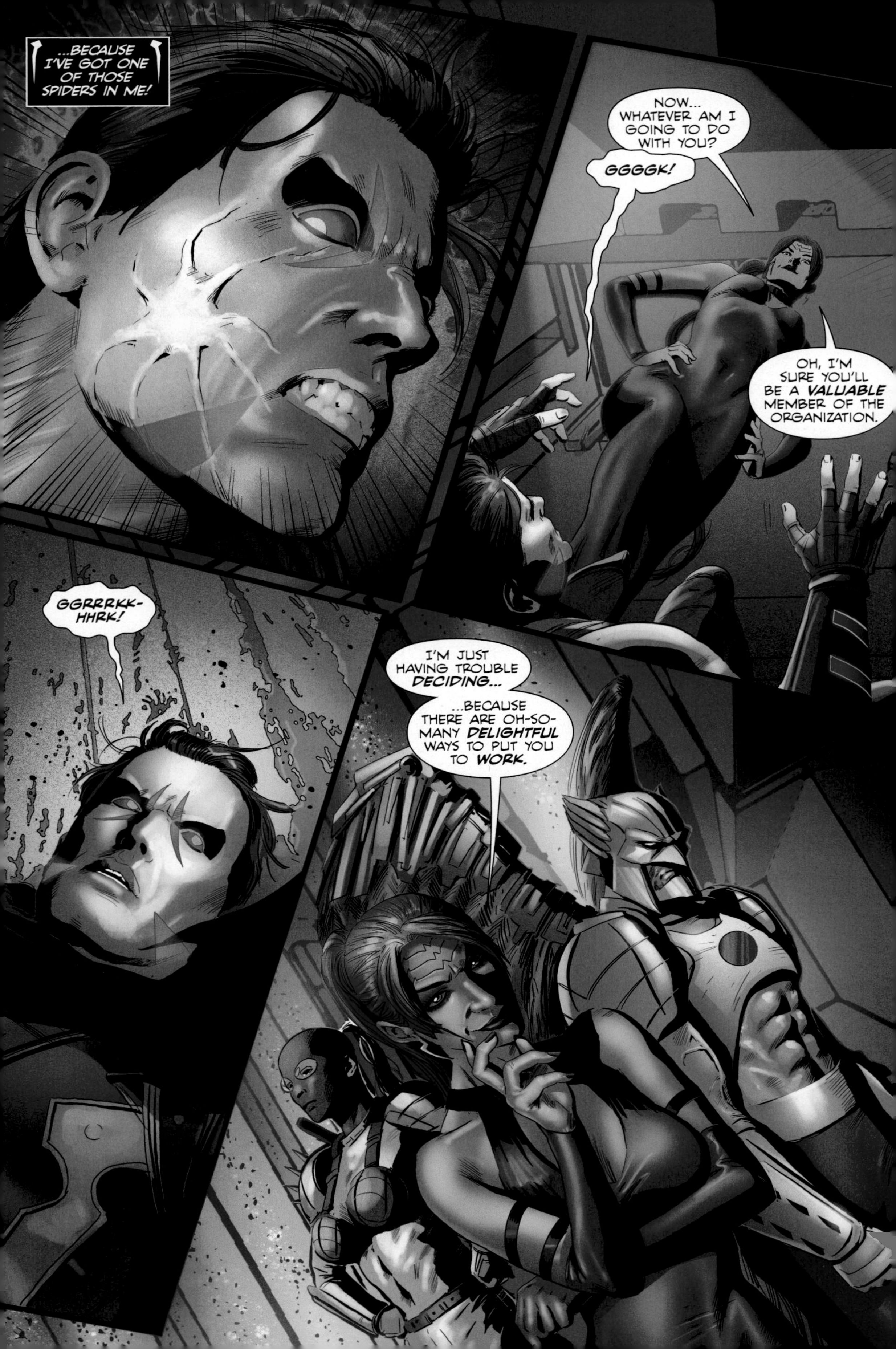
...BECAUSE I'VE GOT ONE OF THOSE SPIDERS IN ME!
NOW... WHATEVER AM I GOING TO DO WITH YOU?
GGGGK!
OH, I'M SURE YOU'LL BE A **VALUABLE** MEMBER OF THE ORGANIZATION.
GGRRRKK-HHRK!
I'M JUST HAVING TROUBLE **DECIDING...**
...BECAUSE THERE ARE OH-SO-MANY **DELIGHTFUL** WAYS TO PUT YOU TO **WORK.**

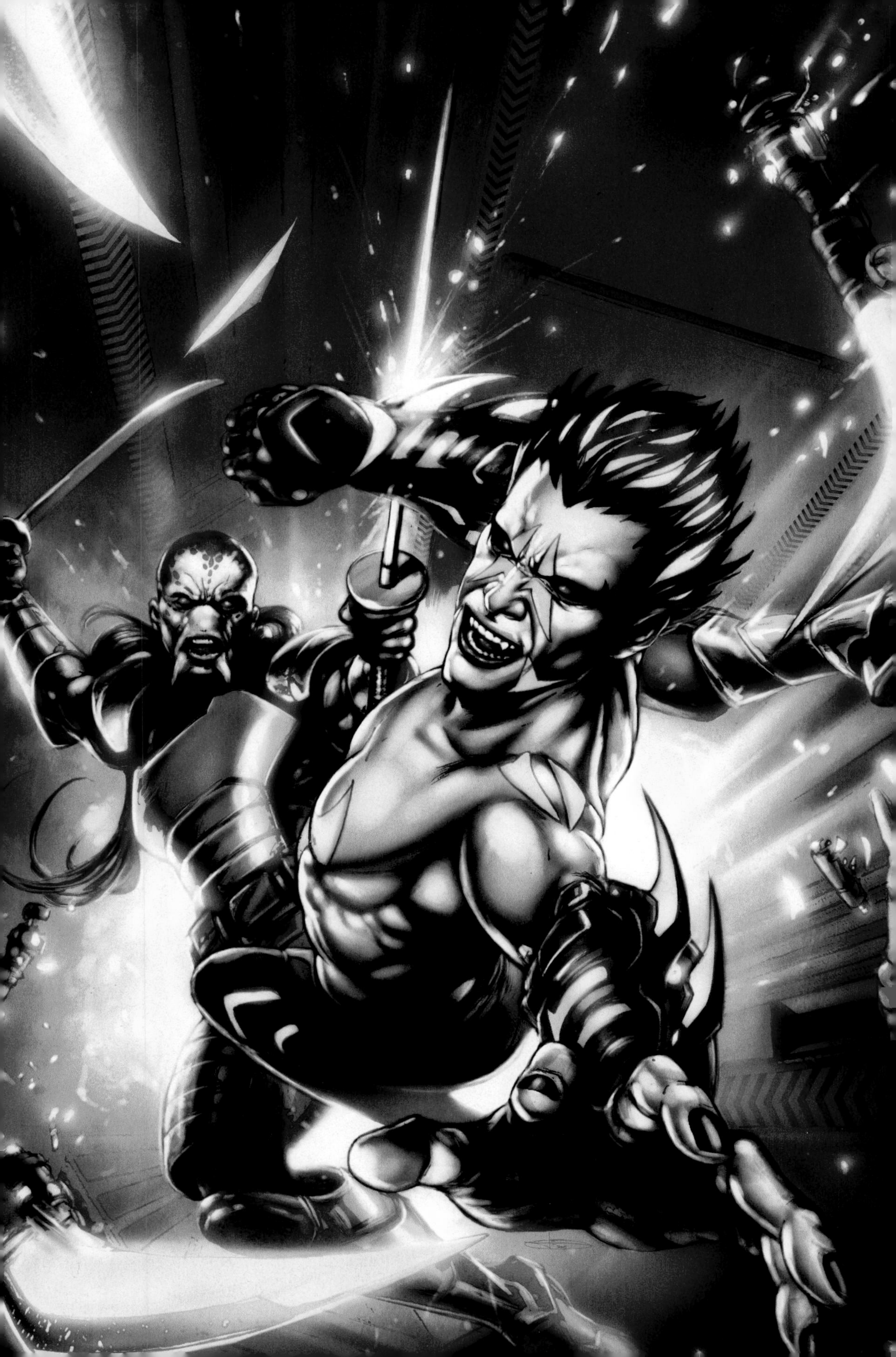

CULLEN BUNN FRANK BARBIERE writers SZYMON KUDRANSKI artist BLOND colorist TRAVIS LANHAM letterer cover art by LEONARDO MANCO

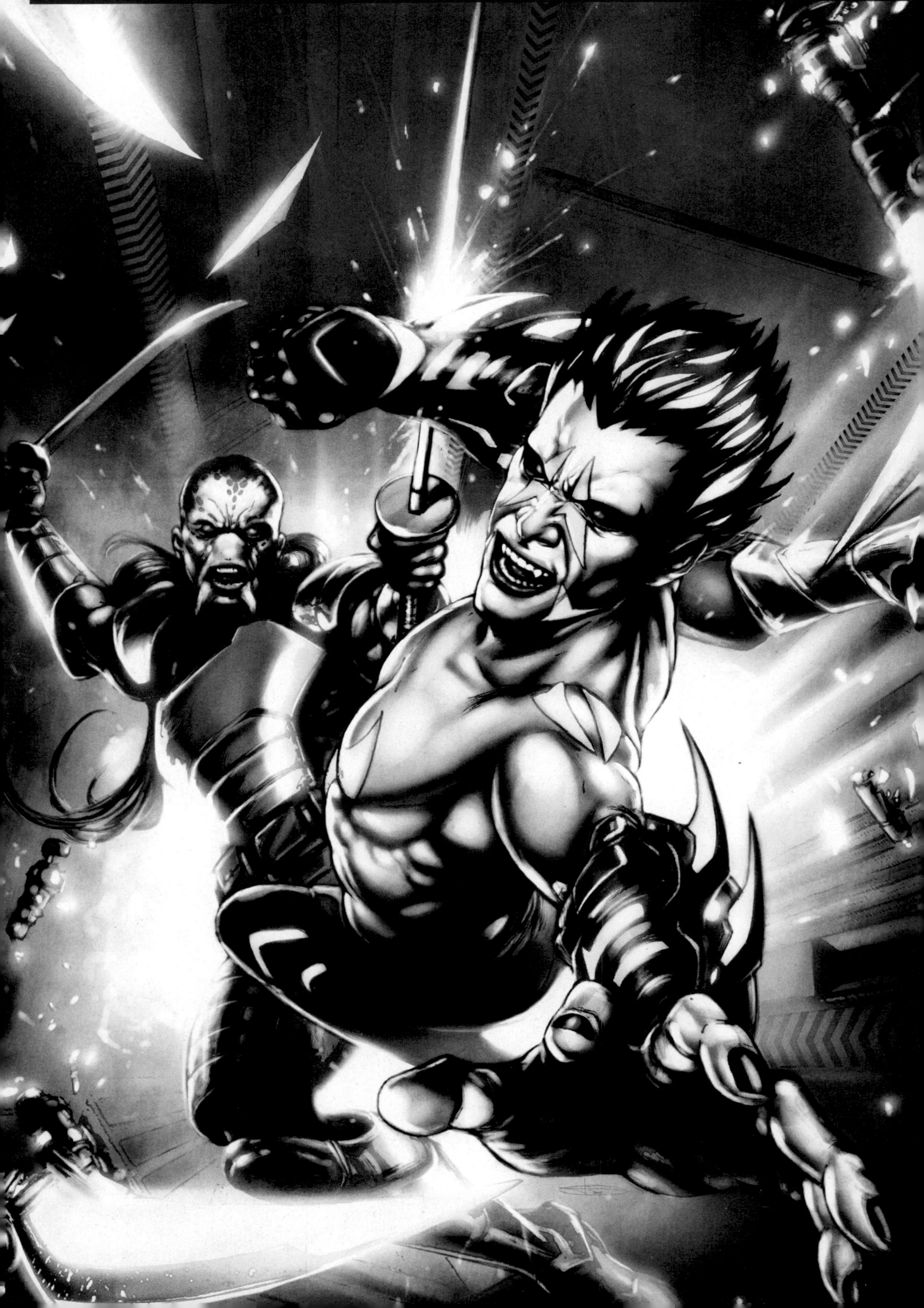

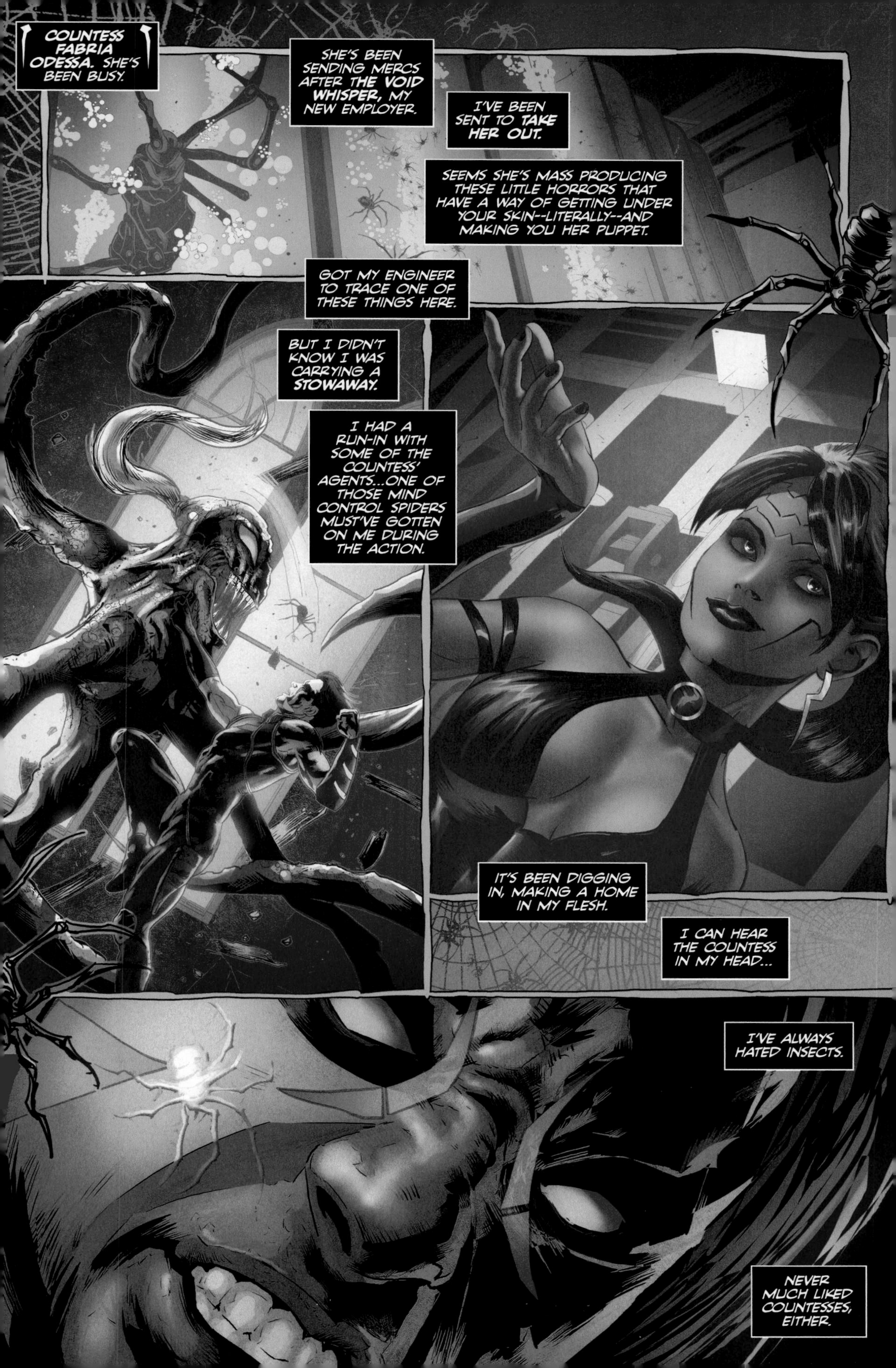
COUNTESS FABRIA ODESSA. SHE'S BEEN BUSY.
SHE'S BEEN SENDING MERCS AFTER THE VOID WHISPER, MY NEW EMPLOYER.
I'VE BEEN SENT TO TAKE HER OUT.
SEEMS SHE'S MASS PRODUCING THESE LITTLE HORRORS THAT HAVE A WAY OF GETTING UNDER YOUR SKIN--LITERALLY--AND MAKING YOU HER PUPPET.
GOT MY ENGINEER TO TRACE ONE OF THESE THINGS HERE.
BUT I DIDN'T KNOW I WAS CARRYING A STOWAWAY.
I HAD A RUN-IN WITH SOME OF THE COUNTESS' AGENTS...ONE OF THOSE MIND CONTROL SPIDERS MUST'VE GOTTEN ON ME DURING THE ACTION.
IT'S BEEN DIGGING IN, MAKING A HOME IN MY FLESH.
I CAN HEAR THE COUNTESS IN MY HEAD...
I'VE ALWAYS HATED INSECTS.
NEVER MUCH LIKED COUNTESSES, EITHER.

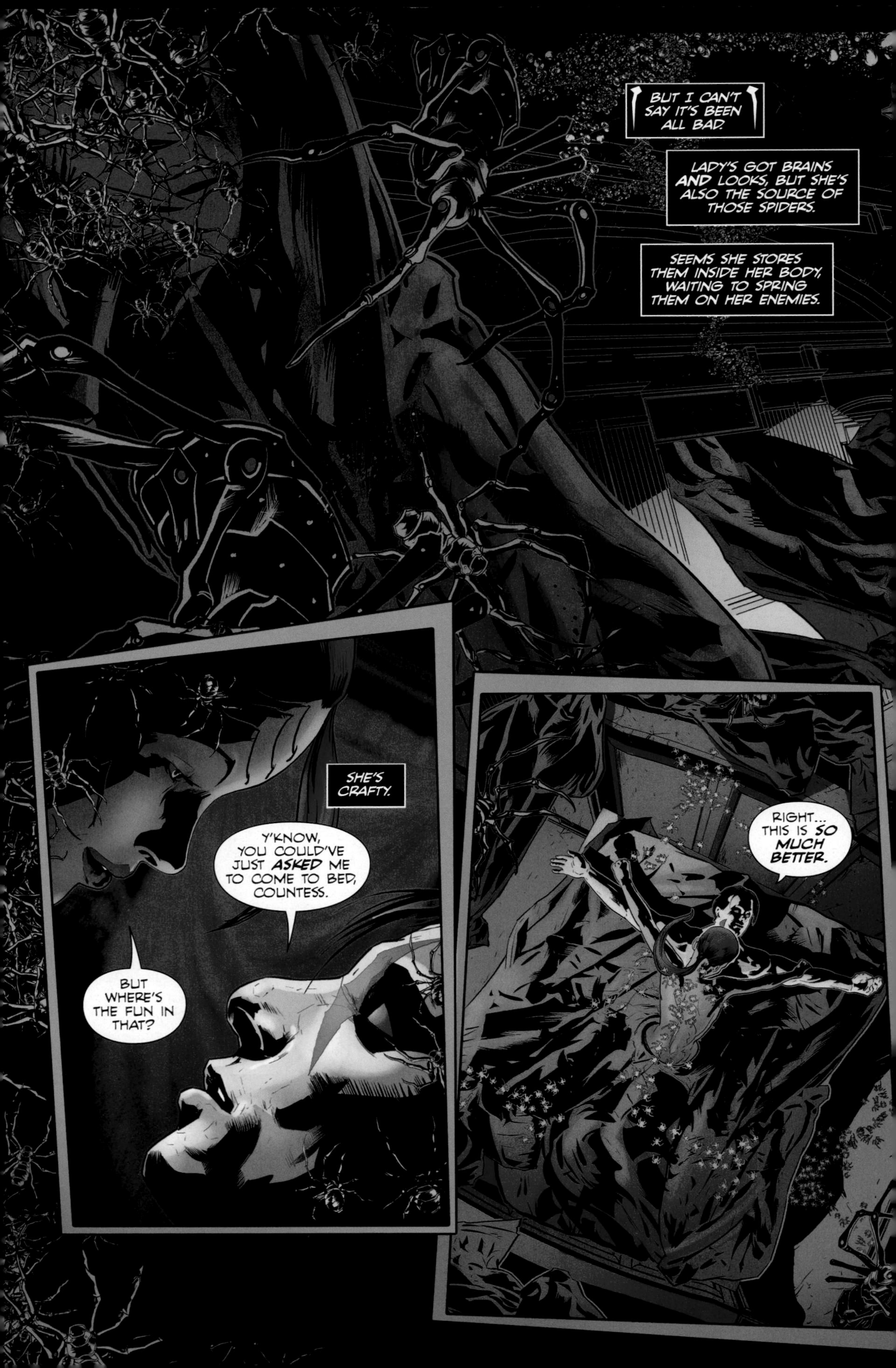
BUT I CAN'T SAY IT'S BEEN ALL BAD.
LADY'S GOT BRAINS AND LOOKS, BUT SHE'S ALSO THE SOURCE OF THOSE SPIDERS.
SEEMS SHE STORES THEM INSIDE HER BODY, WAITING TO SPRING THEM ON HER ENEMIES.
SHE'S CRAFTY.
Y'KNOW, YOU COULD'VE JUST ASKED ME TO COME TO BED, COUNTESS.
BUT WHERE'S THE FUN IN THAT?
RIGHT... THIS IS SO MUCH BETTER.

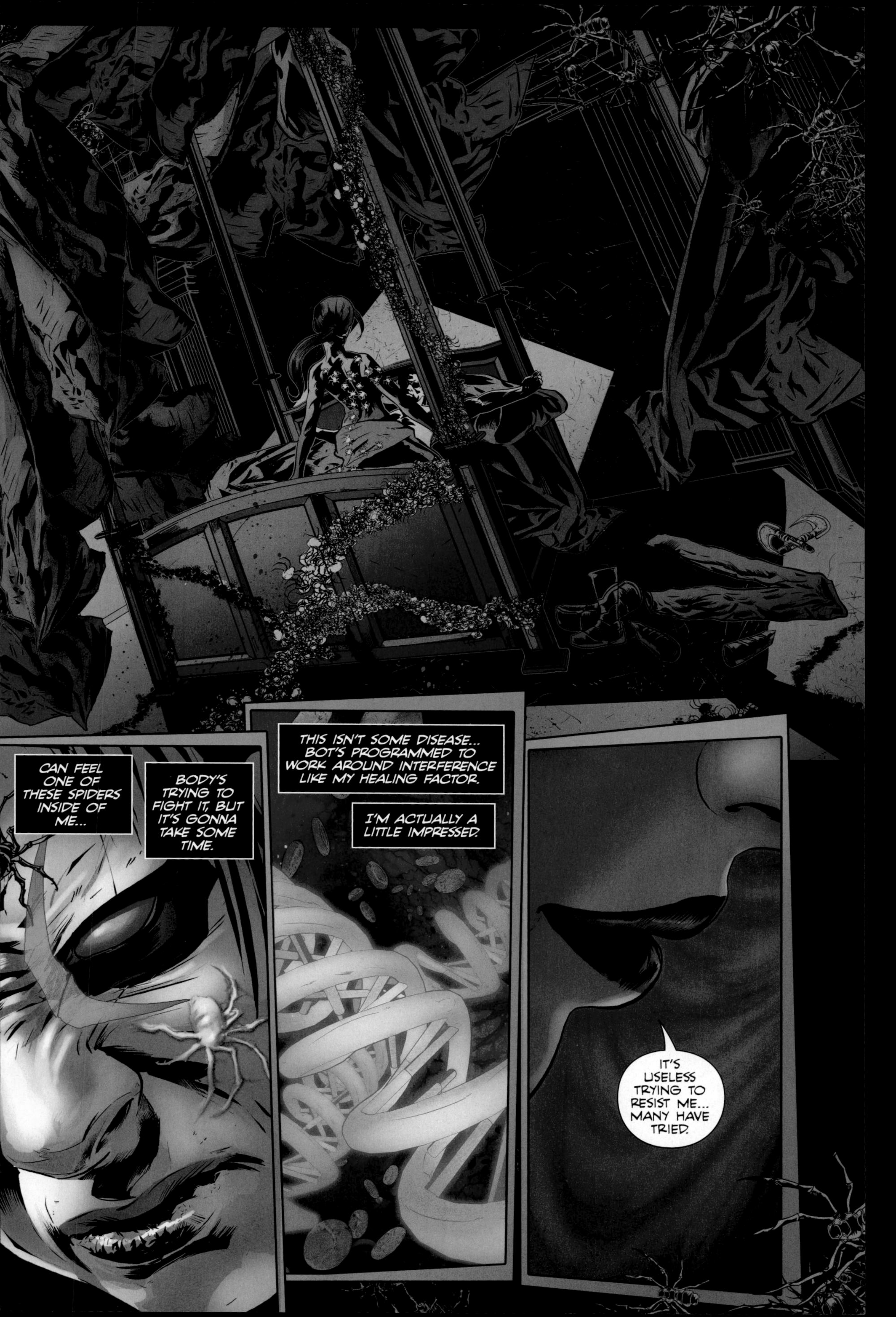
CAN FEEL ONE OF THESE SPIDERS INSIDE OF ME...
BODY'S TRYING TO FIGHT IT, BUT IT'S GONNA TAKE SOME TIME.
THIS ISN'T SOME DISEASE... BOT'S PROGRAMMED TO WORK AROUND INTERFERENCE LIKE MY HEALING FACTOR.
I'M ACTUALLY A LITTLE IMPRESSED.
IT'S USELESS TRYING TO RESIST ME... MANY HAVE TRIED.

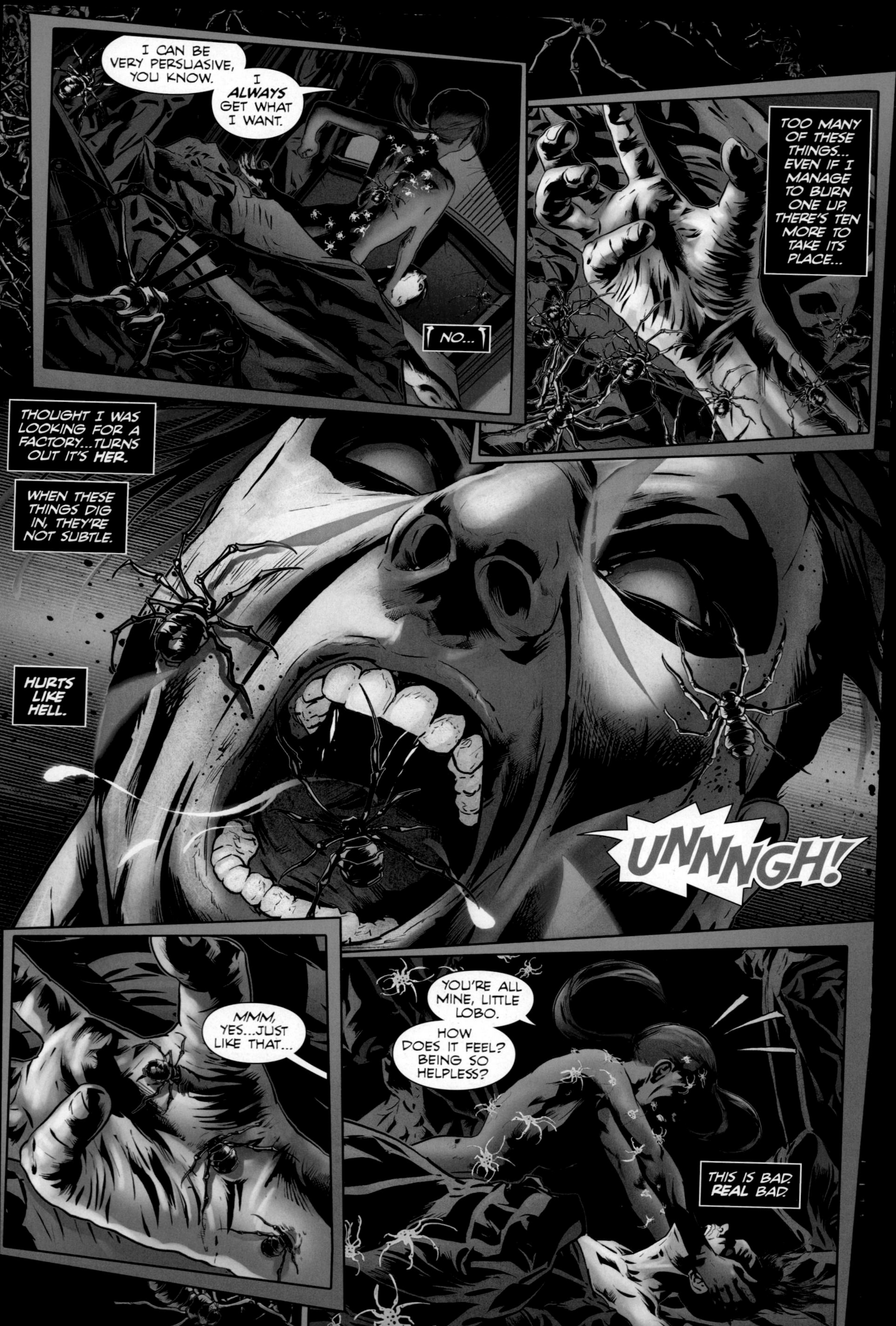
I CAN BE VERY PERSUASIVE, YOU KNOW.
I **ALWAYS** GET WHAT I WANT.
"NO..."
TOO MANY OF THESE THINGS... EVEN IF I MANAGE TO BURN ONE UP, THERE'S TEN MORE TO TAKE ITS PLACE...
THOUGHT I WAS LOOKING FOR A FACTORY...TURNS OUT IT'S **HER**.
WHEN THESE THINGS DIG IN, THEY'RE NOT SUBTLE.
HURTS LIKE HELL.
UNNNGH!
MMM, YES...JUST LIKE THAT...
YOU'RE ALL MINE, LITTLE LOBO.
HOW DOES IT FEEL? BEING SO HELPLESS?
THIS IS BAD. **REAL** BAD.

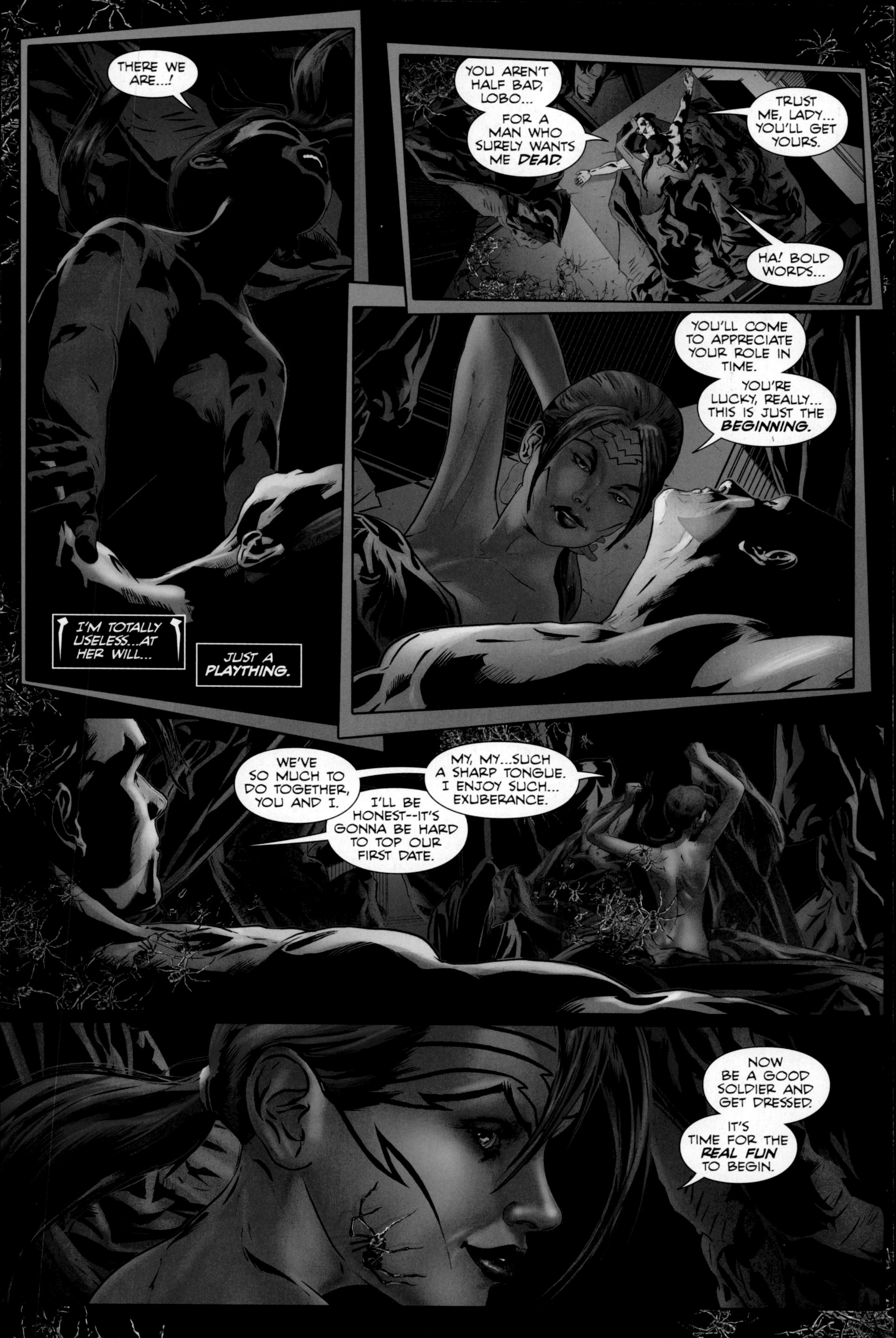
THERE WE ARE...!
YOU AREN'T HALF BAD, LOBO...
FOR A MAN WHO SURELY WANTS ME DEAD.
TRUST ME, LADY... YOU'LL GET YOURS.
HA! BOLD WORDS...
I'M TOTALLY USELESS...AT HER WILL...
JUST A PLAYTHING.
YOU'LL COME TO APPRECIATE YOUR ROLE IN TIME.
YOU'RE LUCKY, REALLY... THIS IS JUST THE BEGINNING.
WE'VE SO MUCH TO DO TOGETHER, YOU AND I.
I'LL BE HONEST--IT'S GONNA BE HARD TO TOP OUR FIRST DATE.
MY, MY...SUCH A SHARP TONGUE. I ENJOY SUCH... EXUBERANCE.
NOW BE A GOOD SOLDIER AND GET DRESSED.
IT'S TIME FOR THE REAL FUN TO BEGIN.

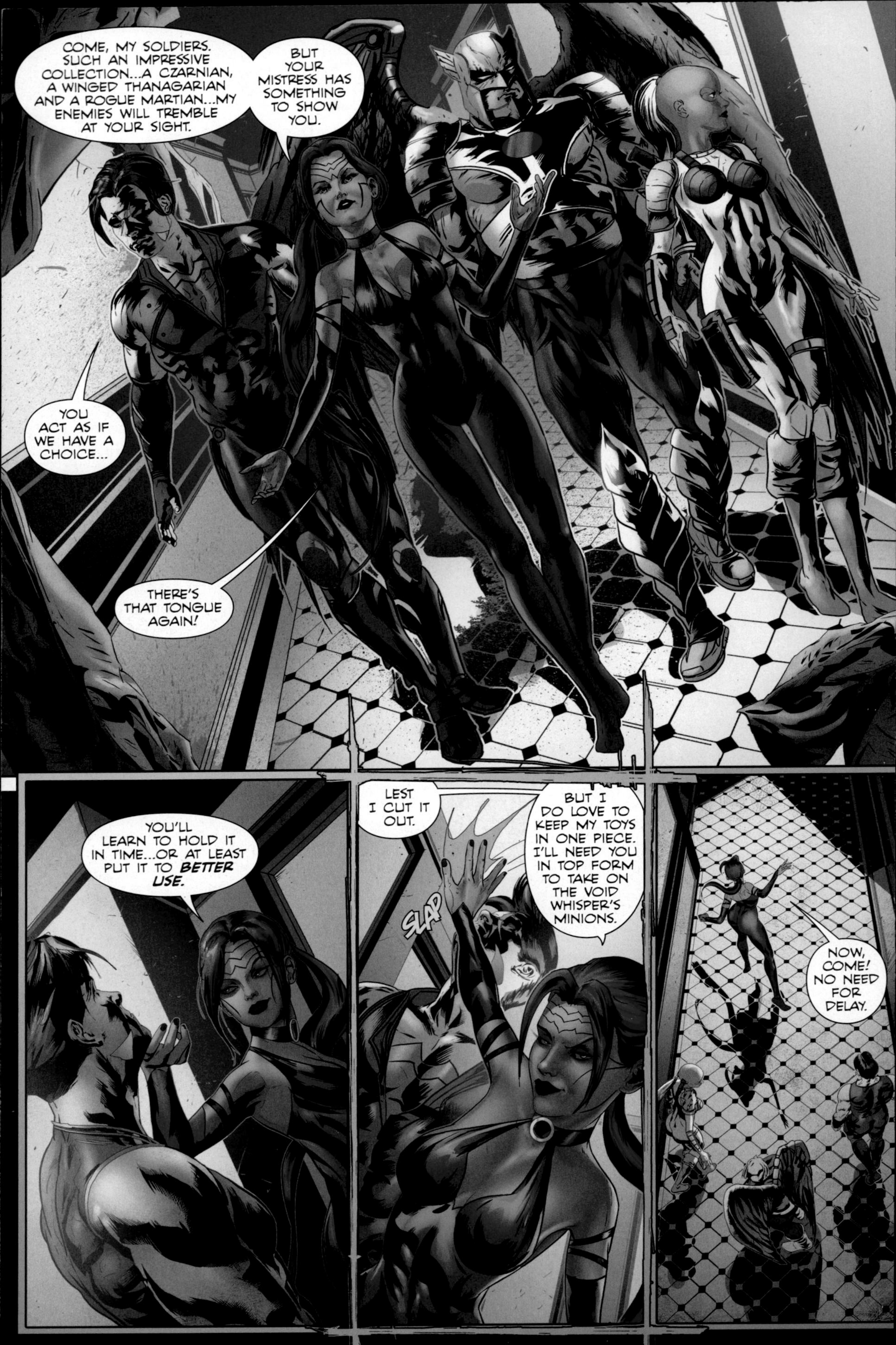
COME, MY SOLDIERS. SUCH AN IMPRESSIVE COLLECTION...A CZARNIAN, A WINGED THANAGARIAN AND A ROGUE MARTIAN...MY ENEMIES WILL TREMBLE AT YOUR SIGHT.
BUT YOUR MISTRESS HAS SOMETHING TO SHOW YOU.
YOU ACT AS IF WE HAVE A CHOICE...
THERE'S THAT TONGUE AGAIN!
YOU'LL LEARN TO HOLD IT IN TIME...OR AT LEAST PUT IT TO BETTER USE.
LEST I CUT IT OUT.
SLAP
BUT I DO LOVE TO KEEP MY TOYS IN ONE PIECE. I'LL NEED YOU IN TOP FORM TO TAKE ON THE VOID WHISPER'S MINIONS.
NOW, COME! NO NEED FOR DELAY.

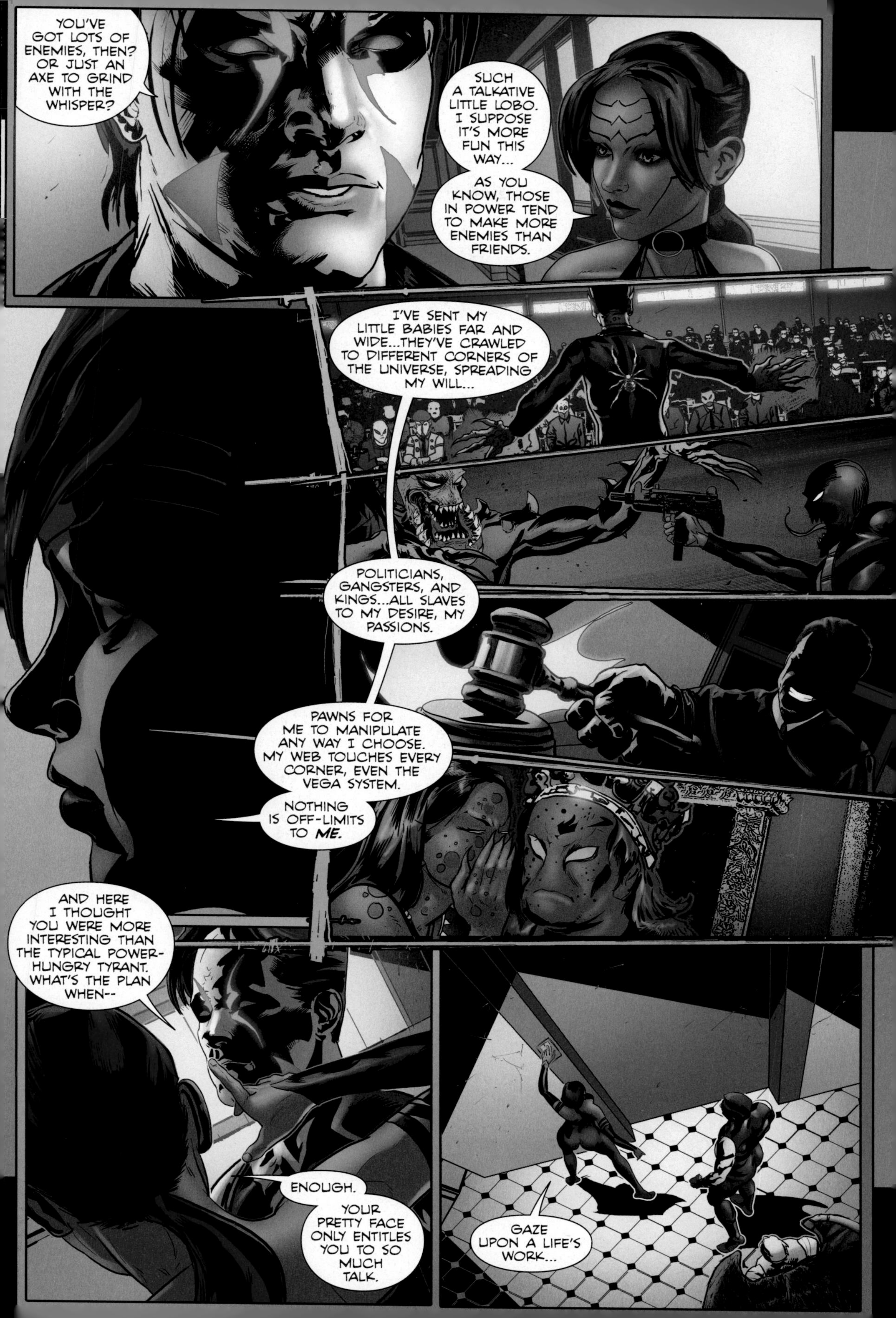
YOU'VE GOT LOTS OF ENEMIES, THEN? OR JUST AN AXE TO GRIND WITH THE WHISPER?
SUCH A TALKATIVE LITTLE LOBO. I SUPPOSE IT'S MORE FUN THIS WAY...
AS YOU KNOW, THOSE IN POWER TEND TO MAKE MORE ENEMIES THAN FRIENDS.
I'VE SENT MY LITTLE BABIES FAR AND WIDE...THEY'VE CRAWLED TO DIFFERENT CORNERS OF THE UNIVERSE, SPREADING MY WILL...
POLITICIANS, GANGSTERS, AND KINGS...ALL SLAVES TO MY DESIRE, MY PASSIONS.
PAWNS FOR ME TO MANIPULATE ANY WAY I CHOOSE. MY WEB TOUCHES EVERY CORNER, EVEN THE VEGA SYSTEM.
NOTHING IS OFF-LIMITS TO ***ME.***
AND HERE I THOUGHT YOU WERE MORE INTERESTING THAN THE TYPICAL POWER-HUNGRY TYRANT. WHAT'S THE PLAN WHEN--
ENOUGH.
YOUR PRETTY FACE ONLY ENTITLES YOU TO SO MUCH TALK.
GAZE UPON A LIFE'S WORK...

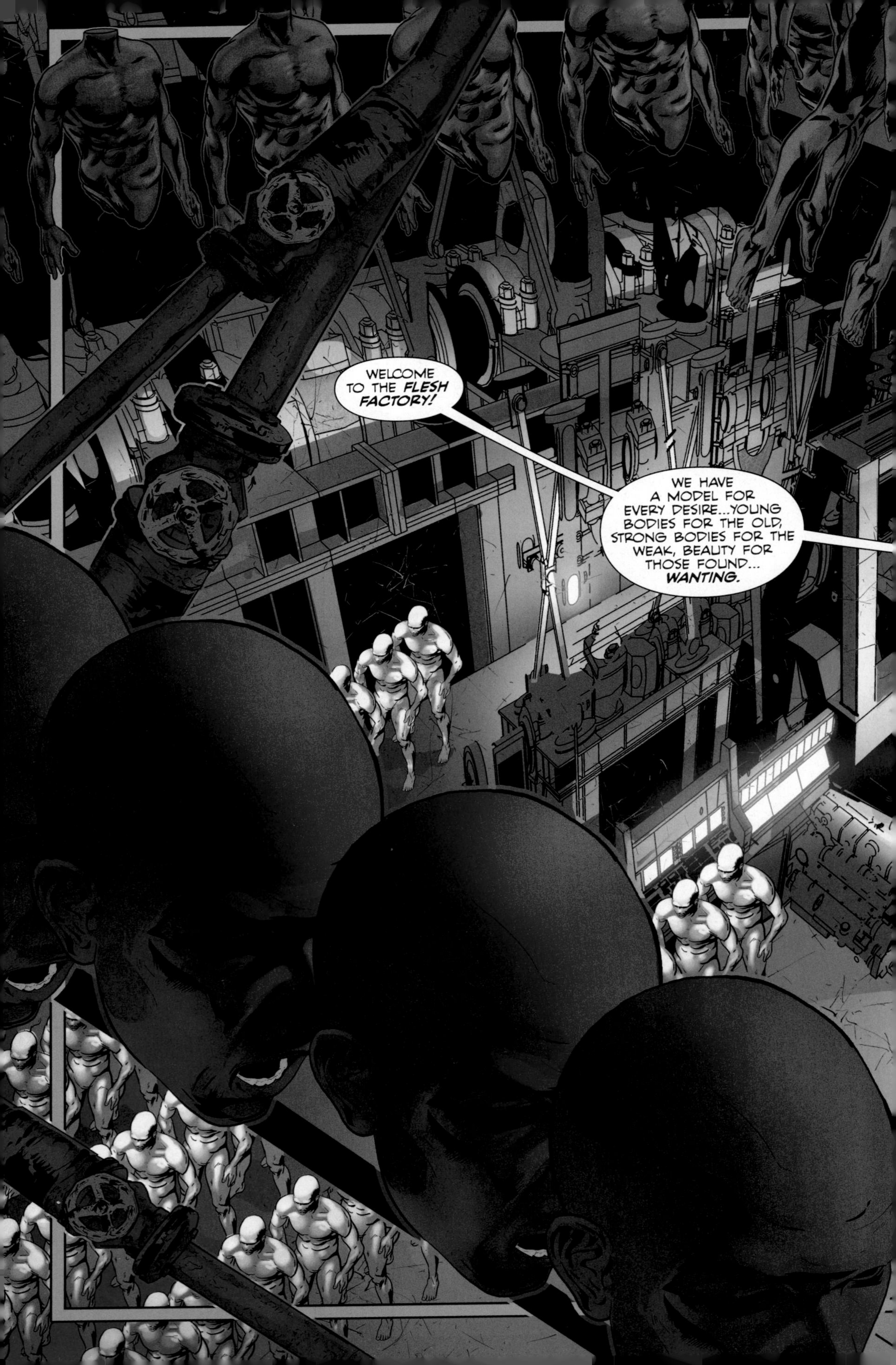
WELCOME TO THE FLESH FACTORY!
WE HAVE A MODEL FOR EVERY DESIRE...YOUNG BODIES FOR THE OLD, STRONG BODIES FOR THE WEAK, BEAUTY FOR THOSE FOUND... WANTING.

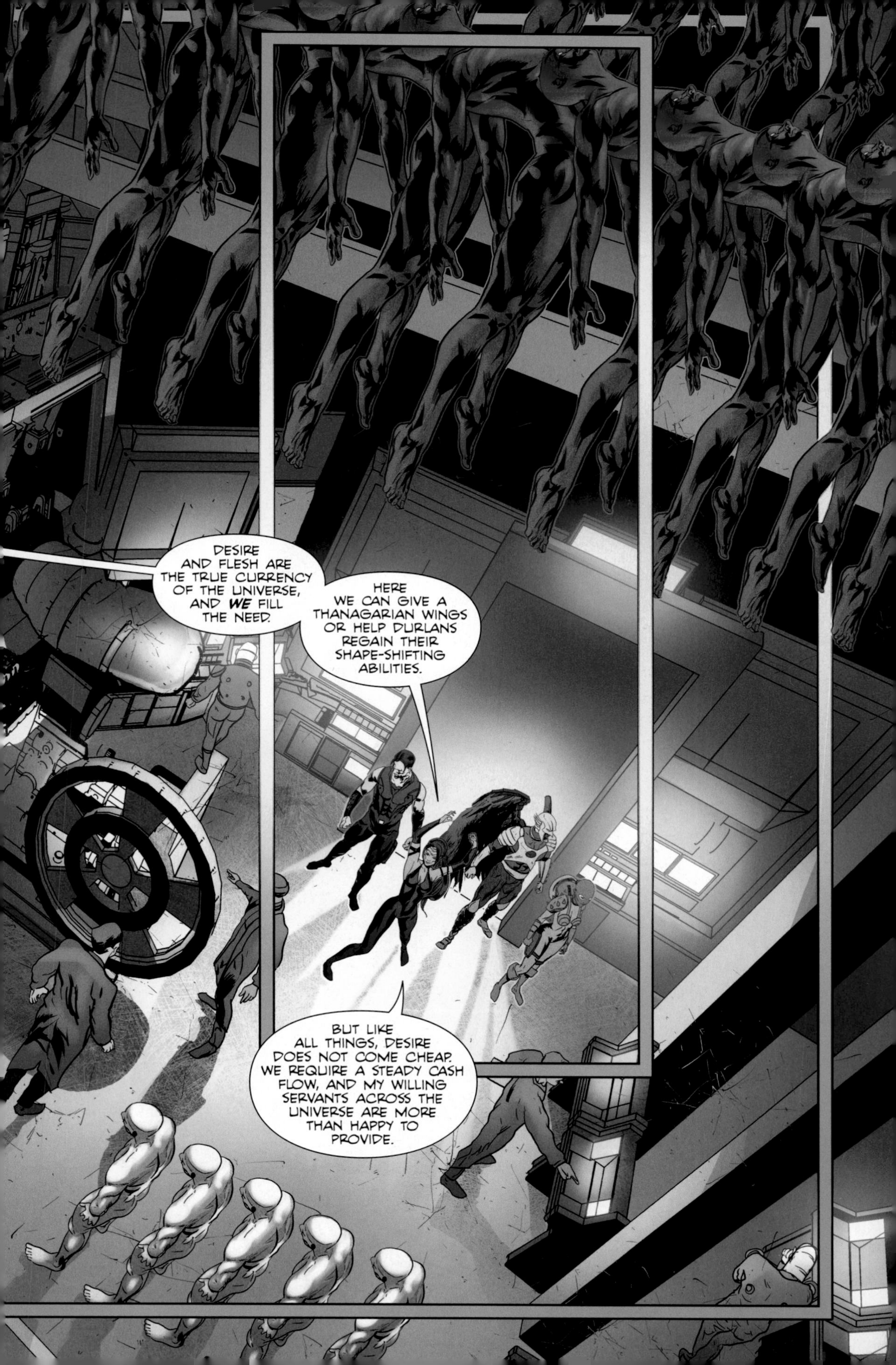
DESIRE AND FLESH ARE THE TRUE CURRENCY OF THE UNIVERSE, AND *WE* FILL THE NEED.
HERE WE CAN GIVE A THANAGARIAN WINGS OR HELP DURLANS REGAIN THEIR SHAPE-SHIFTING ABILITIES.
BUT LIKE ALL THINGS, DESIRE DOES NOT COME CHEAP. WE REQUIRE A STEADY CASH FLOW, AND MY WILLING SERVANTS ACROSS THE UNIVERSE ARE MORE THAN HAPPY TO PROVIDE.

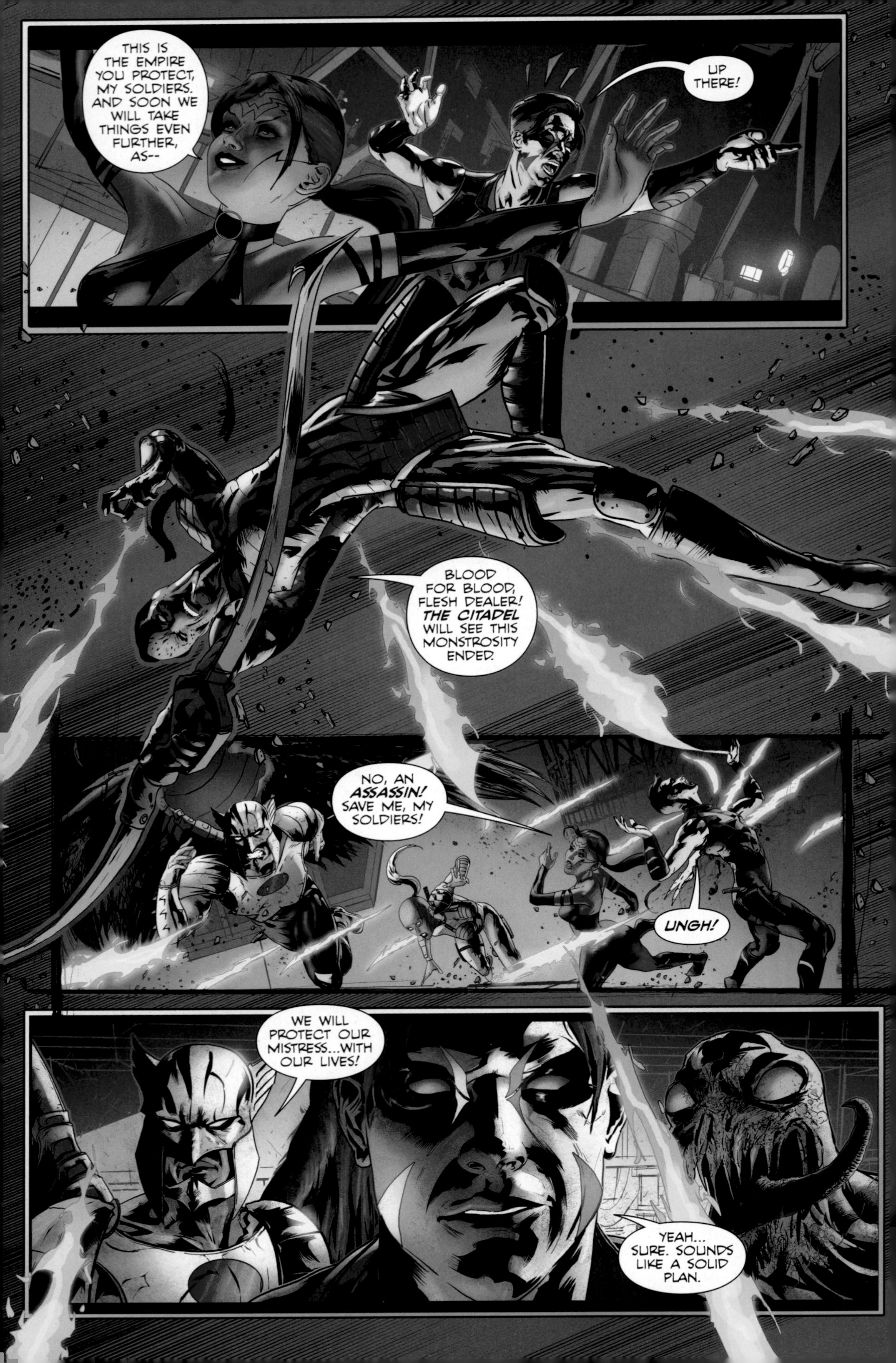
THIS IS THE EMPIRE YOU PROTECT, MY SOLDIERS. AND SOON WE WILL TAKE THINGS EVEN FURTHER, AS--
UP THERE!
BLOOD FOR BLOOD, FLESH DEALER! *THE CITADEL* WILL SEE THIS MONSTROSITY ENDED.
NO, AN *ASSASSIN!* SAVE ME, MY SOLDIERS!
UNGH!
WE WILL PROTECT OUR MISTRESS...WITH OUR LIVES!
YEAH... SURE. SOUNDS LIKE A SOLID PLAN.

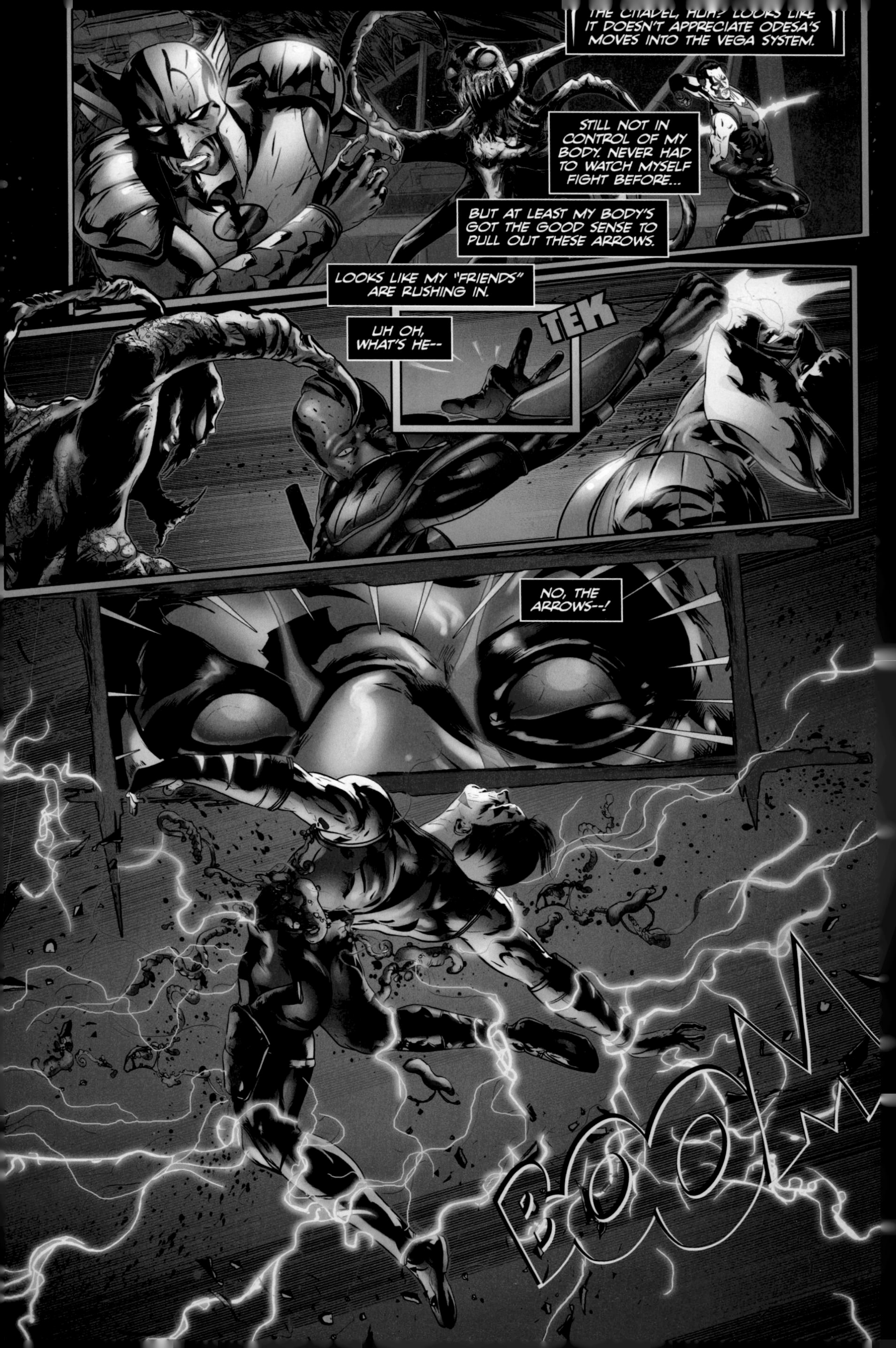
THE CITADEL, HUH? LOOKS LIKE IT DOESN'T APPRECIATE ODESA'S MOVES INTO THE VEGA SYSTEM.
STILL NOT IN CONTROL OF MY BODY. NEVER HAD TO WATCH MYSELF FIGHT BEFORE...
BUT AT LEAST MY BODY'S GOT THE GOOD SENSE TO PULL OUT THESE ARROWS.
LOOKS LIKE MY "FRIENDS" ARE RUSHING IN.
UH OH, WHAT'S HE--
TEK
NO, THE ARROWS--!
BOOOM

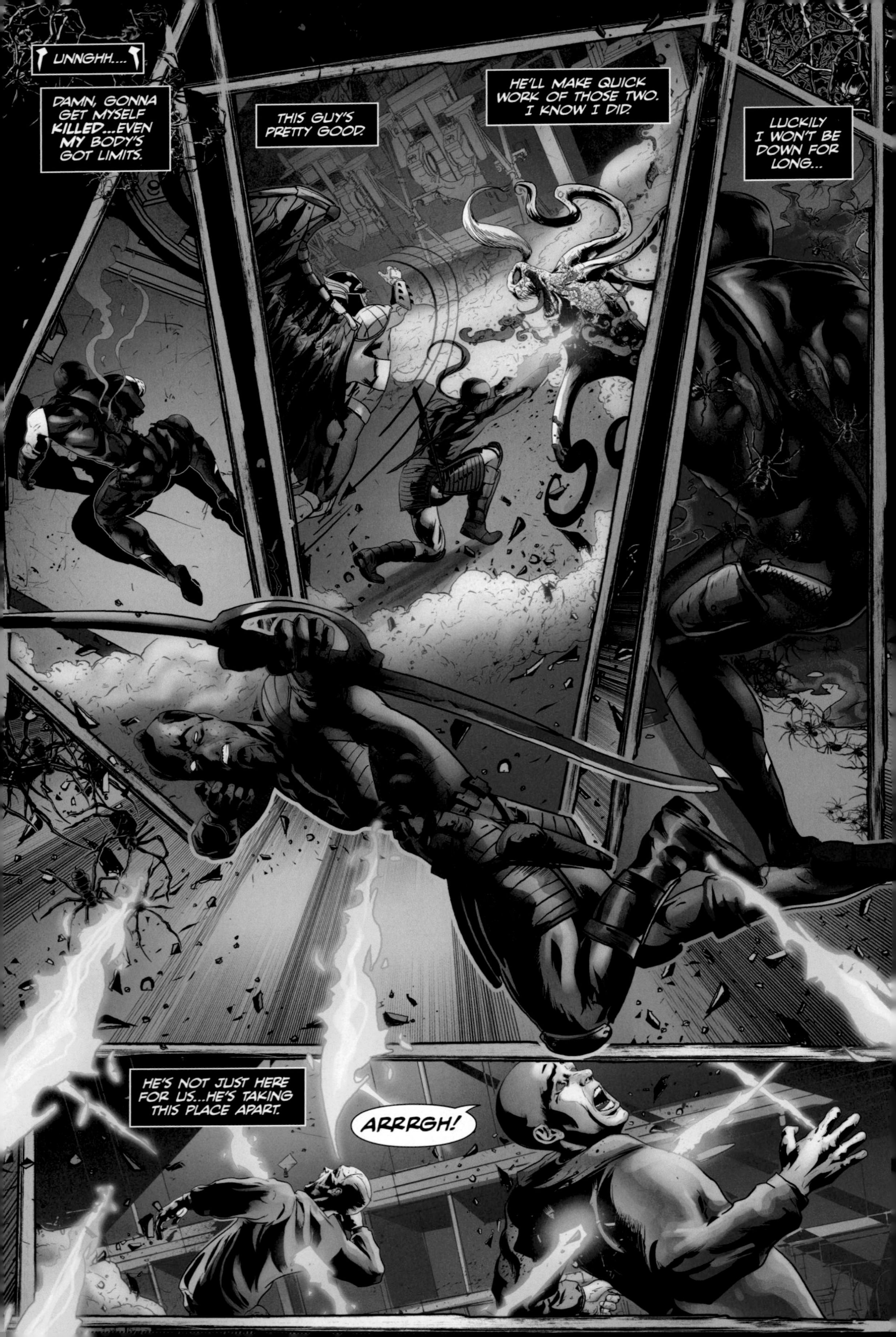
UNNGHH....
DAMN, GONNA GET MYSELF KILLED...EVEN MY BODY'S GOT LIMITS.
THIS GUY'S PRETTY GOOD.
HE'LL MAKE QUICK WORK OF THOSE TWO. I KNOW I DID.
LUCKILY I WON'T BE DOWN FOR LONG...
HE'S NOT JUST HERE FOR US...HE'S TAKING THIS PLACE APART.
ARRRGH!

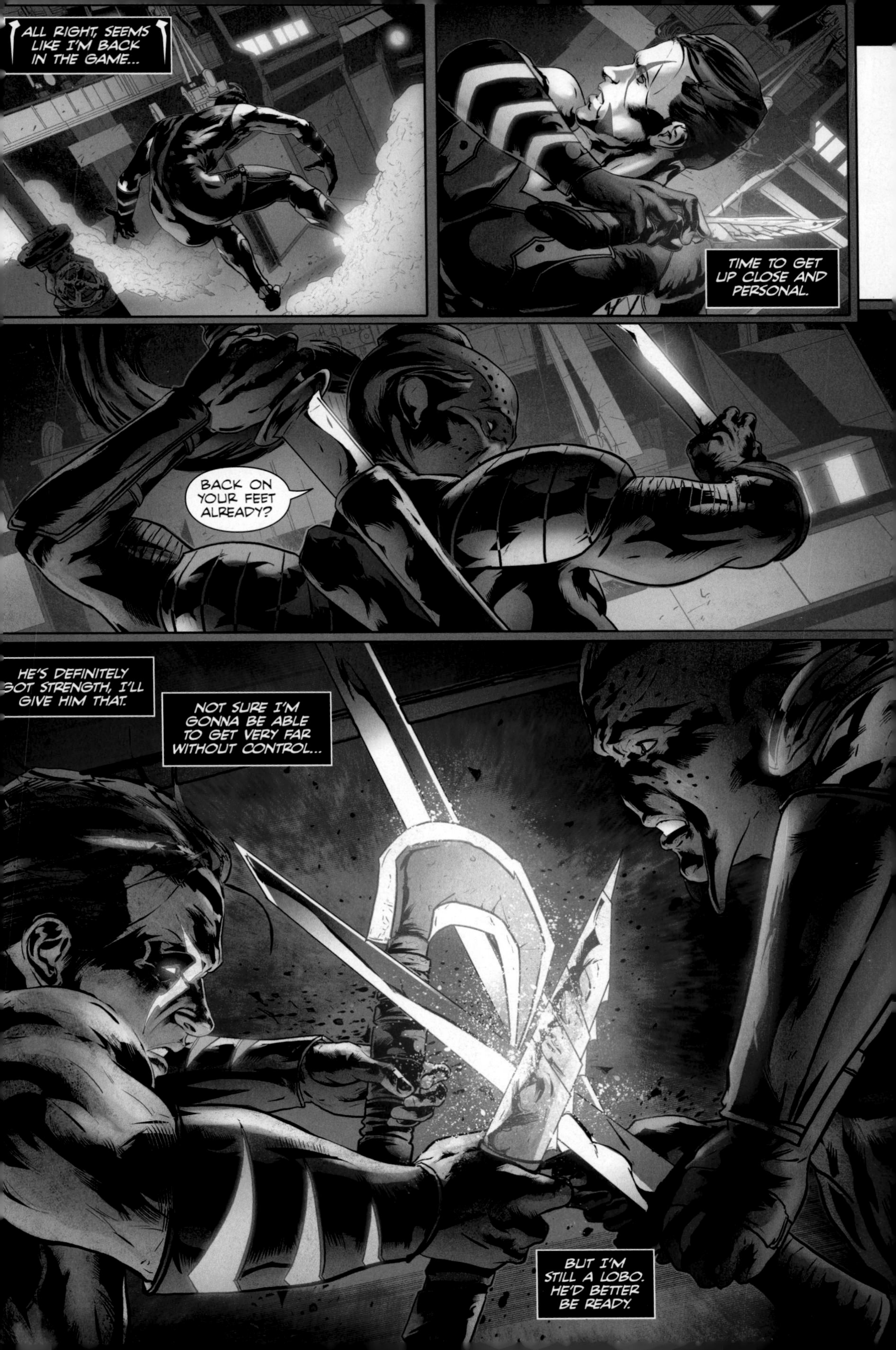
ALL RIGHT, SEEMS LIKE I'M BACK IN THE GAME...
TIME TO GET UP CLOSE AND PERSONAL.
BACK ON YOUR FEET ALREADY?
HE'S DEFINITELY GOT STRENGTH, I'LL GIVE HIM THAT.
NOT SURE I'M GONNA BE ABLE TO GET VERY FAR WITHOUT CONTROL...
BUT I'M STILL A LOBO. HE'D BETTER BE READY.

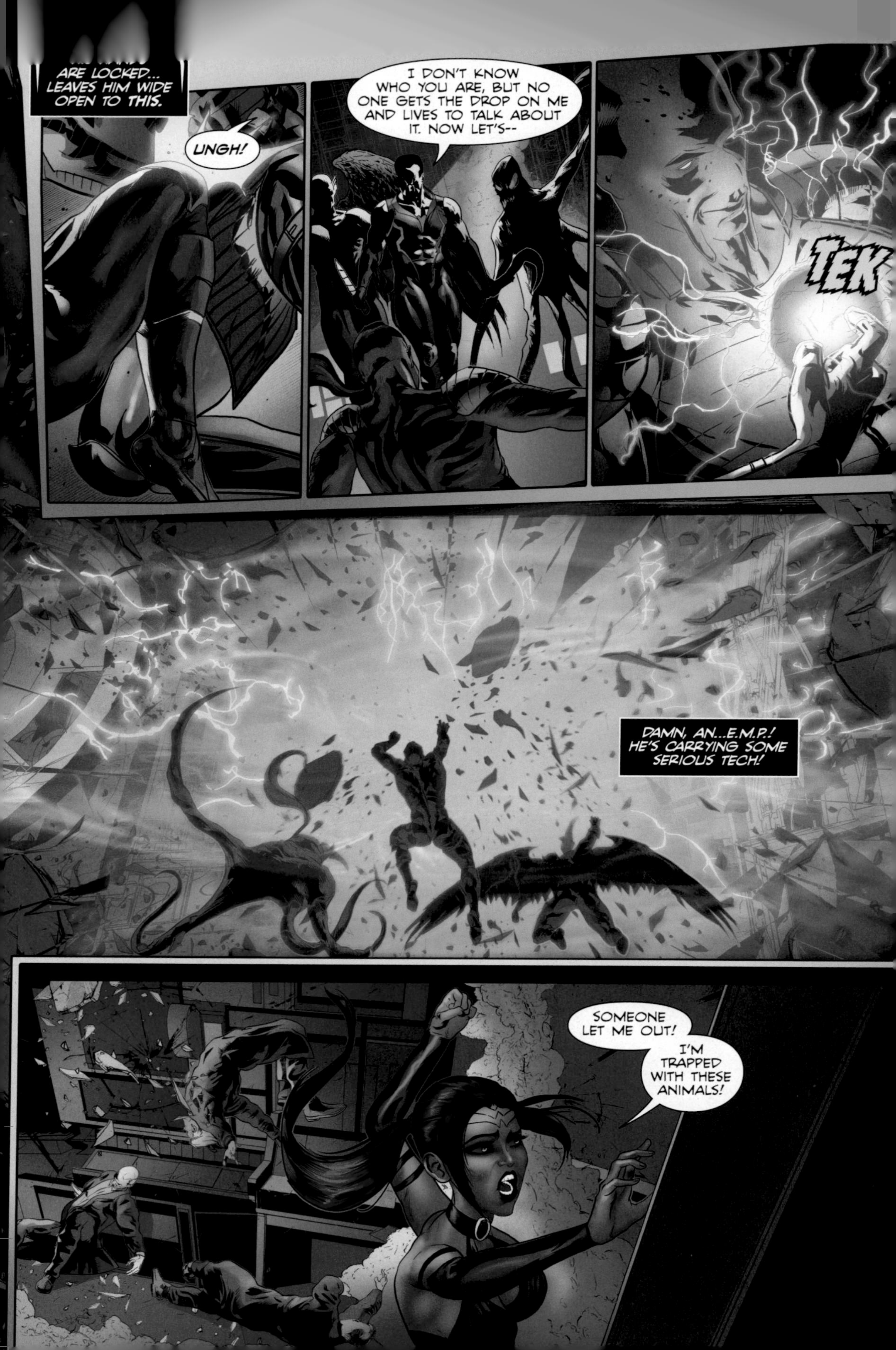
ARE LOCKED... LEAVES HIM WIDE OPEN TO THIS.
UNGH!
I DON'T KNOW WHO YOU ARE, BUT NO ONE GETS THE DROP ON ME AND LIVES TO TALK ABOUT IT. NOW LET'S--
TEK
DAMN, AN...E.M.P.! HE'S CARRYING SOME SERIOUS TECH!
SOMEONE LET ME OUT!
I'M TRAPPED WITH THESE ANIMALS!

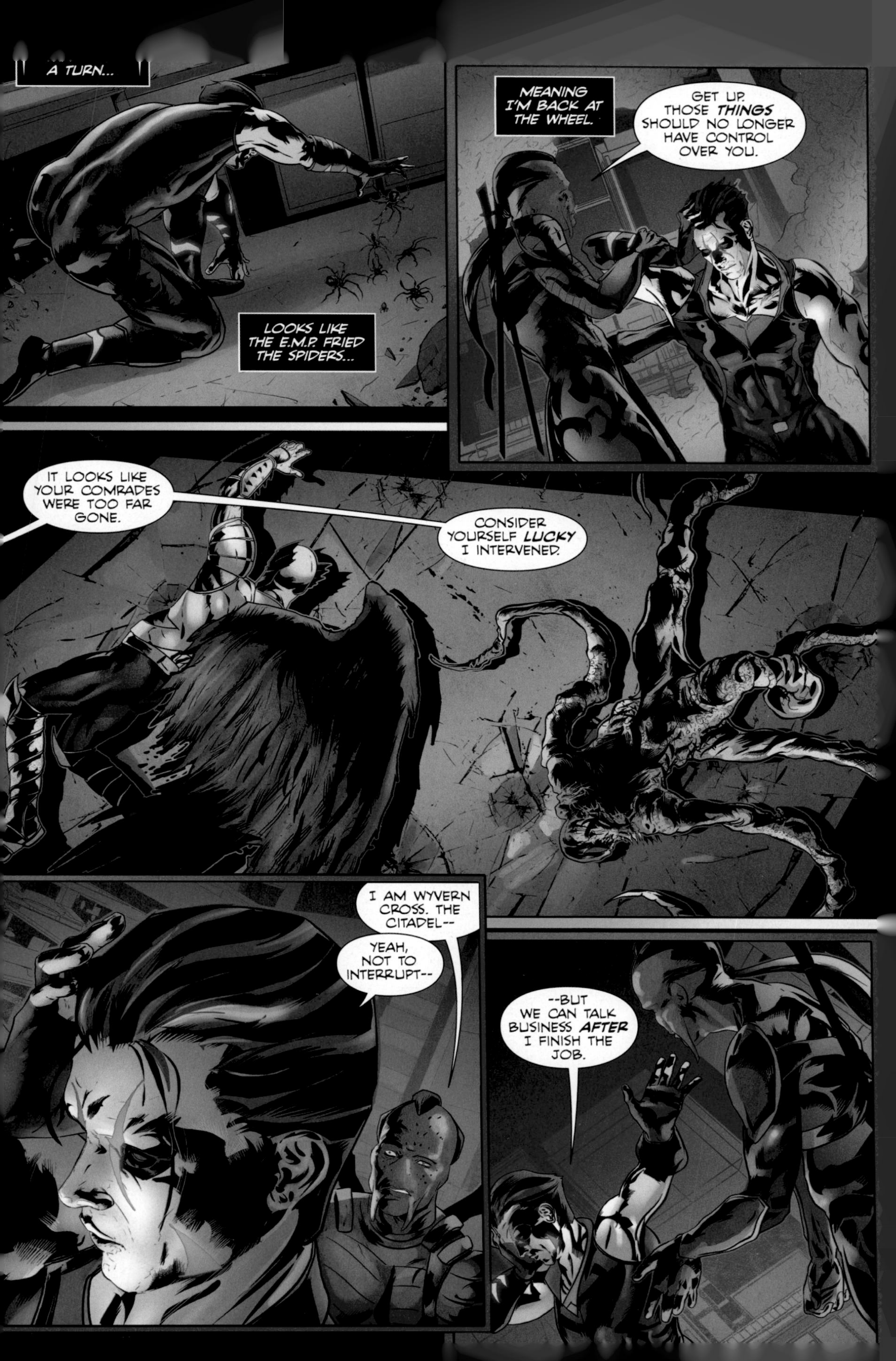
A TURN...
LOOKS LIKE THE E.M.P. FRIED THE SPIDERS...
MEANING I'M BACK AT THE WHEEL.
GET UP. THOSE THINGS SHOULD NO LONGER HAVE CONTROL OVER YOU.
IT LOOKS LIKE YOUR COMRADES WERE TOO FAR GONE.
CONSIDER YOURSELF LUCKY I INTERVENED.
I AM WYVERN CROSS. THE CITADEL--
YEAH, NOT TO INTERRUPT--
--BUT WE CAN TALK BUSINESS AFTER I FINISH THE JOB.

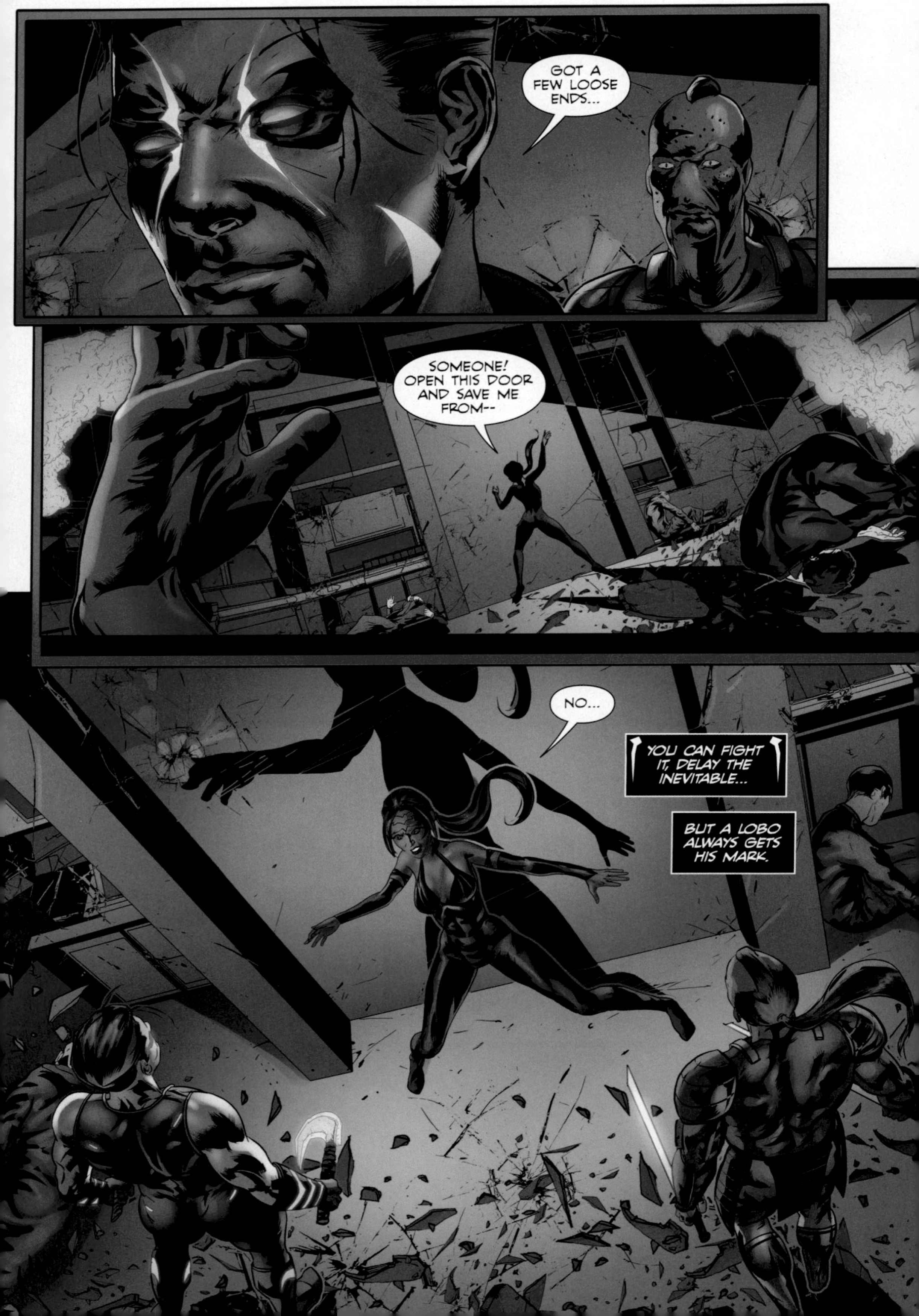
GOT A FEW LOOSE ENDS...
SOMEONE! OPEN THIS DOOR AND SAVE ME FROM--
NO...
YOU CAN FIGHT IT, DELAY THE INEVITABLE...
BUT A LOBO ALWAYS GETS HIS MARK.

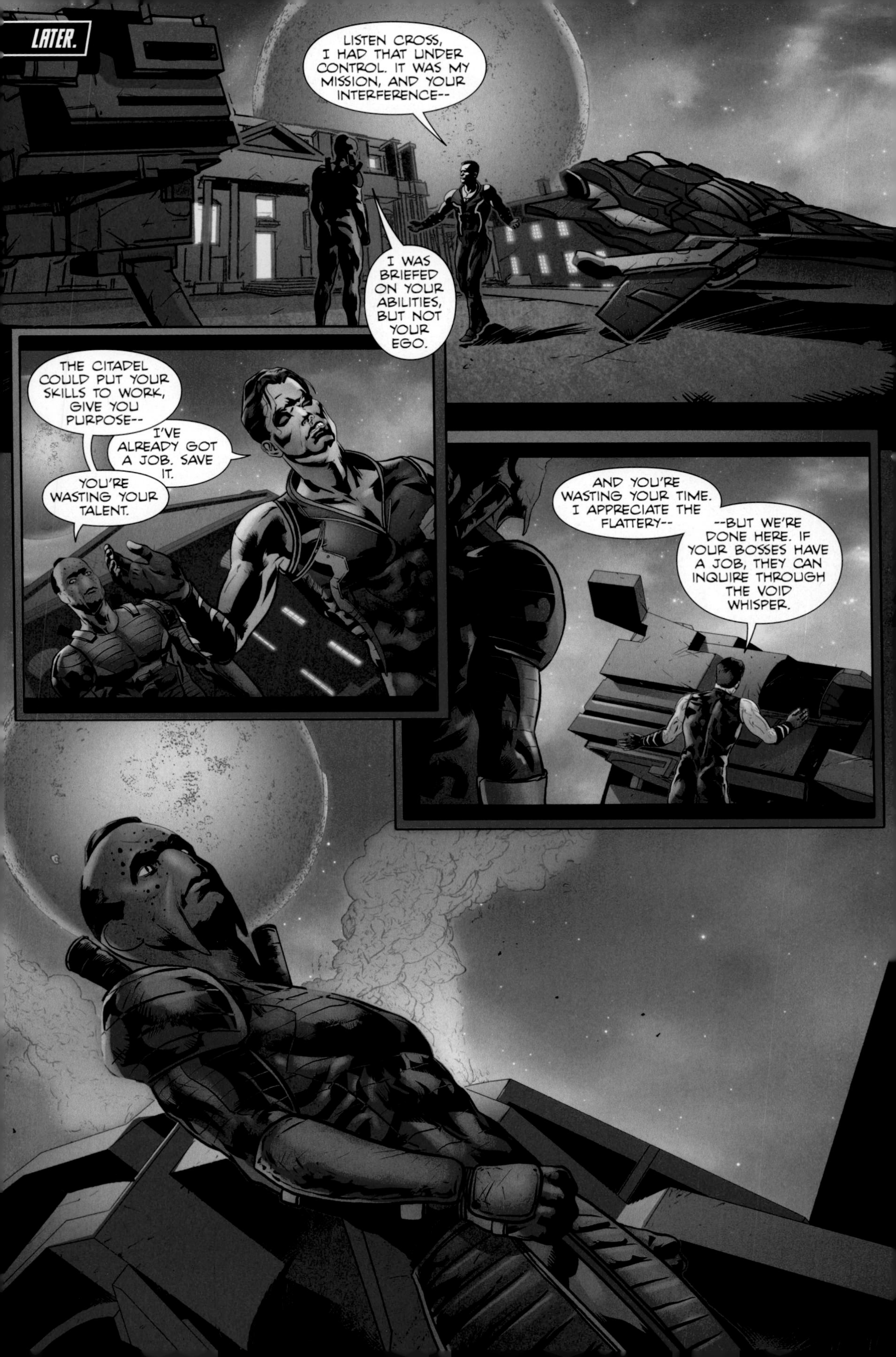
LATER.
LISTEN CROSS, I HAD THAT UNDER CONTROL. IT WAS MY MISSION, AND YOUR INTERFERENCE--
I WAS BRIEFED ON YOUR ABILITIES, BUT NOT YOUR EGO.
THE CITADEL COULD PUT YOUR SKILLS TO WORK, GIVE YOU PURPOSE--
I'VE ALREADY GOT A JOB. SAVE IT.
YOU'RE WASTING YOUR TALENT.
AND YOU'RE WASTING YOUR TIME. I APPRECIATE THE FLATTERY--
--BUT WE'RE DONE HERE. IF YOUR BOSSES HAVE A JOB, THEY CAN INQUIRE THROUGH THE VOID WHISPER.

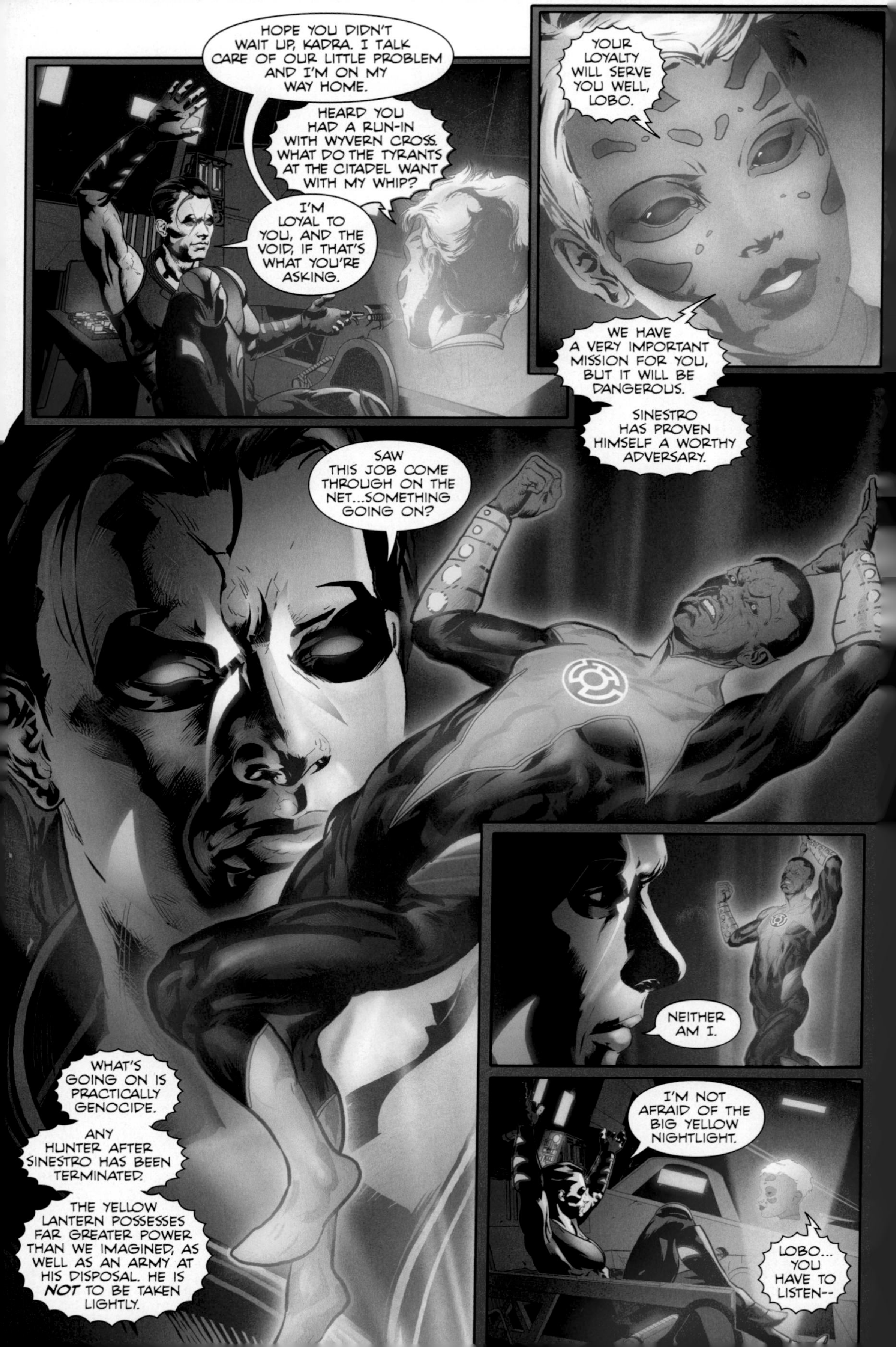
HOPE YOU DIDN'T WAIT UP, KADRA. I TALK CARE OF OUR LITTLE PROBLEM AND I'M ON MY WAY HOME.
HEARD YOU HAD A RUN-IN WITH WYVERN CROSS. WHAT DO THE TYRANTS AT THE CITADEL WANT WITH MY WHIP?
I'M LOYAL TO YOU, AND THE VOID, IF THAT'S WHAT YOU'RE ASKING.
YOUR LOYALTY WILL SERVE YOU WELL, LOBO.
WE HAVE A VERY IMPORTANT MISSION FOR YOU, BUT IT WILL BE DANGEROUS.
SINESTRO HAS PROVEN HIMSELF A WORTHY ADVERSARY.
SAW THIS JOB COME THROUGH ON THE NET...SOMETHING GOING ON?
WHAT'S GOING ON IS PRACTICALLY GENOCIDE.
ANY HUNTER AFTER SINESTRO HAS BEEN TERMINATED.
THE YELLOW LANTERN POSSESSES FAR GREATER POWER THAN WE IMAGINED, AS WELL AS AN ARMY AT HIS DISPOSAL. HE IS NOT TO BE TAKEN LIGHTLY.
NEITHER AM I.
I'M NOT AFRAID OF THE BIG YELLOW NIGHTLIGHT.
LOBO... YOU HAVE TO LISTEN--

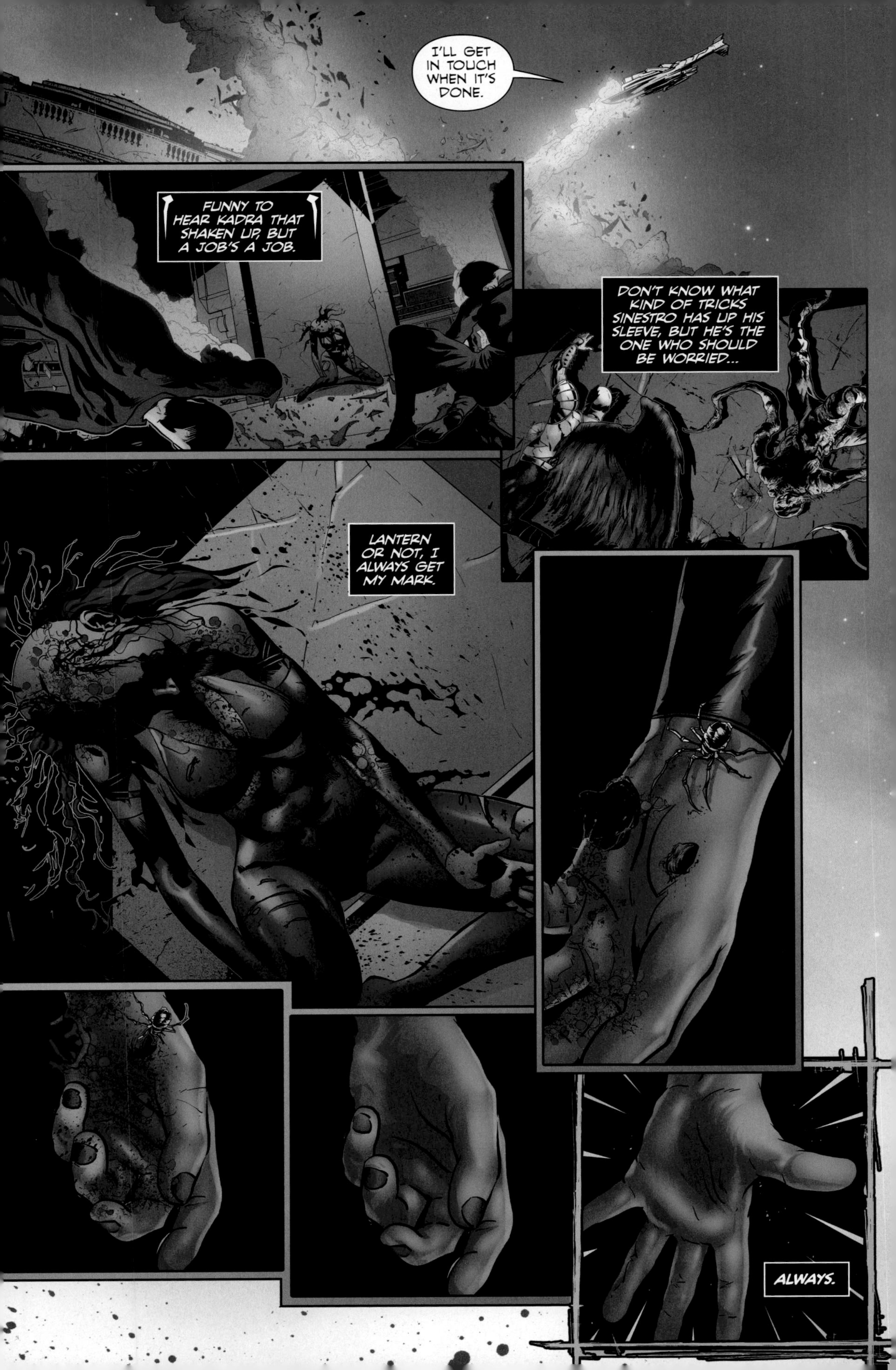
I'LL GET IN TOUCH WHEN IT'S DONE.
FUNNY TO HEAR KADRA THAT SHAKEN UP, BUT A JOB'S A JOB.
DON'T KNOW WHAT KIND OF TRICKS SINESTRO HAS UP HIS SLEEVE, BUT HE'S THE ONE WHO SHOULD BE WORRIED...
LANTERN OR NOT, I ALWAYS GET MY MARK.
ALWAYS.

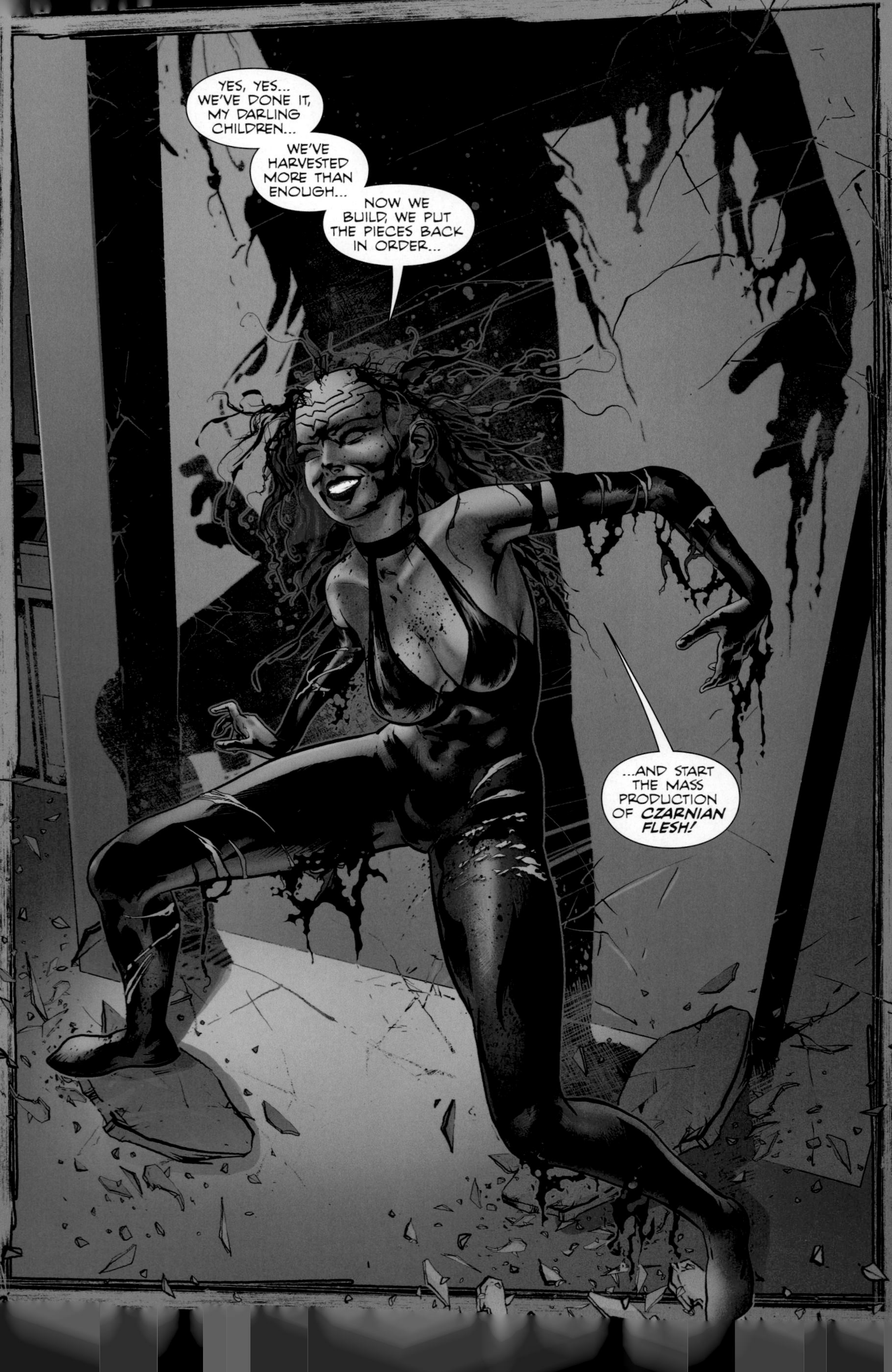
YES, YES... WE'VE DONE IT, MY DARLING CHILDREN...
WE'VE HARVESTED MORE THAN ENOUGH...
NOW WE BUILD, WE PUT THE PIECES BACK IN ORDER...
...AND START THE MASS PRODUCTION OF *CZARNIAN FLESH!*

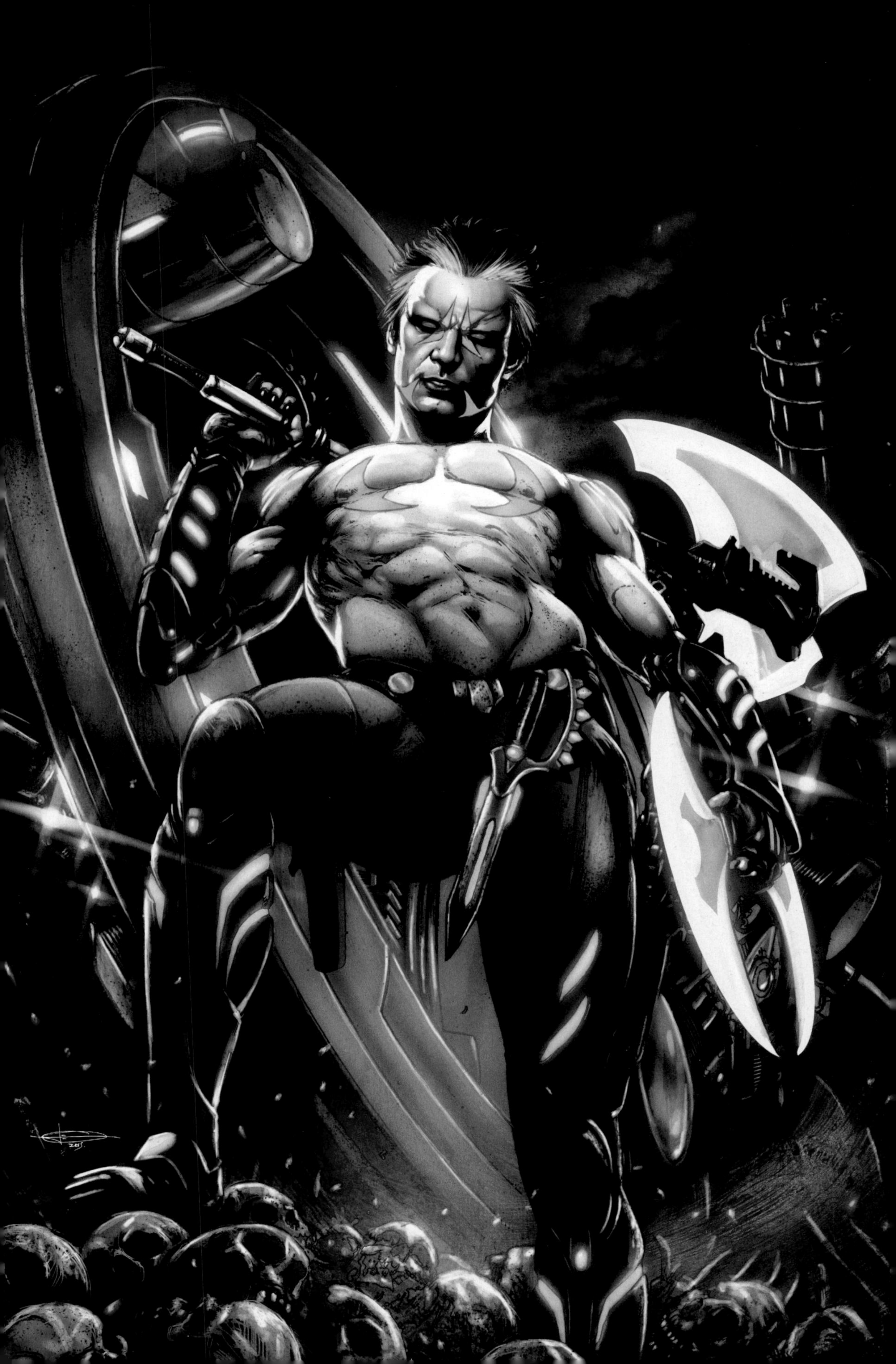

BEWARE HIS MIGHT

CULLEN BUNN writer **ROBSON ROCHA** penciller **GUILLERMO ORTEGO** inker **BLOND** colorist **TRAVIS LANHAM** letterer cover art by **LEONARDO MANCO**

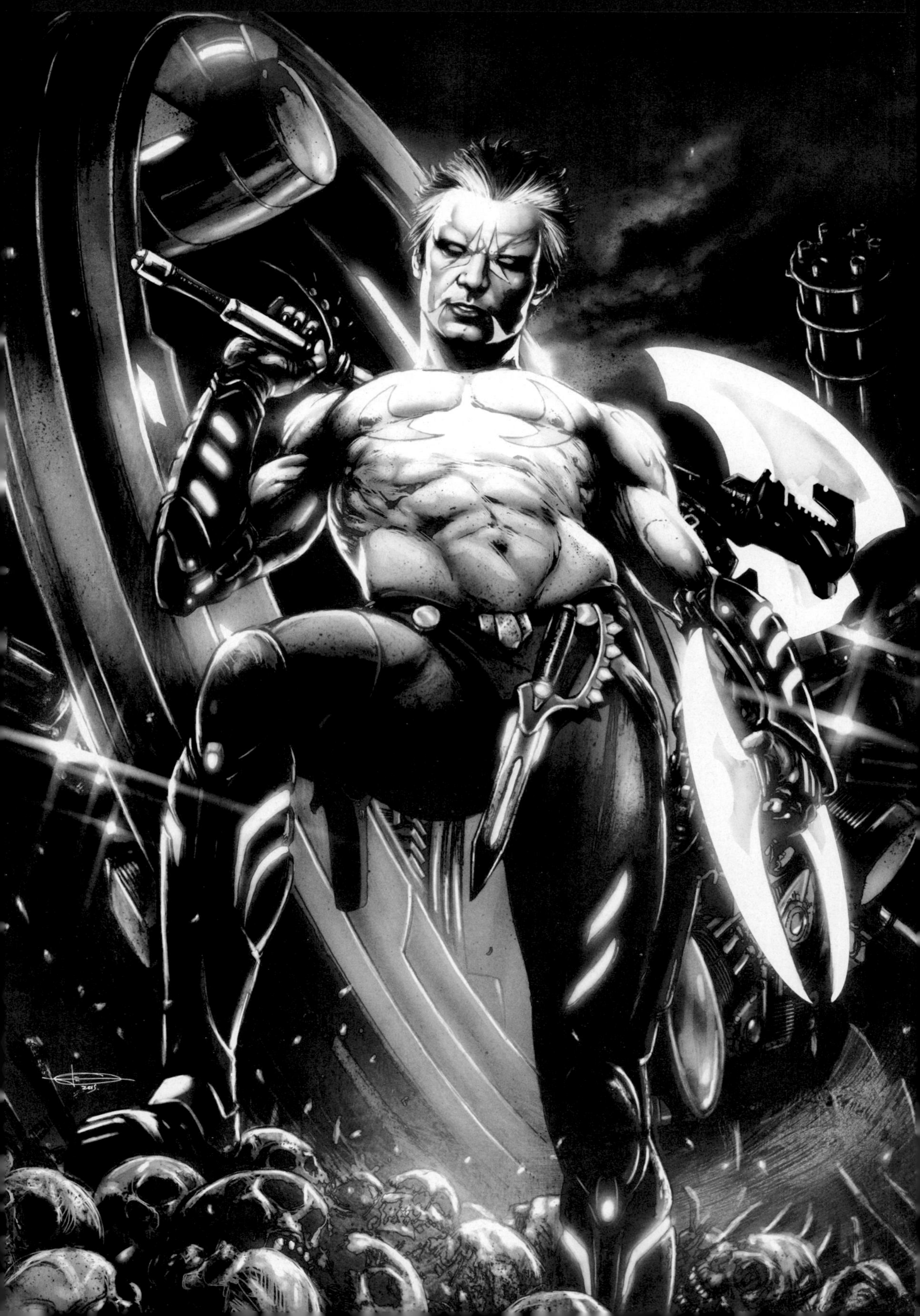

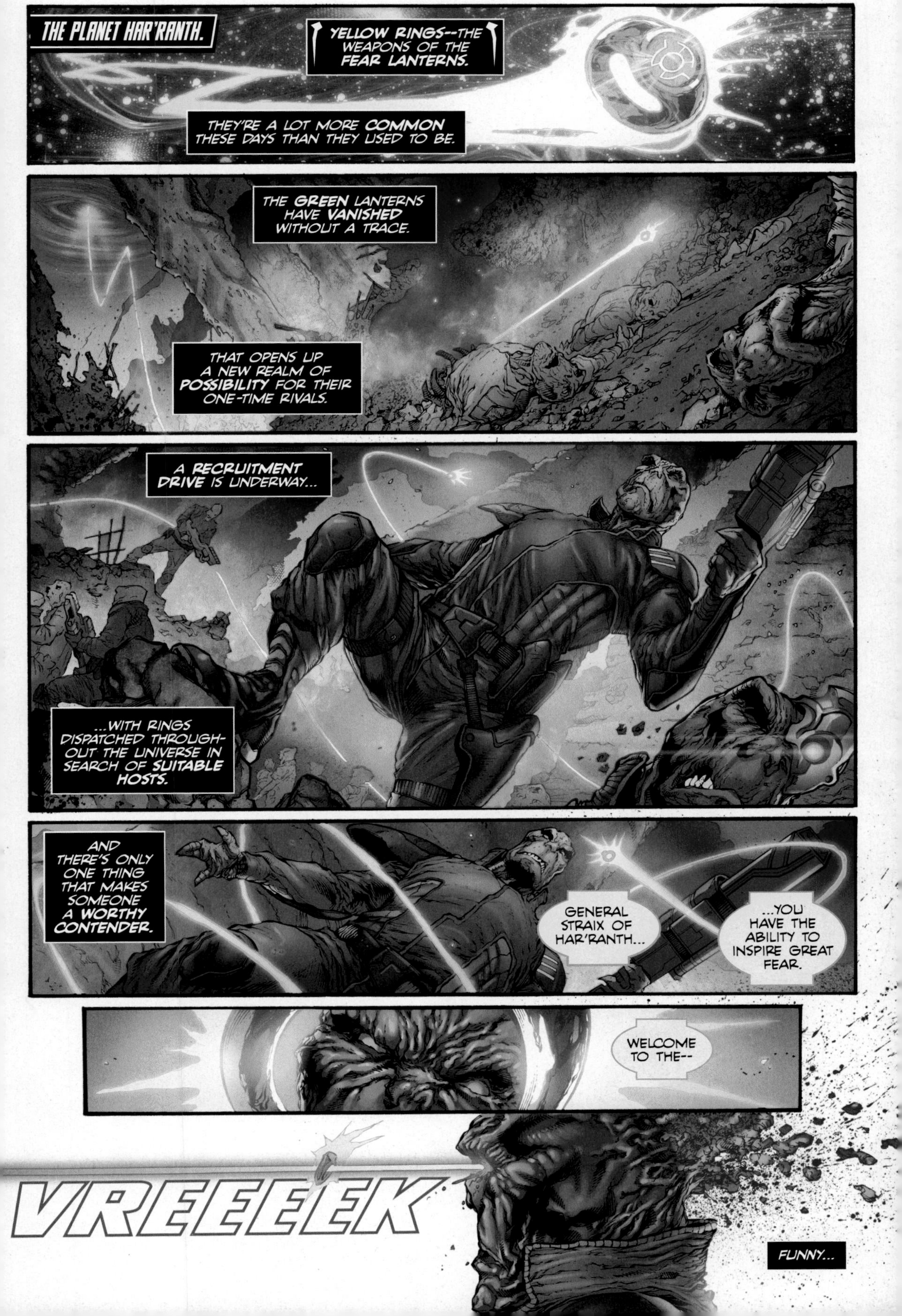
THE PLANET HAR'RANTH.
YELLOW RINGS--THE WEAPONS OF THE FEAR LANTERNS.
THEY'RE A LOT MORE COMMON THESE DAYS THAN THEY USED TO BE.
THE GREEN LANTERNS HAVE VANISHED WITHOUT A TRACE.
THAT OPENS UP A NEW REALM OF POSSIBILITY FOR THEIR ONE-TIME RIVALS.
A RECRUITMENT DRIVE IS UNDERWAY...
...WITH RINGS DISPATCHED THROUGH-OUT THE UNIVERSE IN SEARCH OF SUITABLE HOSTS.
AND THERE'S ONLY ONE THING THAT MAKES SOMEONE A WORTHY CONTENDER.
GENERAL STRAIX OF HAR'RANTH...
...YOU HAVE THE ABILITY TO INSPIRE GREAT FEAR.
WELCOME TO THE--
VREEEEK
FUNNY...

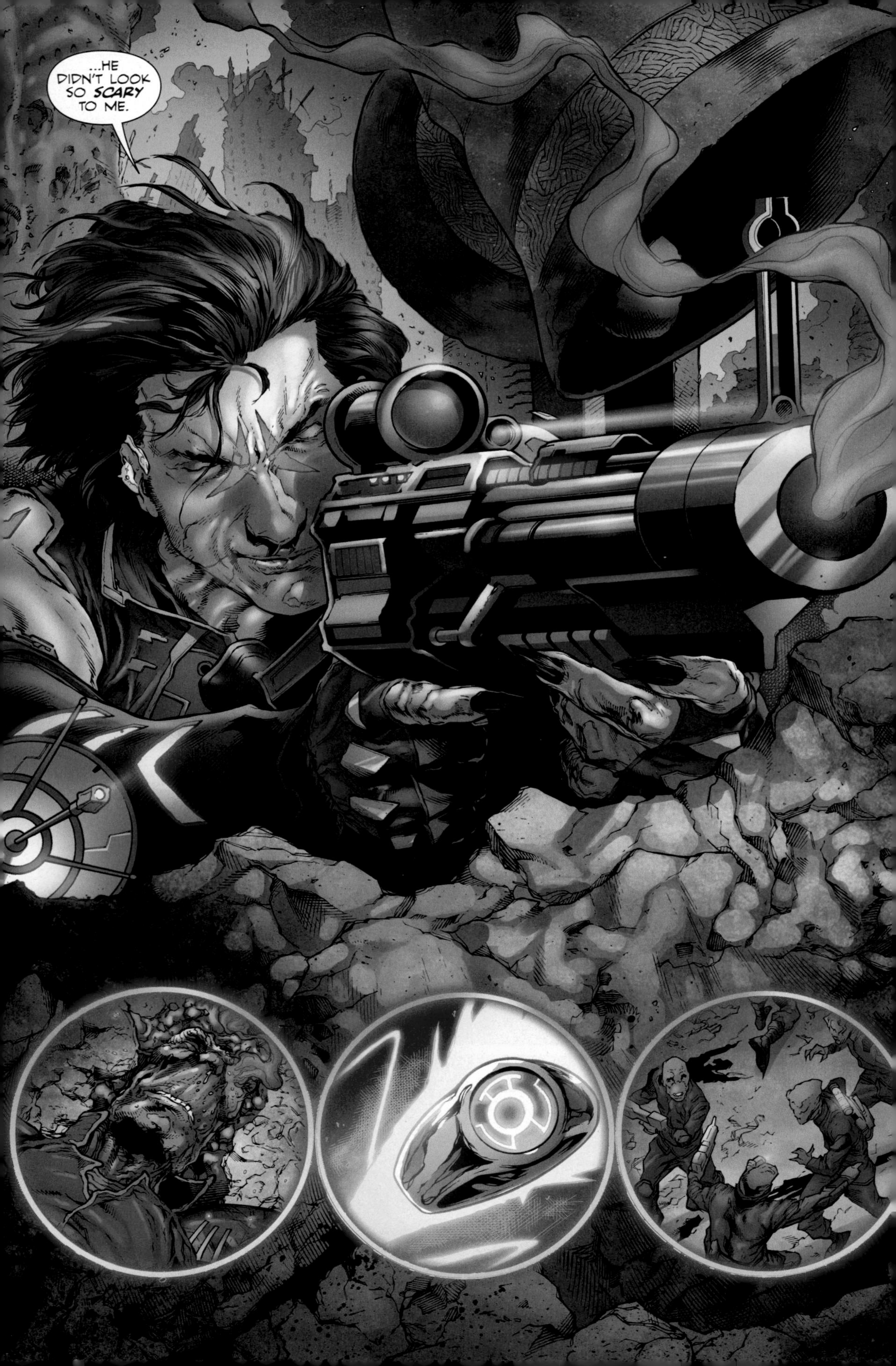
...HE DIDN'T LOOK SO SCARY TO ME.

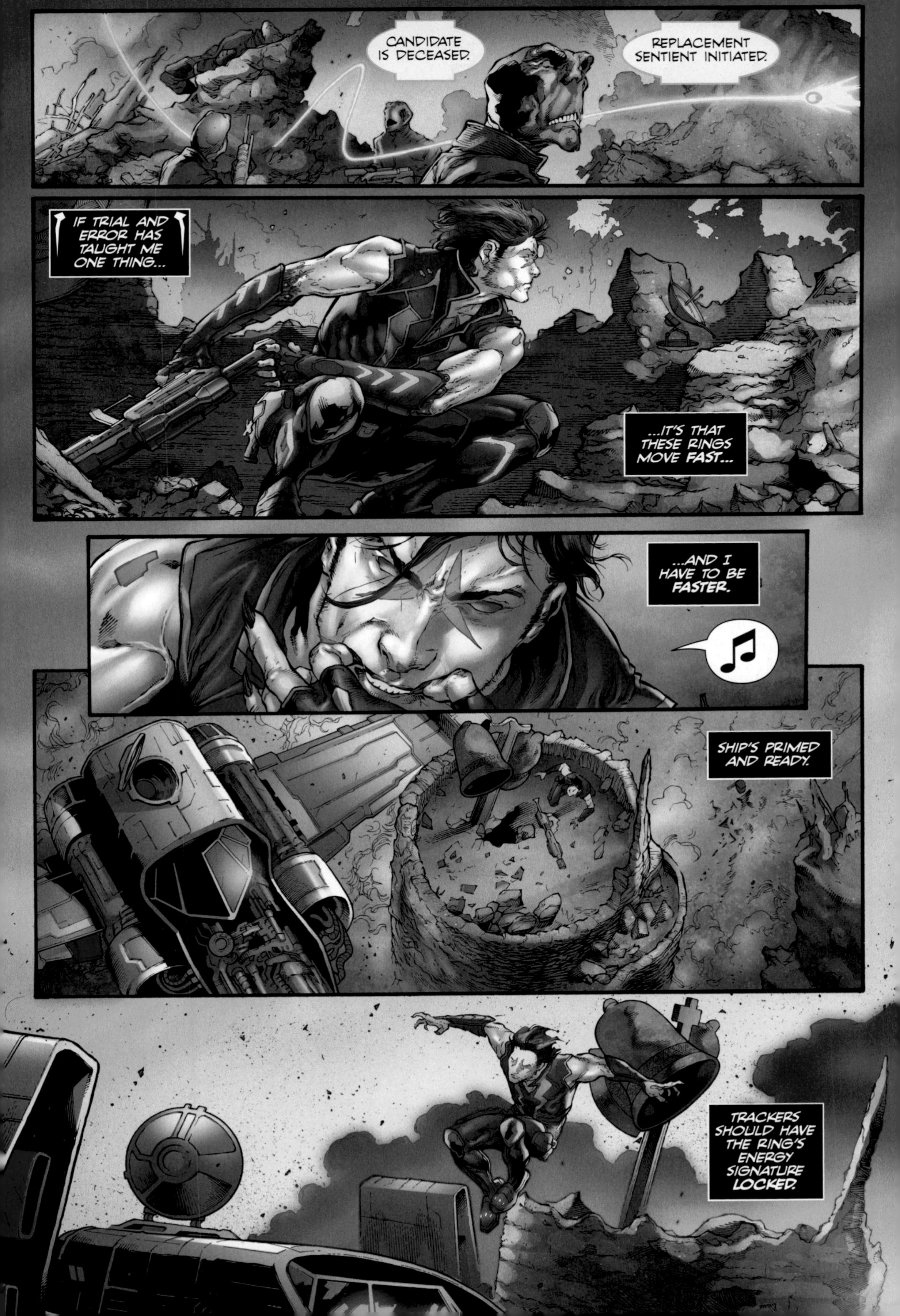
CANDIDATE IS DECEASED.
REPLACEMENT SENTIENT INITIATED.
IF TRIAL AND ERROR HAS TAUGHT ME ONE THING...
...IT'S THAT THESE RINGS MOVE FAST...
...AND I HAVE TO BE FASTER.
SHIP'S PRIMED AND READY.
TRACKERS SHOULD HAVE THE RING'S ENERGY SIGNATURE LOCKED.

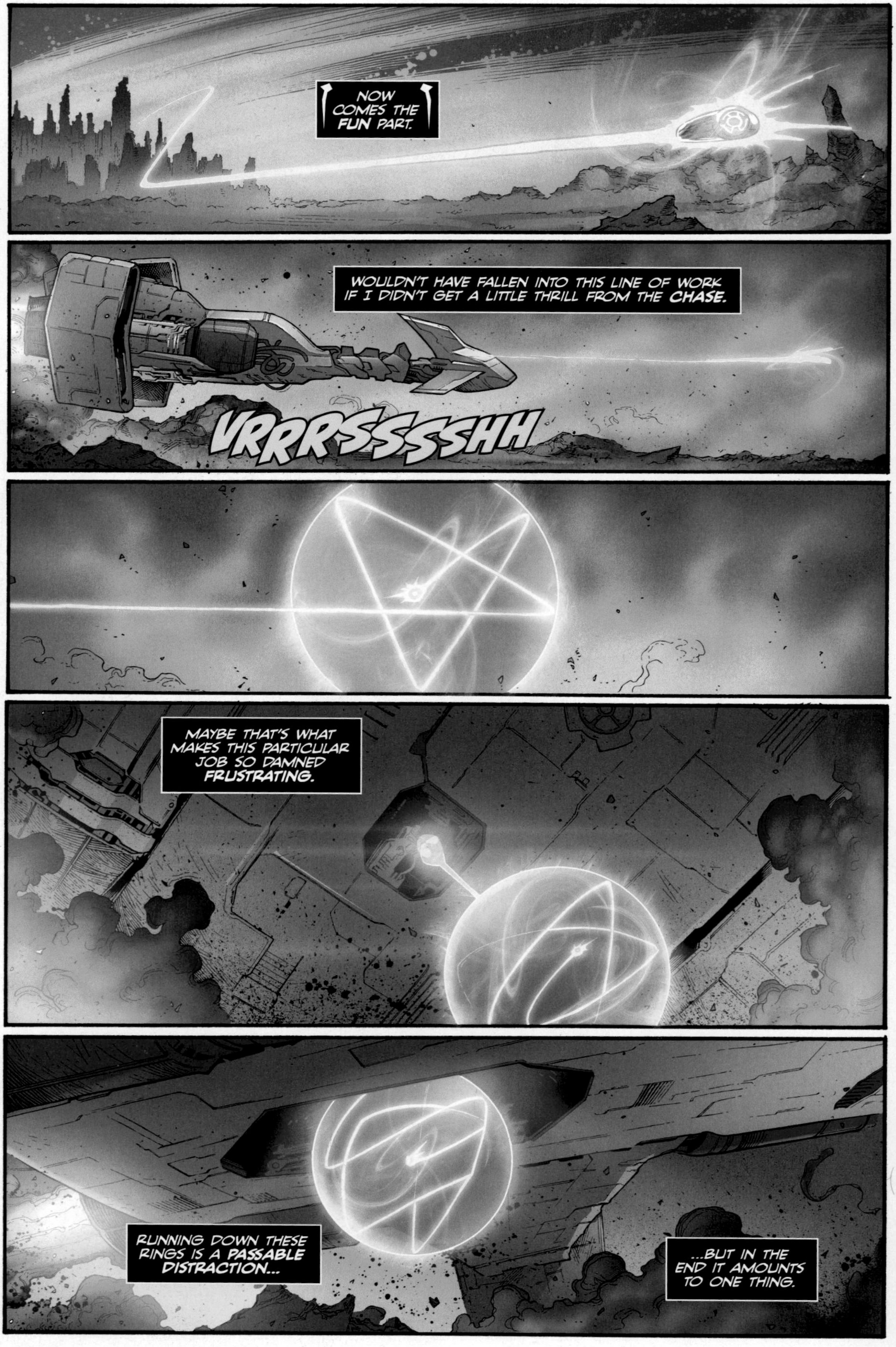
NOW COMES THE FUN PART.
WOULDN'T HAVE FALLEN INTO THIS LINE OF WORK IF I DIDN'T GET A LITTLE THRILL FROM THE CHASE.
VRRRSSSSSHH
MAYBE THAT'S WHAT MAKES THIS PARTICULAR JOB SO DAMNED FRUSTRATING.
RUNNING DOWN THESE RINGS IS A PASSABLE DISTRACTION...
...BUT IN THE END IT AMOUNTS TO ONE THING.

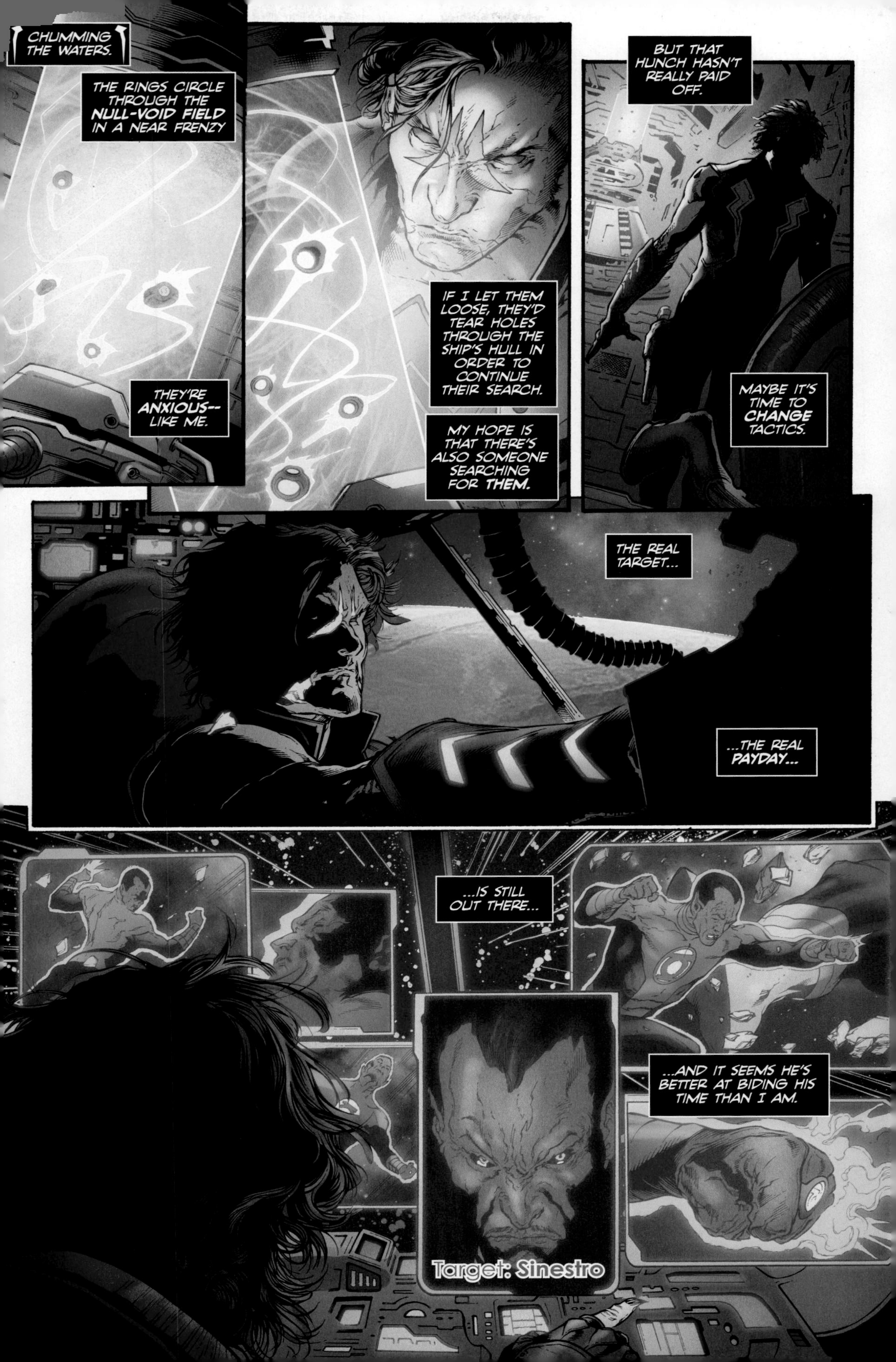
CHUMMING THE WATERS.
THE RINGS CIRCLE THROUGH THE NULL-VOID FIELD IN A NEAR FRENZY
THEY'RE ANXIOUS-- LIKE ME.
IF I LET THEM LOOSE, THEY'D TEAR HOLES THROUGH THE SHIP'S HULL IN ORDER TO CONTINUE THEIR SEARCH.
MY HOPE IS THAT THERE'S ALSO SOMEONE SEARCHING FOR THEM.
BUT THAT HUNCH HASN'T REALLY PAID OFF.
MAYBE IT'S TIME TO CHANGE TACTICS.
THE REAL TARGET...
...THE REAL PAYDAY...
...IS STILL OUT THERE...
...AND IT SEEMS HE'S BETTER AT BIDING HIS TIME THAN I AM.
Target: Sinestro

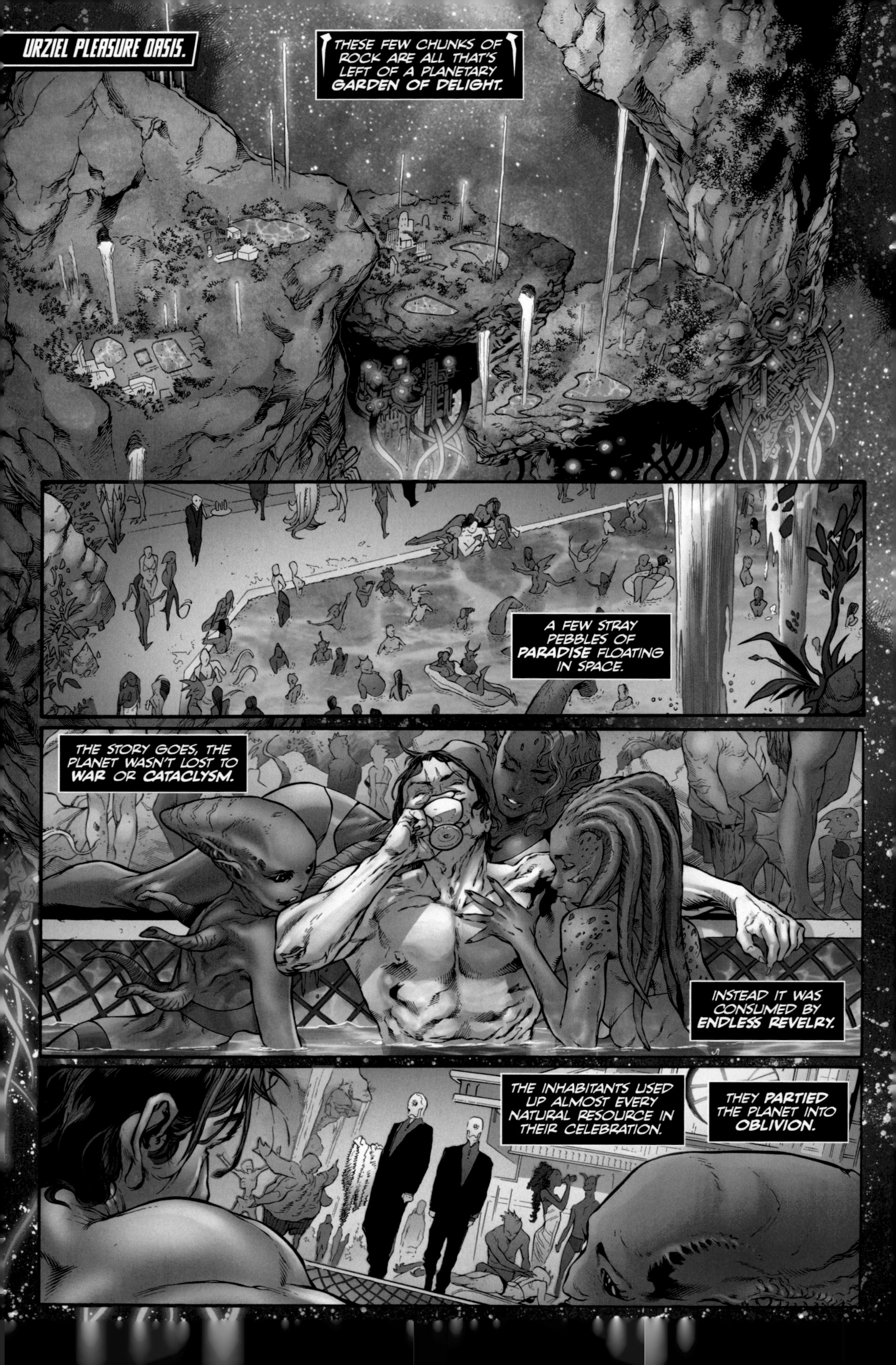
URZIEL PLEASURE OASIS.
THESE FEW CHUNKS OF ROCK ARE ALL THAT'S LEFT OF A PLANETARY GARDEN OF DELIGHT.
A FEW STRAY PEBBLES OF PARADISE FLOATING IN SPACE.
THE STORY GOES, THE PLANET WASN'T LOST TO WAR OR CATACLYSM.
INSTEAD IT WAS CONSUMED BY ENDLESS REVELRY.
THE INHABITANTS USED UP ALMOST EVERY NATURAL RESOURCE IN THEIR CELEBRATION.
THEY PARTIED THE PLANET INTO OBLIVION.

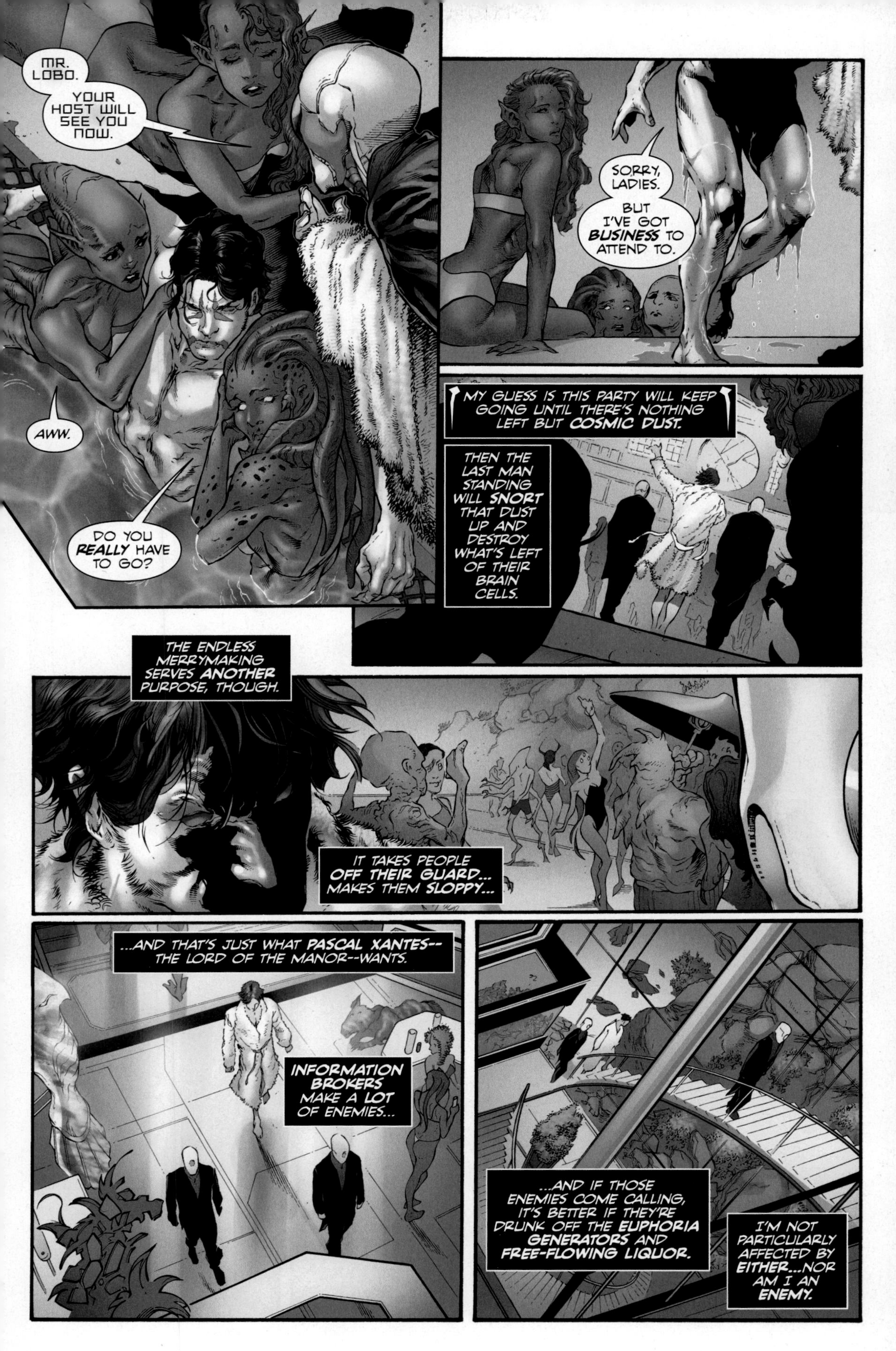
MR. LOBO.
YOUR HOST WILL SEE YOU NOW.
AWW.
DO YOU REALLY HAVE TO GO?
SORRY, LADIES.
BUT I'VE GOT BUSINESS TO ATTEND TO.
MY GUESS IS THIS PARTY WILL KEEP GOING UNTIL THERE'S NOTHING LEFT BUT COSMIC DUST.
THEN THE LAST MAN STANDING WILL SNORT THAT DUST UP AND DESTROY WHAT'S LEFT OF THEIR BRAIN CELLS.
THE ENDLESS MERRYMAKING SERVES ANOTHER PURPOSE, THOUGH.
IT TAKES PEOPLE OFF THEIR GUARD... MAKES THEM SLOPPY...
...AND THAT'S JUST WHAT PASCAL XANTES-- THE LORD OF THE MANOR--WANTS.
INFORMATION BROKERS MAKE A LOT OF ENEMIES...
...AND IF THOSE ENEMIES COME CALLING, IT'S BETTER IF THEY'RE DRUNK OFF THE EUPHORIA GENERATORS AND FREE-FLOWING LIQUOR.
I'M NOT PARTICULARLY AFFECTED BY EITHER...NOR AM I AN ENEMY.

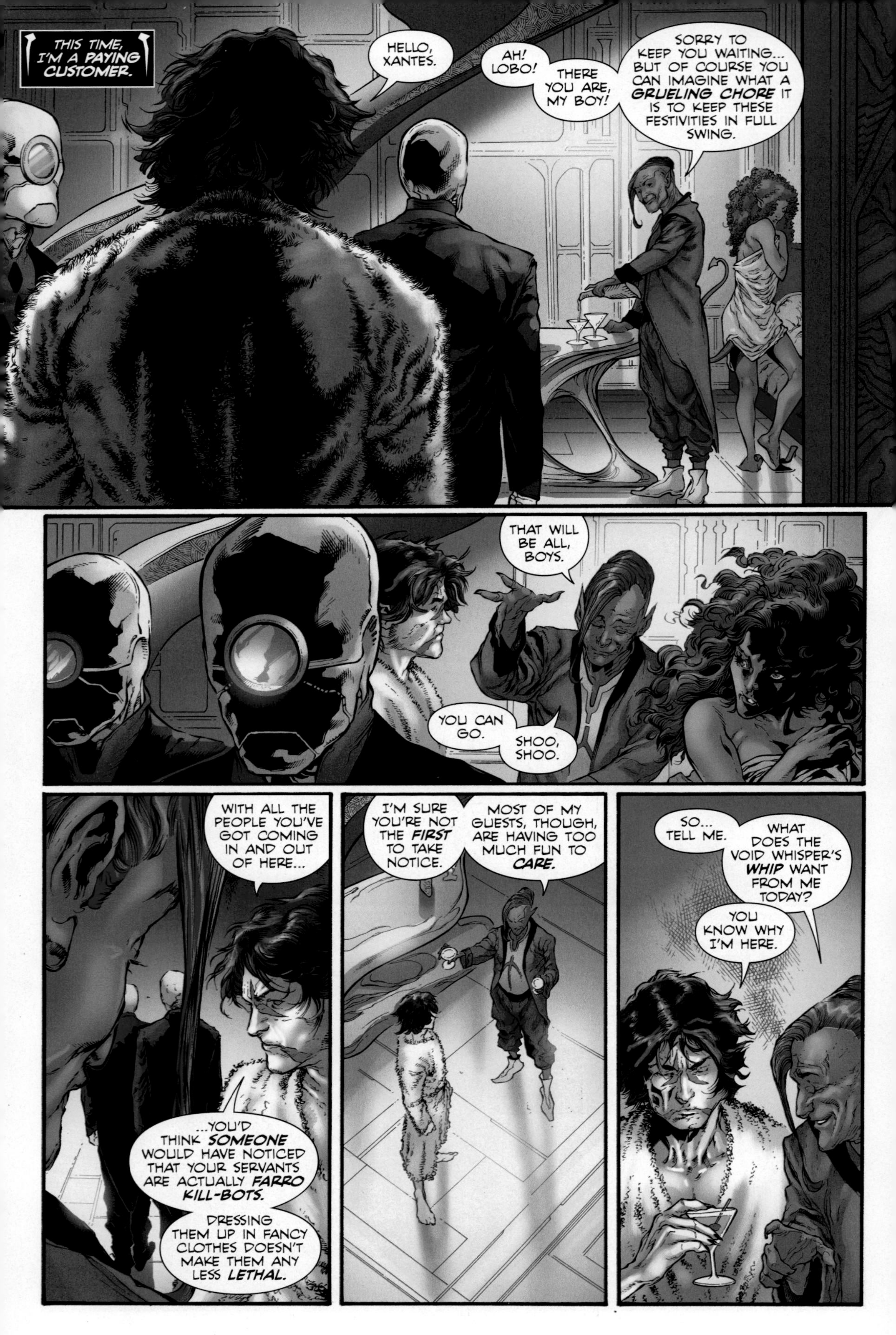
THIS TIME, I'M A PAYING CUSTOMER.
HELLO, XANTES.
AH! LOBO!
THERE YOU ARE, MY BOY!
SORRY TO KEEP YOU WAITING... BUT OF COURSE YOU CAN IMAGINE WHAT A GRUELING CHORE IT IS TO KEEP THESE FESTIVITIES IN FULL SWING.
THAT WILL BE ALL, BOYS.
YOU CAN GO.
SHOO, SHOO.
WITH ALL THE PEOPLE YOU'VE GOT COMING IN AND OUT OF HERE...
...YOU'D THINK SOMEONE WOULD HAVE NOTICED THAT YOUR SERVANTS ARE ACTUALLY FARRO KILL-BOTS.
DRESSING THEM UP IN FANCY CLOTHES DOESN'T MAKE THEM ANY LESS LETHAL.
I'M SURE YOU'RE NOT THE FIRST TO TAKE NOTICE.
MOST OF MY GUESTS, THOUGH, ARE HAVING TOO MUCH FUN TO CARE.
SO... TELL ME.
WHAT DOES THE VOID WHISPER'S WHIP WANT FROM ME TODAY?
YOU KNOW WHY I'M HERE.

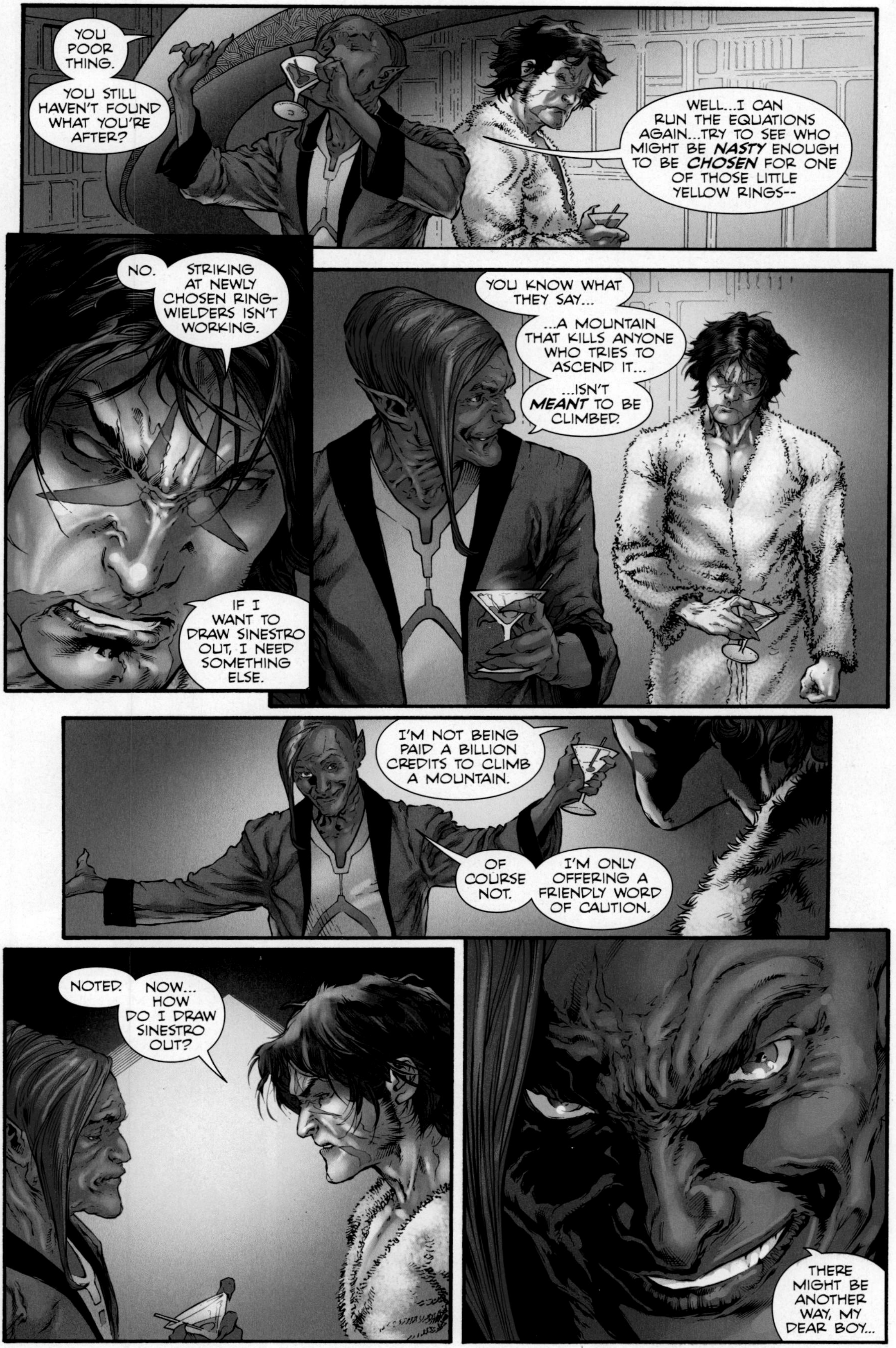

YOU POOR THING.
YOU STILL HAVEN'T FOUND WHAT YOU'RE AFTER?
WELL...I CAN RUN THE EQUATIONS AGAIN...TRY TO SEE WHO MIGHT BE NASTY ENOUGH TO BE CHOSEN FOR ONE OF THOSE LITTLE YELLOW RINGS--
NO.
STRIKING AT NEWLY CHOSEN RING-WIELDERS ISN'T WORKING.
IF I WANT TO DRAW SINESTRO OUT, I NEED SOMETHING ELSE.
YOU KNOW WHAT THEY SAY...
...A MOUNTAIN THAT KILLS ANYONE WHO TRIES TO ASCEND IT...
...ISN'T MEANT TO BE CLIMBED.
I'M NOT BEING PAID A BILLION CREDITS TO CLIMB A MOUNTAIN.
OF COURSE NOT.
I'M ONLY OFFERING A FRIENDLY WORD OF CAUTION.
NOTED.
NOW... HOW DO I DRAW SINESTRO OUT?
THERE MIGHT BE ANOTHER WAY, MY DEAR BOY...

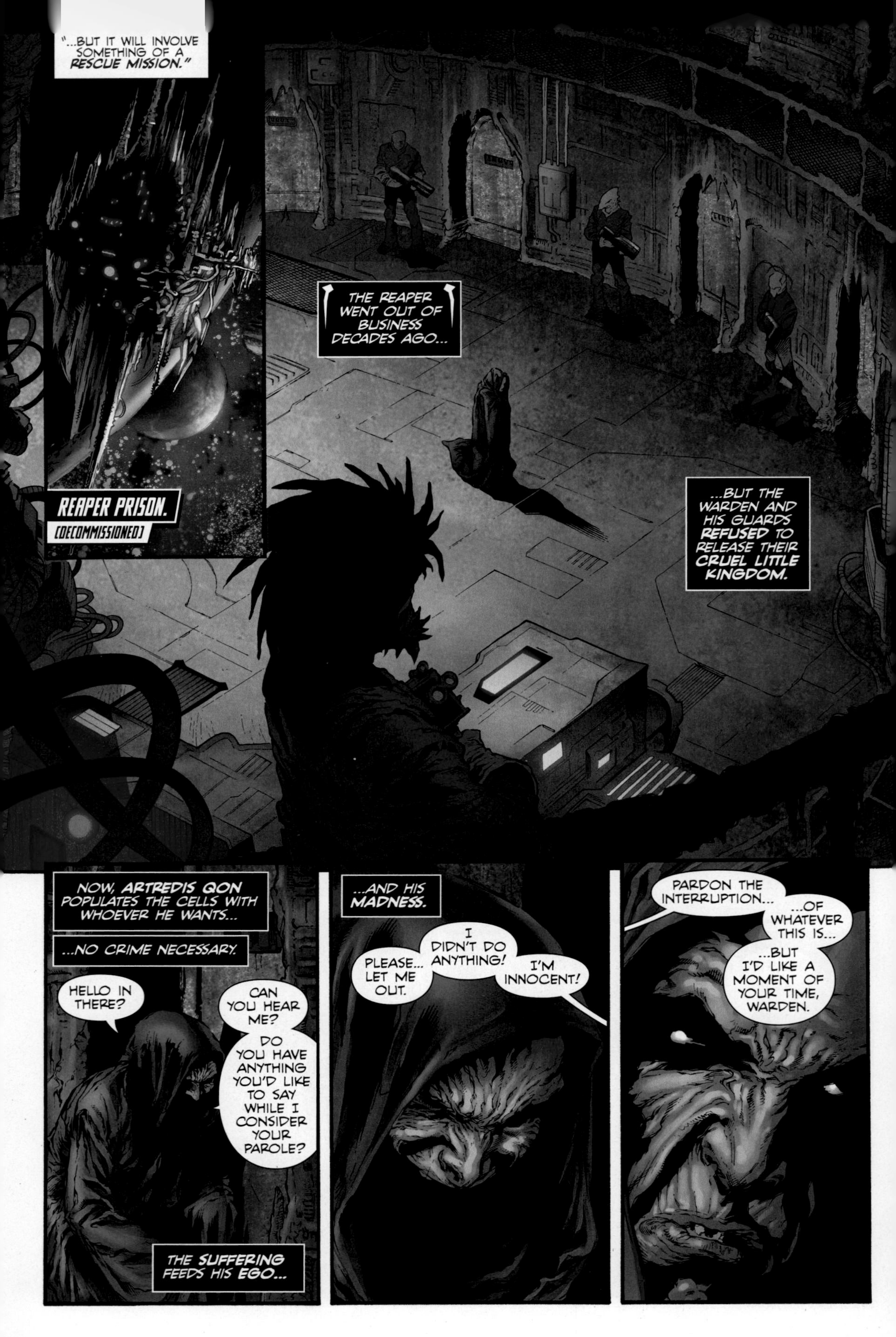
"...BUT IT WILL INVOLVE SOMETHING OF A RESCUE MISSION."
REAPER PRISON.
[DECOMMISSIONED]
THE REAPER WENT OUT OF BUSINESS DECADES AGO...
...BUT THE WARDEN AND HIS GUARDS REFUSED TO RELEASE THEIR CRUEL LITTLE KINGDOM.
NOW, ARTREDIS QON POPULATES THE CELLS WITH WHOEVER HE WANTS...
...NO CRIME NECESSARY.
HELLO IN THERE?
CAN YOU HEAR ME?
DO YOU HAVE ANYTHING YOU'D LIKE TO SAY WHILE I CONSIDER YOUR PAROLE?
THE SUFFERING FEEDS HIS EGO...
...AND HIS MADNESS.
PLEASE... LET ME OUT.
I DIDN'T DO ANYTHING!
I'M INNOCENT!
PARDON THE INTERRUPTION...
...OF WHATEVER THIS IS...
...BUT I'D LIKE A MOMENT OF YOUR TIME, WARDEN.

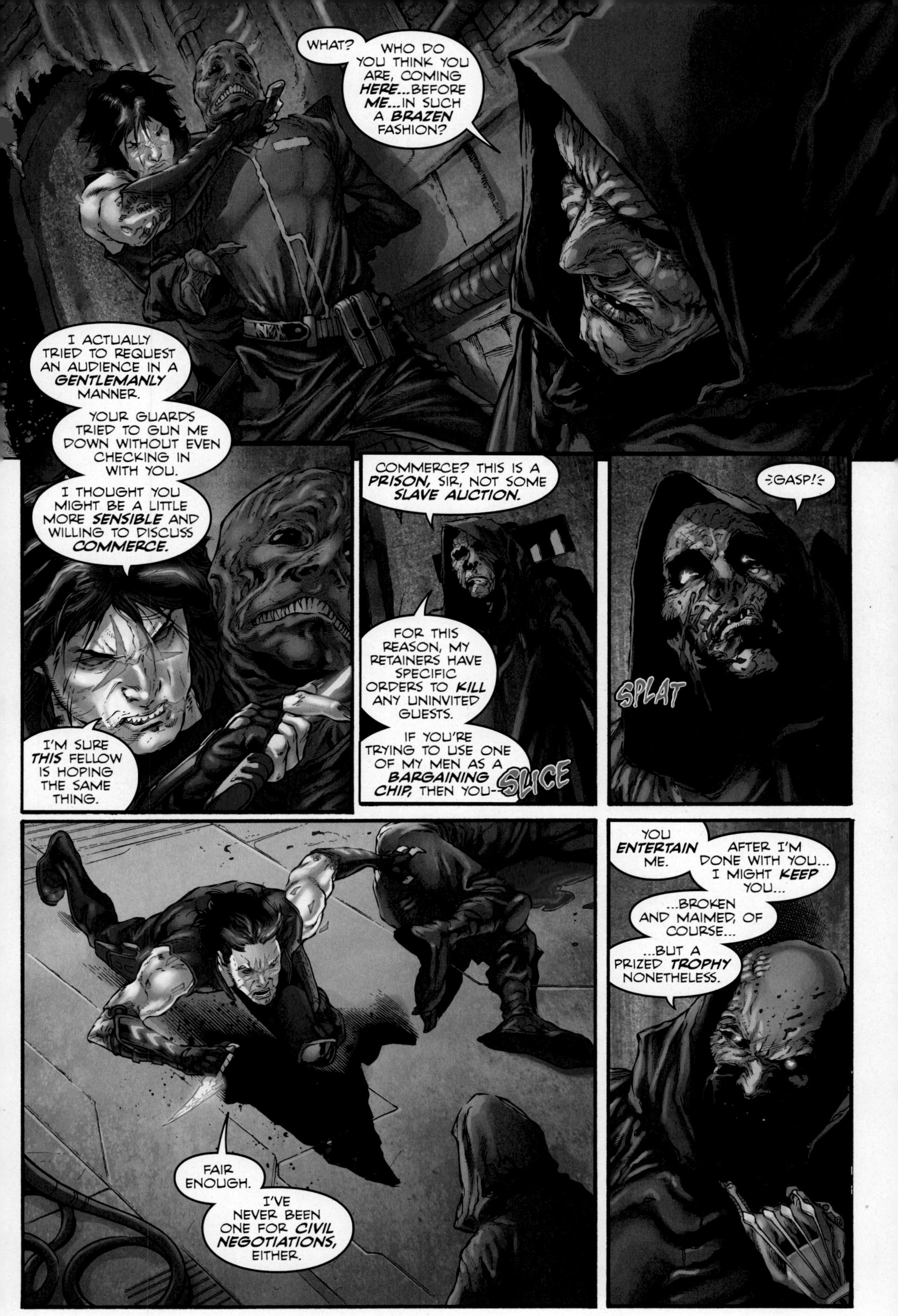
WHAT?
WHO DO YOU THINK YOU ARE, COMING HERE...BEFORE ME...IN SUCH A BRAZEN FASHION?
I ACTUALLY TRIED TO REQUEST AN AUDIENCE IN A GENTLEMANLY MANNER.
YOUR GUARDS TRIED TO GUN ME DOWN WITHOUT EVEN CHECKING IN WITH YOU.
I THOUGHT YOU MIGHT BE A LITTLE MORE SENSIBLE AND WILLING TO DISCUSS COMMERCE.
I'M SURE THIS FELLOW IS HOPING THE SAME THING.
COMMERCE? THIS IS A PRISON, SIR, NOT SOME SLAVE AUCTION.
FOR THIS REASON, MY RETAINERS HAVE SPECIFIC ORDERS TO KILL ANY UNINVITED GUESTS.
IF YOU'RE TRYING TO USE ONE OF MY MEN AS A BARGAINING CHIP, THEN YOU--
SLICE
GASP!
SPLAT
FAIR ENOUGH.
I'VE NEVER BEEN ONE FOR CIVIL NEGOTIATIONS, EITHER.
YOU ENTERTAIN ME.
AFTER I'M DONE WITH YOU... I MIGHT KEEP YOU...
...BROKEN AND MAIMED, OF COURSE...
...BUT A PRIZED TROPHY NONETHELESS.

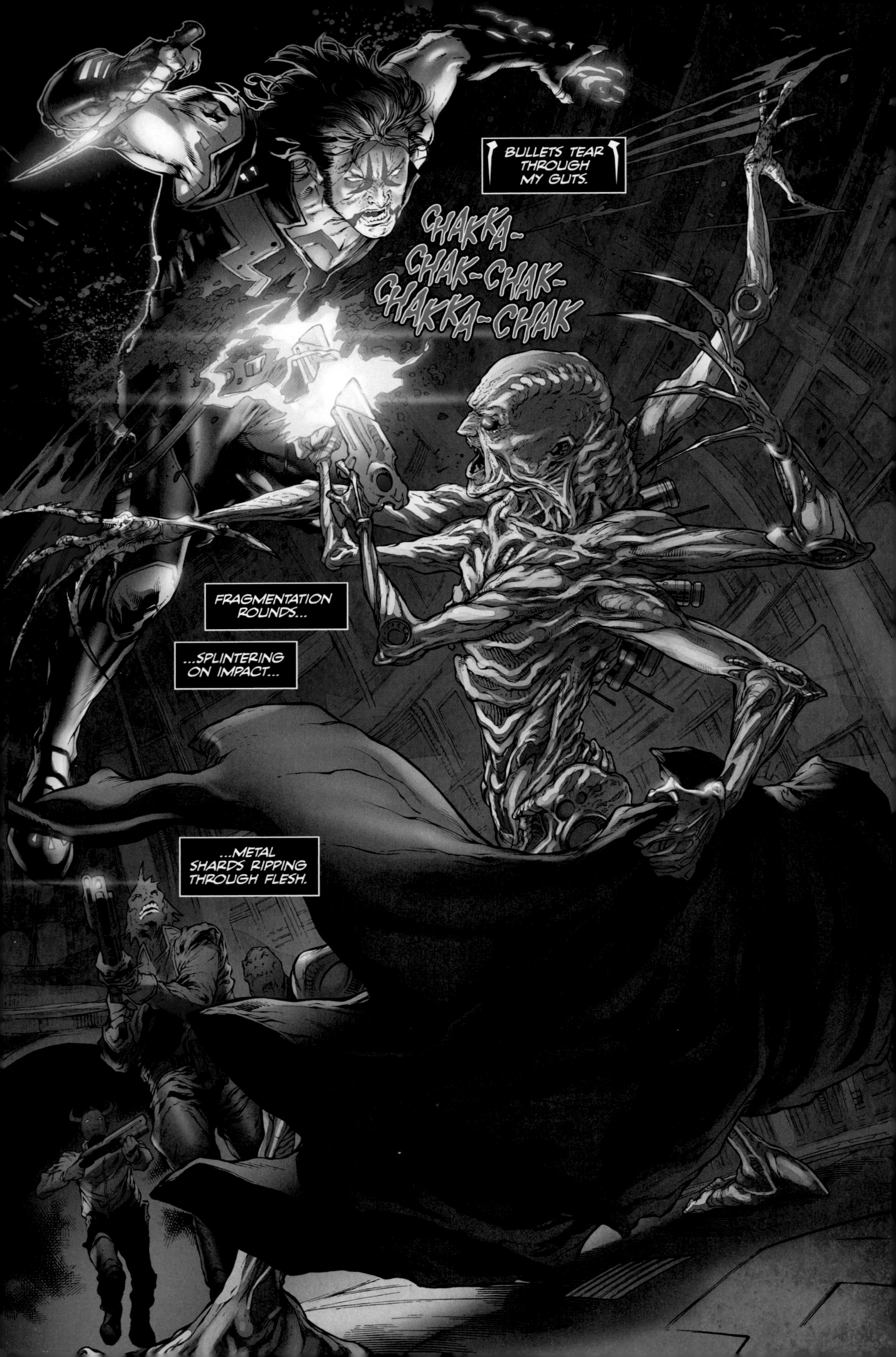
BULLETS TEAR THROUGH MY GUTS.
CHAKKA-CHAK-CHAK-CHAKKA-CHAK
FRAGMENTATION ROUNDS...
...SPLINTERING ON IMPACT...
...METAL SHARDS RIPPING THROUGH FLESH.

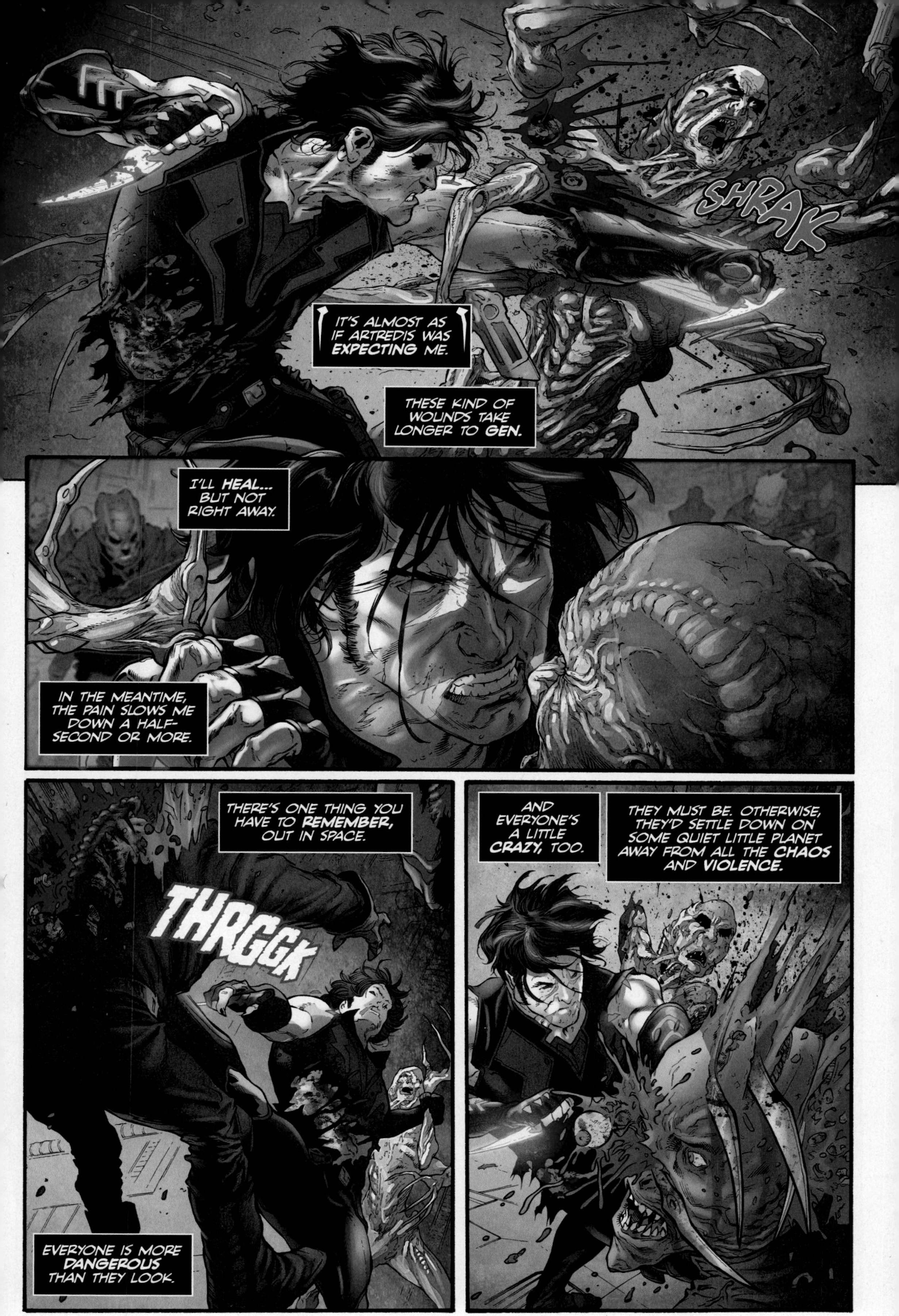
SHRAK
IT'S ALMOST AS IF ARTREDIS WAS EXPECTING ME.
THESE KIND OF WOUNDS TAKE LONGER TO GEN.
I'LL HEAL... BUT NOT RIGHT AWAY.
IN THE MEANTIME, THE PAIN SLOWS ME DOWN A HALF-SECOND OR MORE.
THERE'S ONE THING YOU HAVE TO REMEMBER, OUT IN SPACE.
THRGGK
EVERYONE IS MORE DANGEROUS THAN THEY LOOK.
AND EVERYONE'S A LITTLE CRAZY, TOO.
THEY MUST BE. OTHERWISE, THEY'D SETTLE DOWN ON SOME QUIET LITTLE PLANET AWAY FROM ALL THE CHAOS AND VIOLENCE.

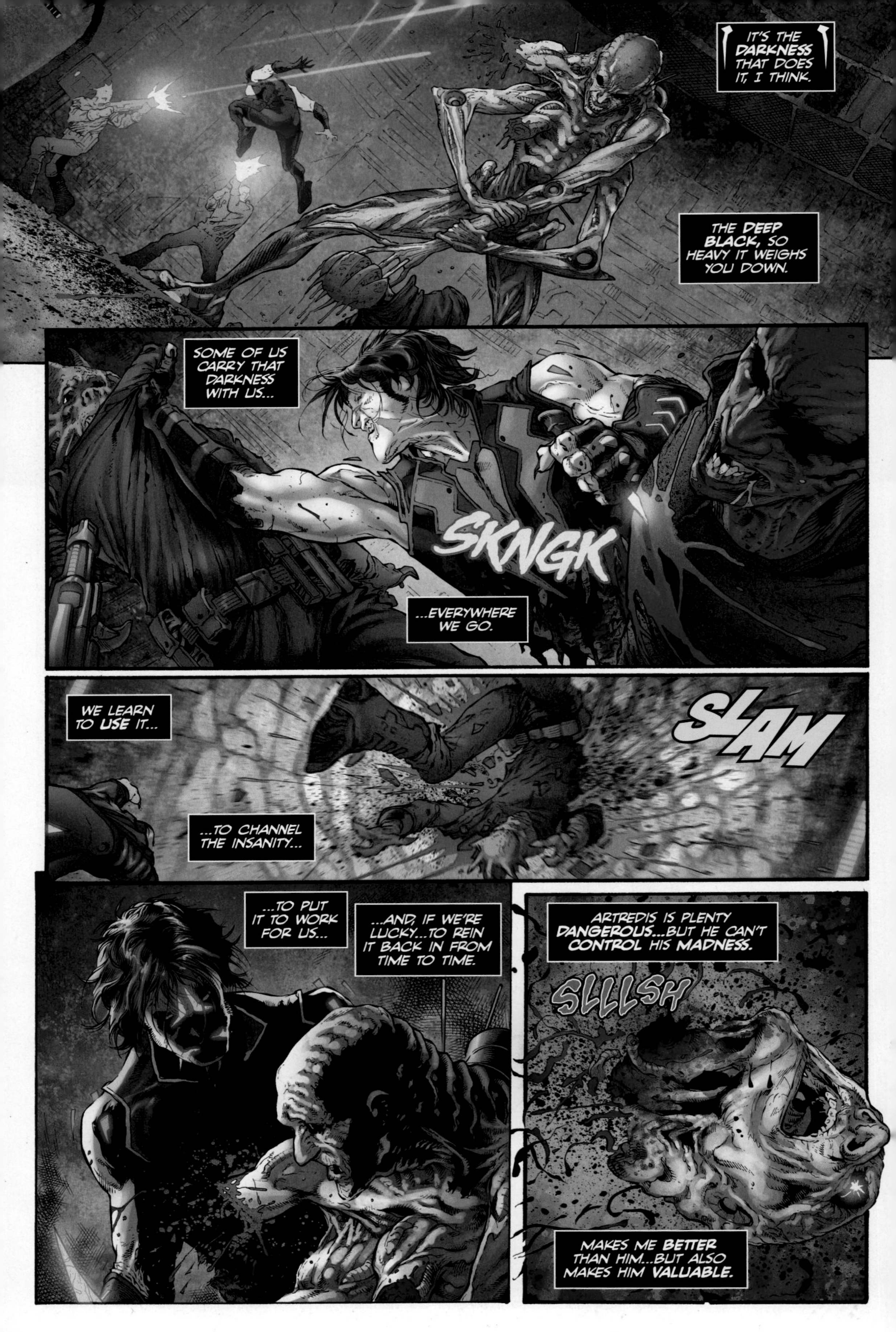
IT'S THE DARKNESS THAT DOES IT, I THINK.
THE DEEP BLACK, SO HEAVY IT WEIGHS YOU DOWN.
SOME OF US CARRY THAT DARKNESS WITH US...
SKNGK
...EVERYWHERE WE GO.
WE LEARN TO USE IT...
SLAM
...TO CHANNEL THE INSANITY...
...TO PUT IT TO WORK FOR US...
...AND, IF WE'RE LUCKY...TO REIN IT BACK IN FROM TIME TO TIME.
ARTREDIS IS PLENTY DANGEROUS...BUT HE CAN'T CONTROL HIS MADNESS.
SLLLSH
MAKES ME BETTER THAN HIM...BUT ALSO MAKES HIM VALUABLE.

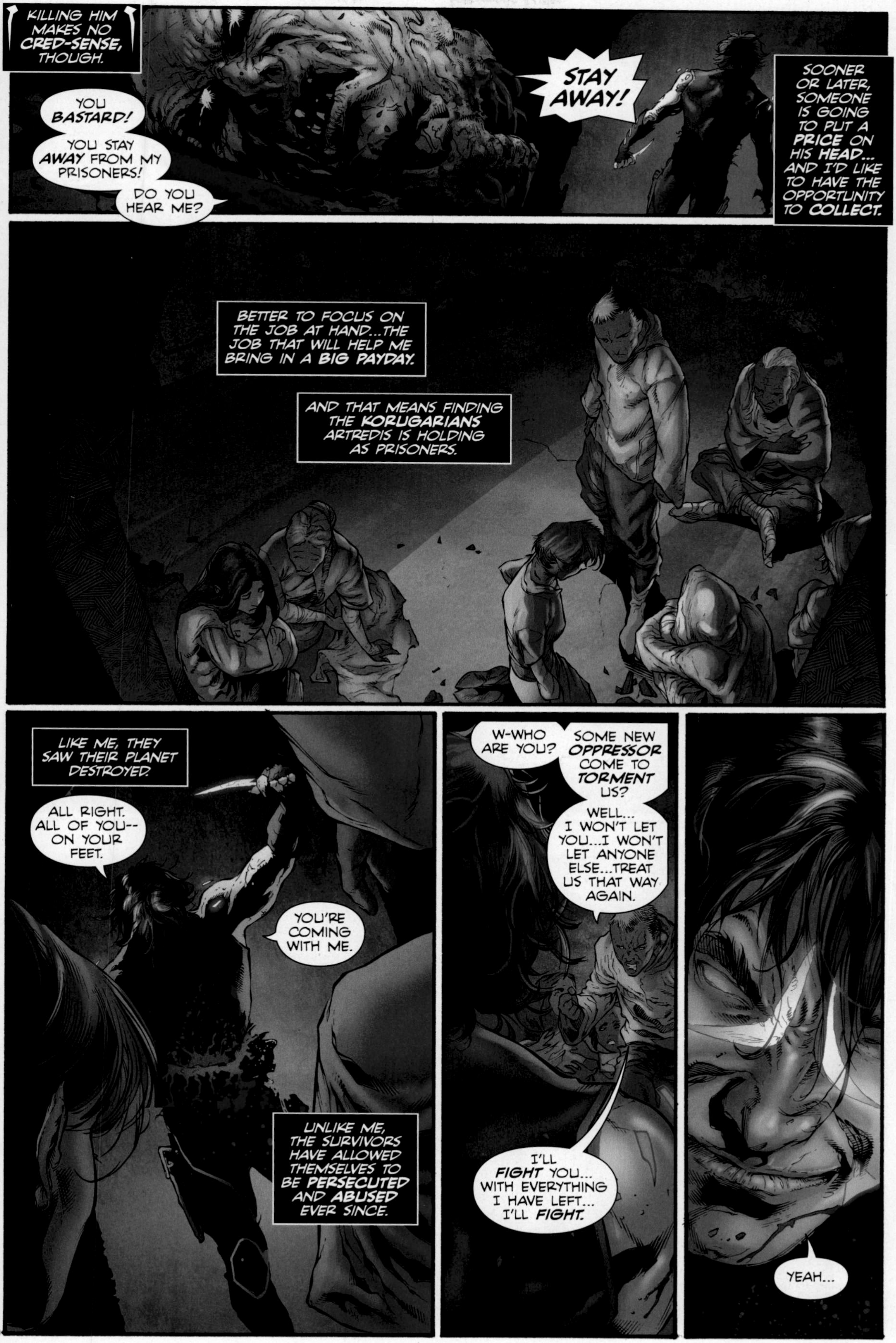
KILLING HIM MAKES NO CRED-SENSE, THOUGH.
YOU BASTARD!
YOU STAY AWAY FROM MY PRISONERS!
DO YOU HEAR ME?
STAY AWAY!
SOONER OR LATER, SOMEONE IS GOING TO PUT A PRICE ON HIS HEAD... AND I'D LIKE TO HAVE THE OPPORTUNITY TO COLLECT.
BETTER TO FOCUS ON THE JOB AT HAND...THE JOB THAT WILL HELP ME BRING IN A BIG PAYDAY.
AND THAT MEANS FINDING THE KORUGARIANS ARTREDIS IS HOLDING AS PRISONERS.
LIKE ME, THEY SAW THEIR PLANET DESTROYED.
ALL RIGHT. ALL OF YOU-- ON YOUR FEET.
YOU'RE COMING WITH ME.
UNLIKE ME, THE SURVIVORS HAVE ALLOWED THEMSELVES TO BE PERSECUTED AND ABUSED EVER SINCE.
W-WHO ARE YOU?
SOME NEW OPPRESSOR COME TO TORMENT US?
WELL... I WON'T LET YOU...I WON'T LET ANYONE ELSE...TREAT US THAT WAY AGAIN.
I'LL FIGHT YOU... WITH EVERYTHING I HAVE LEFT... I'LL FIGHT.
YEAH...

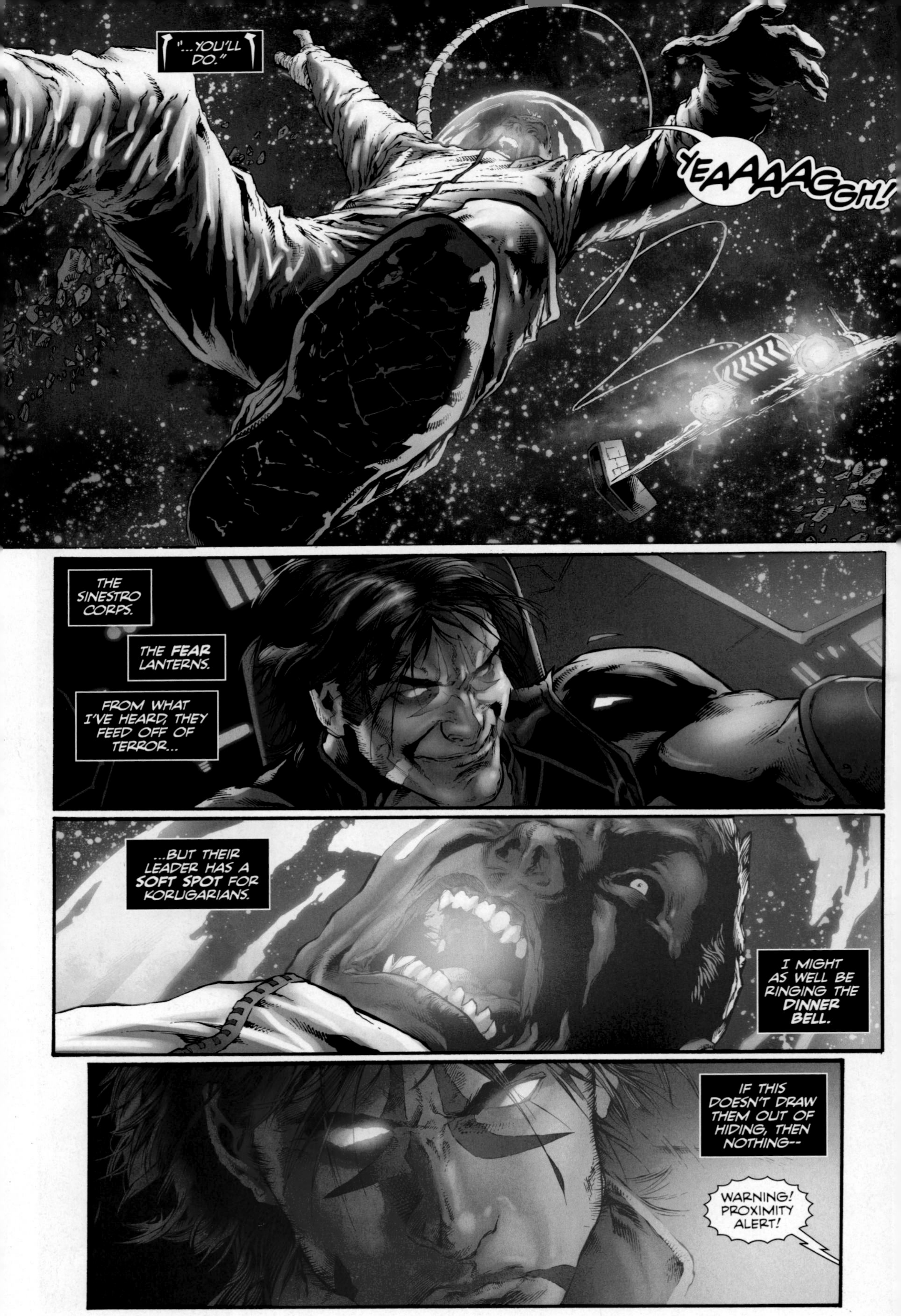
"...YOU'LL DO."
YEAAAAGGH!
THE SINESTRO CORPS.
THE FEAR LANTERNS.
FROM WHAT I'VE HEARD, THEY FEED OFF OF TERROR...
...BUT THEIR LEADER HAS A SOFT SPOT FOR KORUGARIANS.
I MIGHT AS WELL BE RINGING THE DINNER BELL.
IF THIS DOESN'T DRAW THEM OUT OF HIDING, THEN NOTHING--
WARNING! PROXIMITY ALERT!

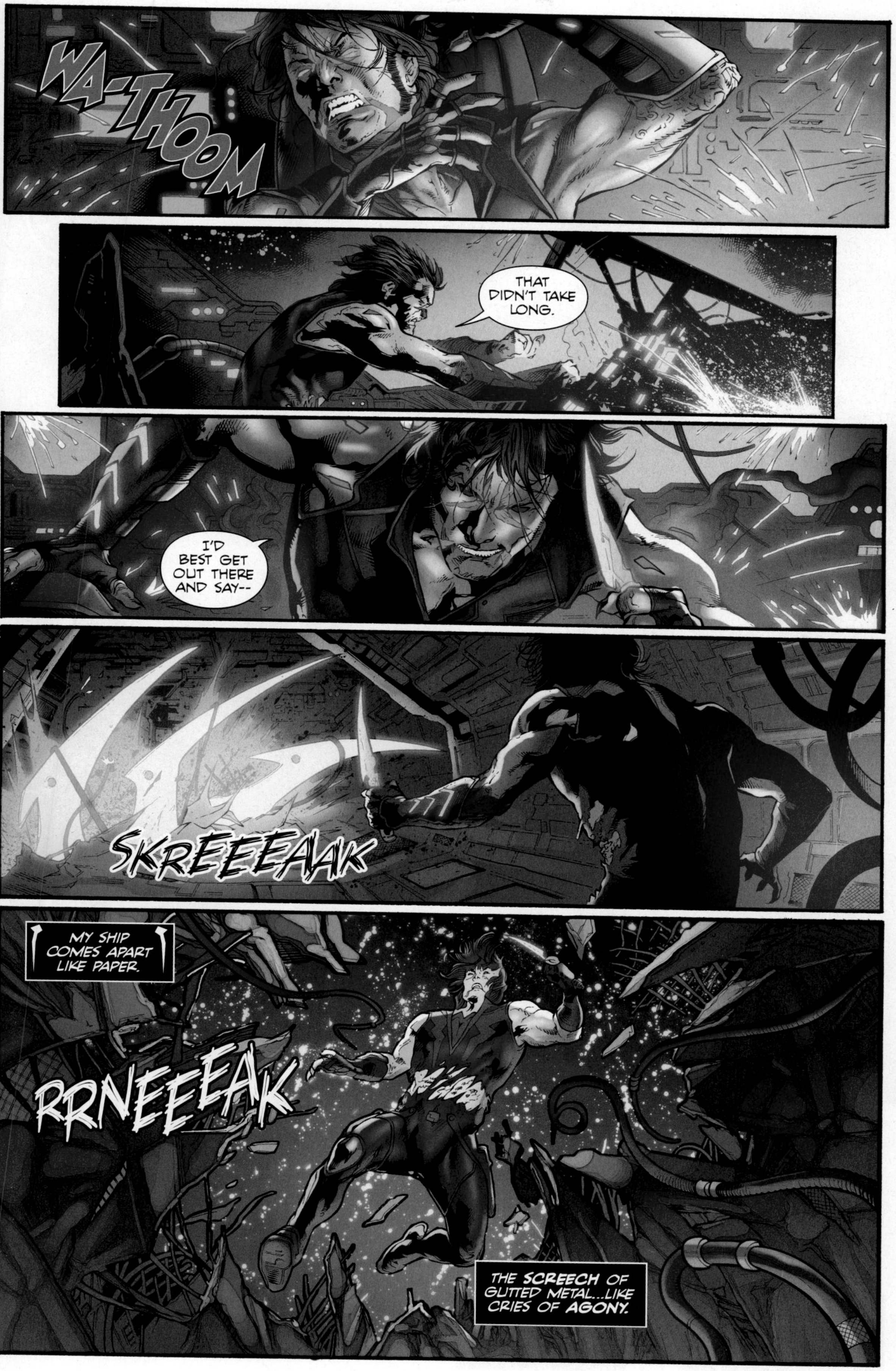
WA-THOOM
THAT DIDN'T TAKE LONG.
I'D BEST GET OUT THERE AND SAY--
SKREEEEAAK
MY SHIP COMES APART LIKE PAPER.
RRNEEEEAK
THE SCREECH OF GUTTED METAL...LIKE CRIES OF AGONY.

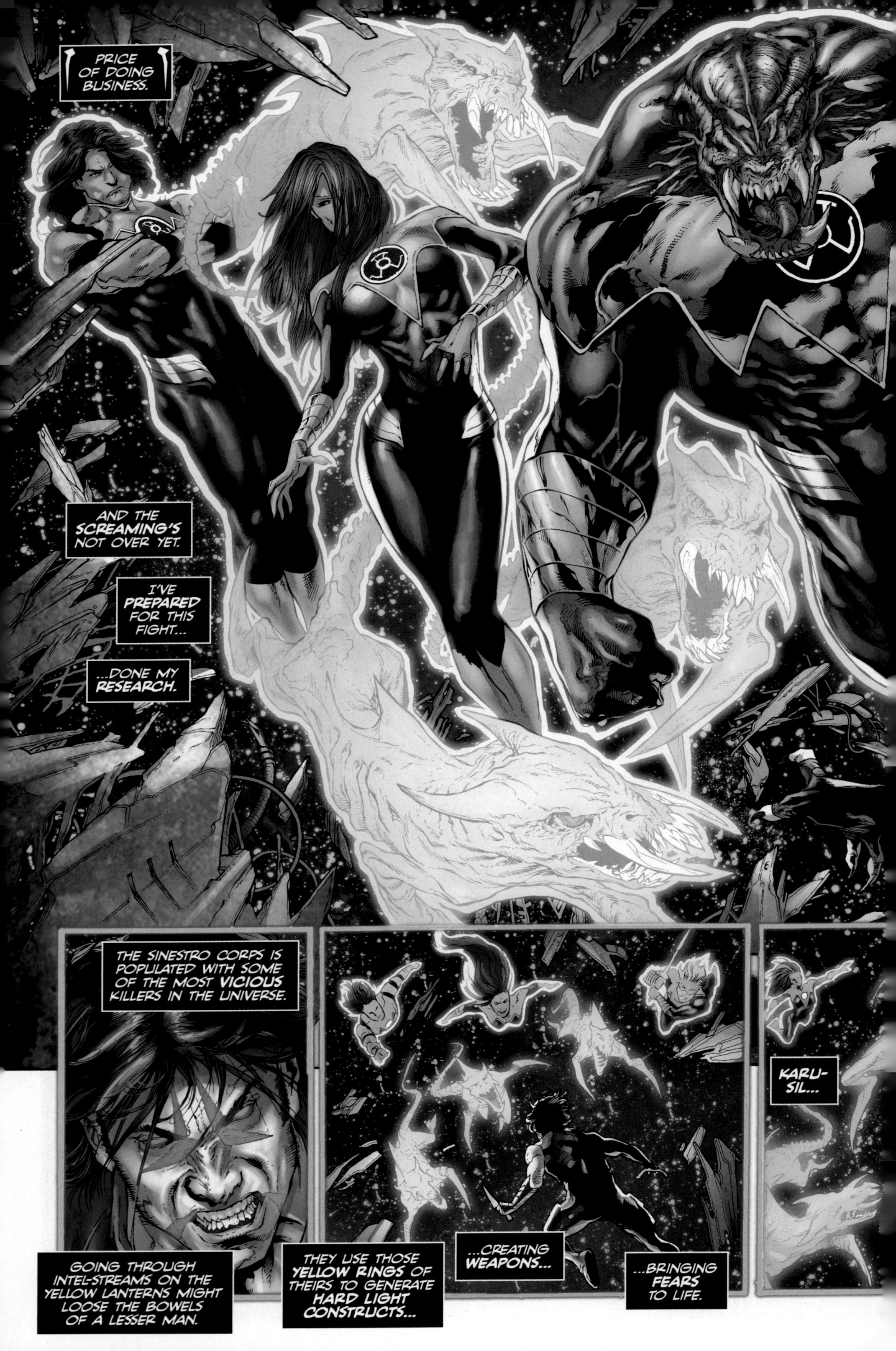
PRICE OF DOING BUSINESS.
AND THE SCREAMING'S NOT OVER YET.
I'VE PREPARED FOR THIS FIGHT...
...DONE MY RESEARCH.
THE SINESTRO CORPS IS POPULATED WITH SOME OF THE MOST VICIOUS KILLERS IN THE UNIVERSE.
GOING THROUGH INTEL-STREAMS ON THE YELLOW LANTERNS MIGHT LOOSE THE BOWELS OF A LESSER MAN.
THEY USE THOSE YELLOW RINGS OF THEIRS TO GENERATE HARD LIGHT CONSTRUCTS...
...CREATING WEAPONS...
...BRINGING FEARS TO LIFE.
KARU-SIL...

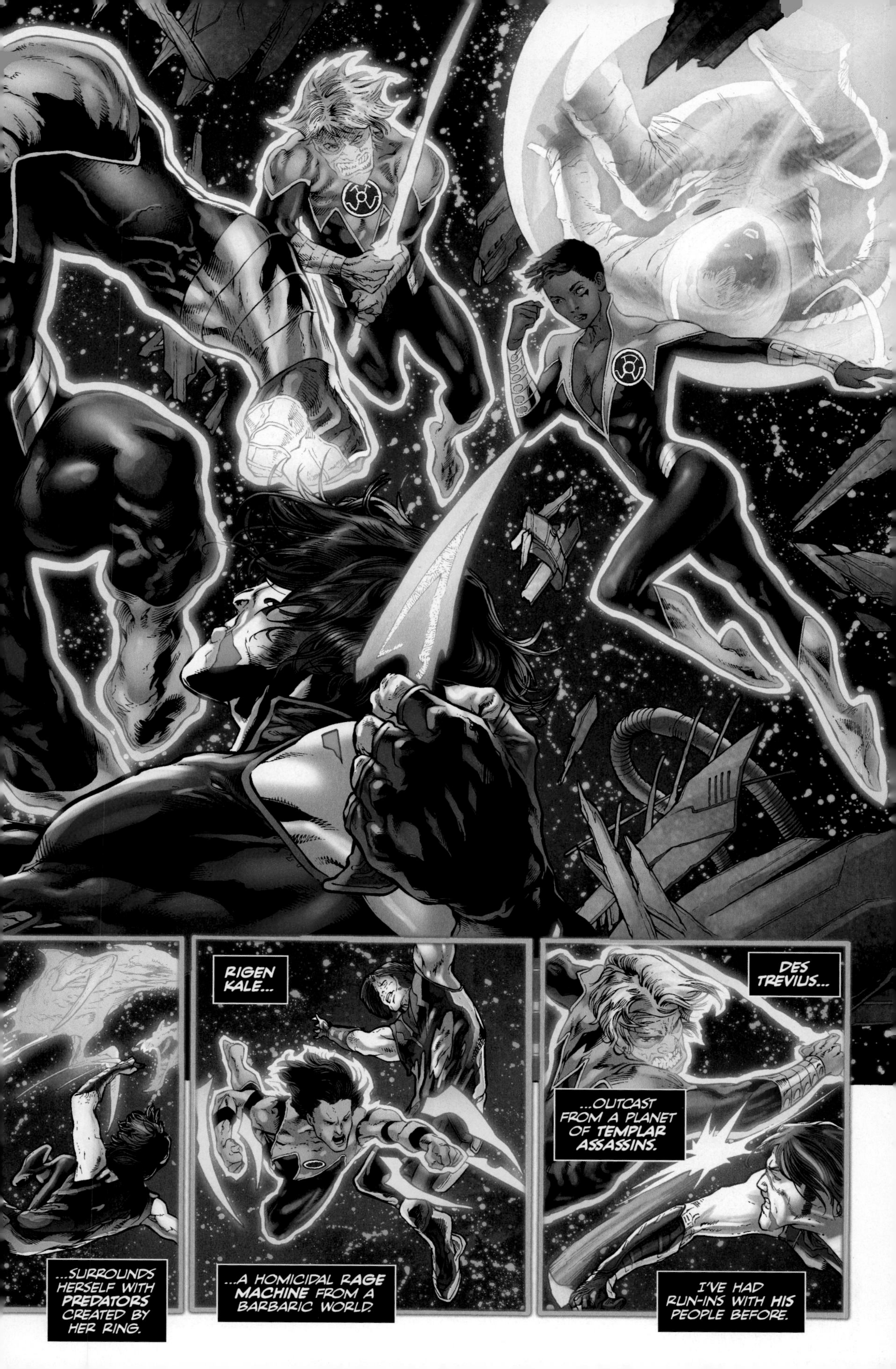
...SURROUNDS HERSELF WITH PREDATORS CREATED BY HER RING.
RIGEN KALE...
...A HOMICIDAL RAGE MACHINE FROM A BARBARIC WORLD.
DES TREVIUS...
...OUTCAST FROM A PLANET OF TEMPLAR ASSASSINS.
I'VE HAD RUN-INS WITH HIS PEOPLE BEFORE.

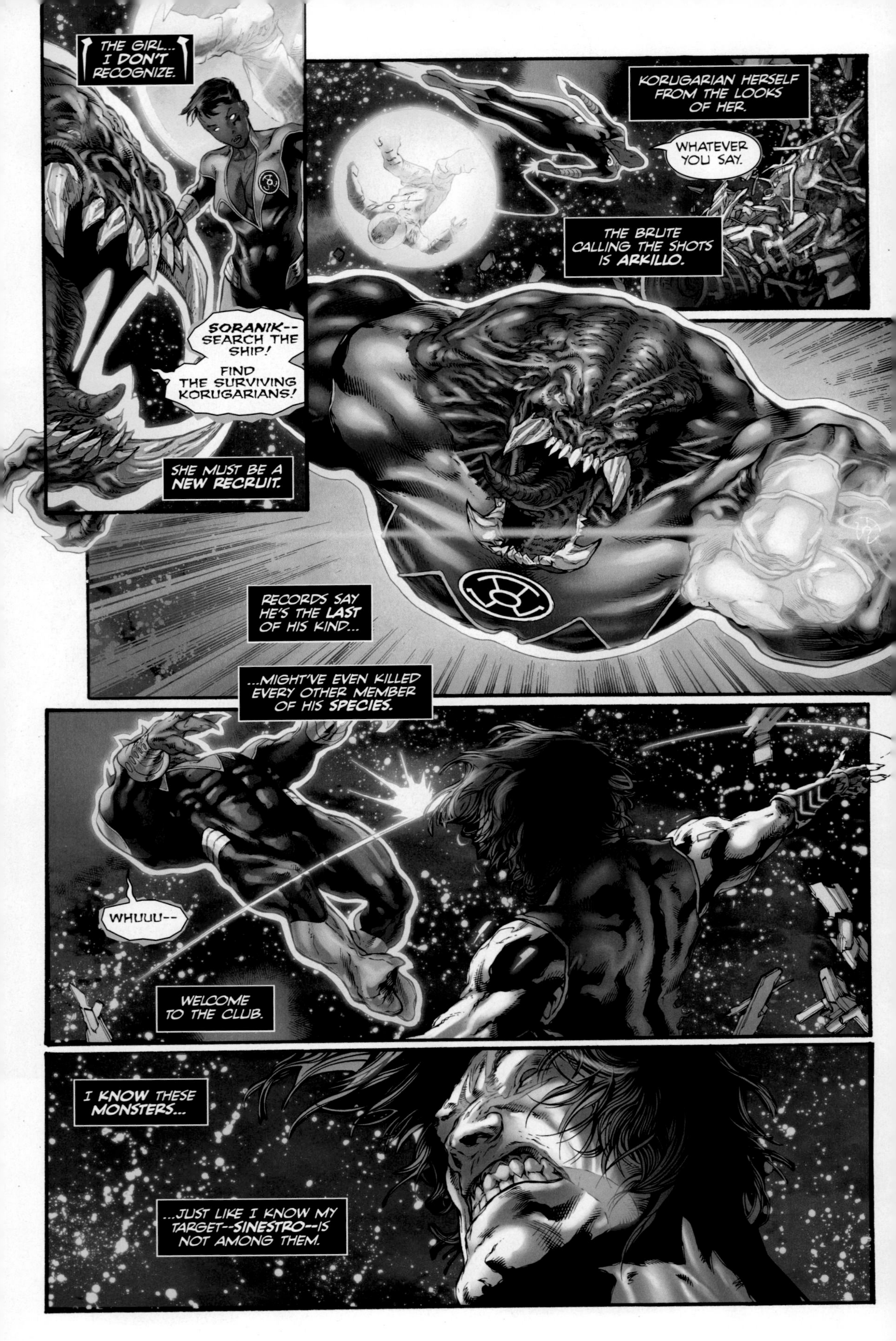
THE GIRL... I DON'T RECOGNIZE.
SORANIK-- SEARCH THE SHIP! FIND THE SURVIVING KORUGARIANS!
SHE MUST BE A NEW RECRUIT.
KORUGARIAN HERSELF FROM THE LOOKS OF HER.
WHATEVER YOU SAY.
THE BRUTE CALLING THE SHOTS IS ARKILLO.
RECORDS SAY HE'S THE LAST OF HIS KIND...
...MIGHT'VE EVEN KILLED EVERY OTHER MEMBER OF HIS SPECIES.
WHUUU--
WELCOME TO THE CLUB.
I KNOW THESE MONSTERS...
...JUST LIKE I KNOW MY TARGET--SINESTRO--IS NOT AMONG THEM.

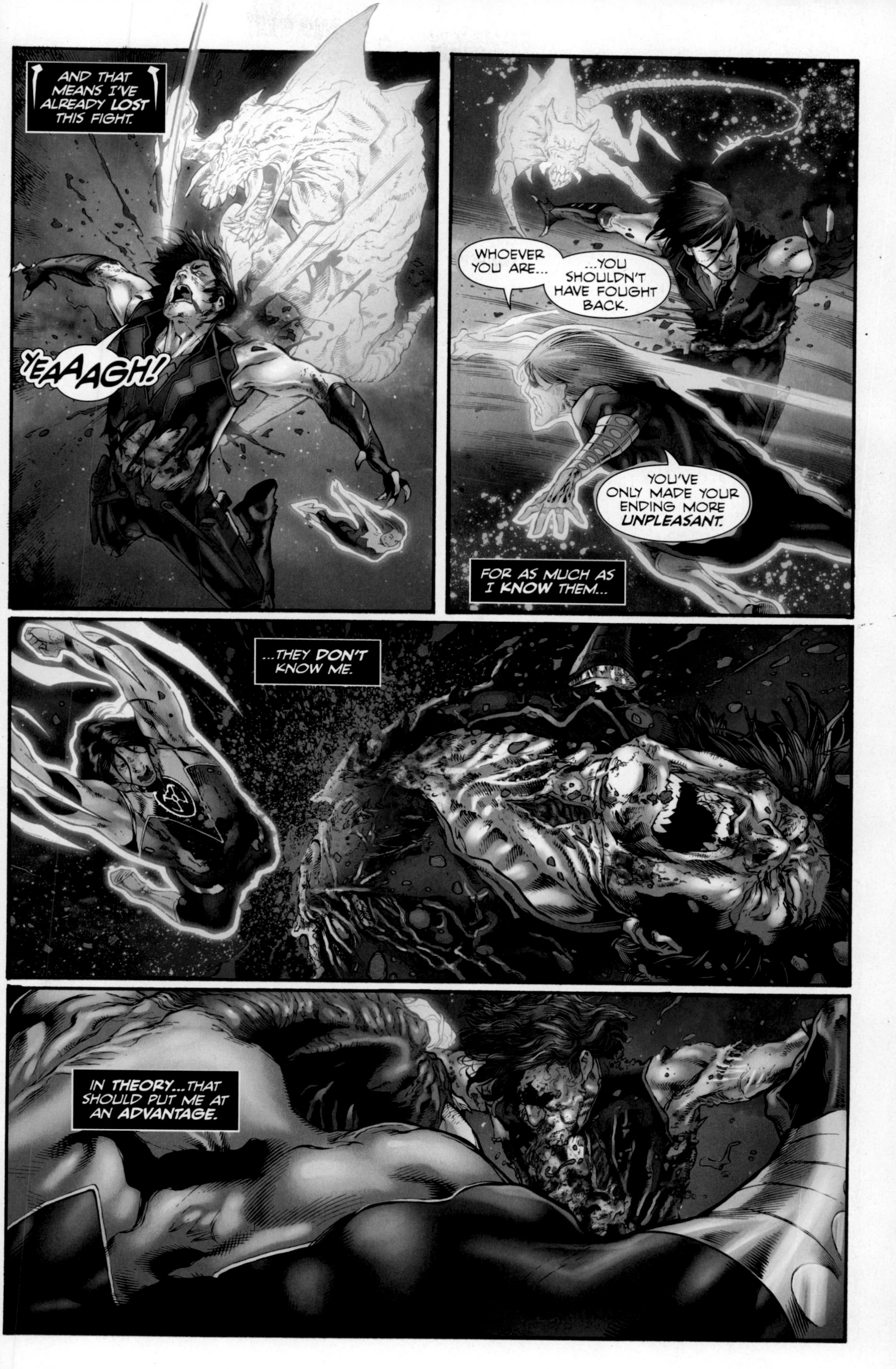

AND THAT MEANS I'VE ALREADY LOST THIS FIGHT.
YEAAAGH!
WHOEVER YOU ARE...
...YOU SHOULDN'T HAVE FOUGHT BACK.
YOU'VE ONLY MADE YOUR ENDING MORE UNPLEASANT.
FOR AS MUCH AS I KNOW THEM...
...THEY DON'T KNOW ME.
IN THEORY...THAT SHOULD PUT ME AT AN ADVANTAGE.

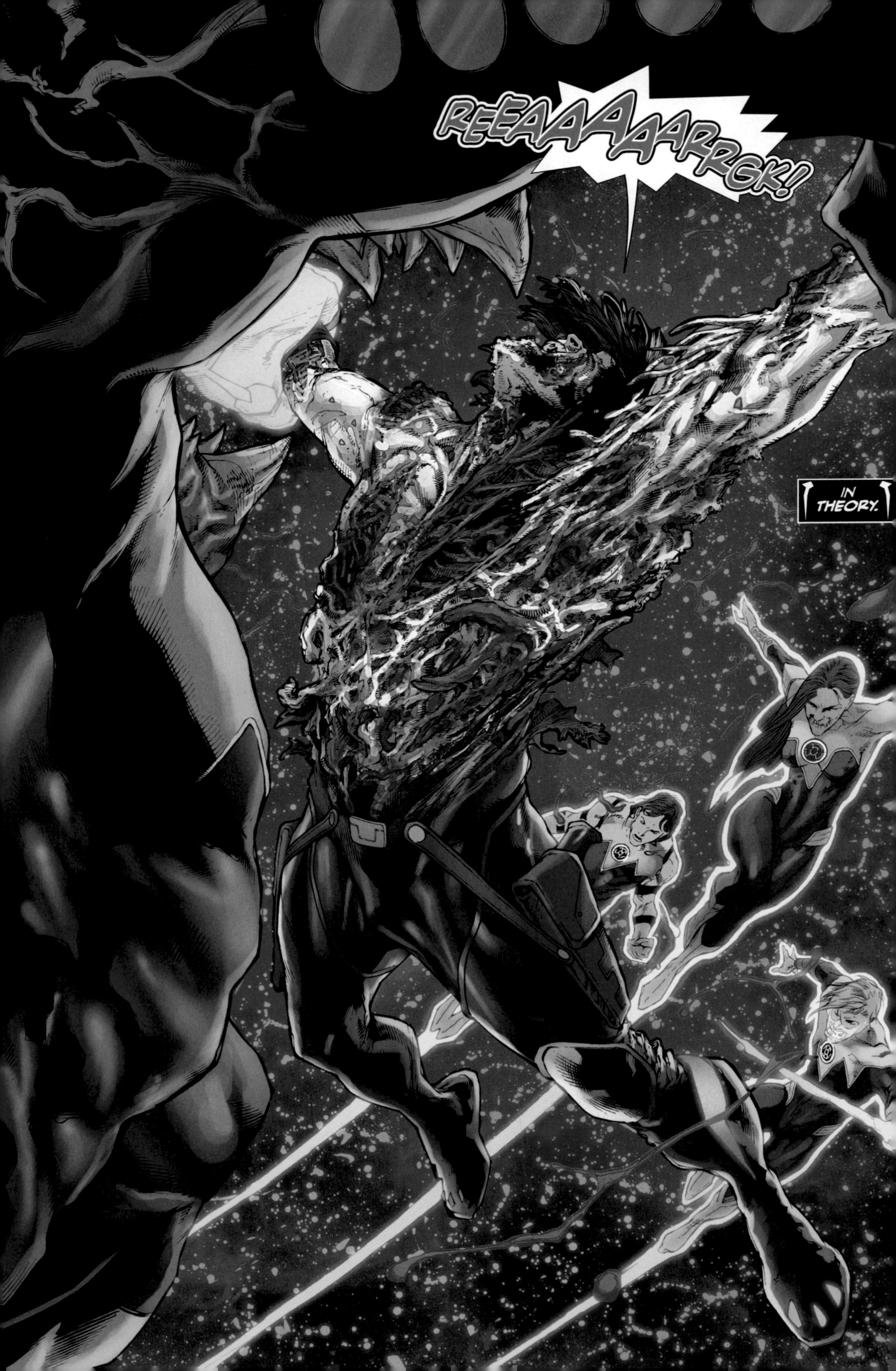
REEAAAAAARRGK!
IN THEORY.

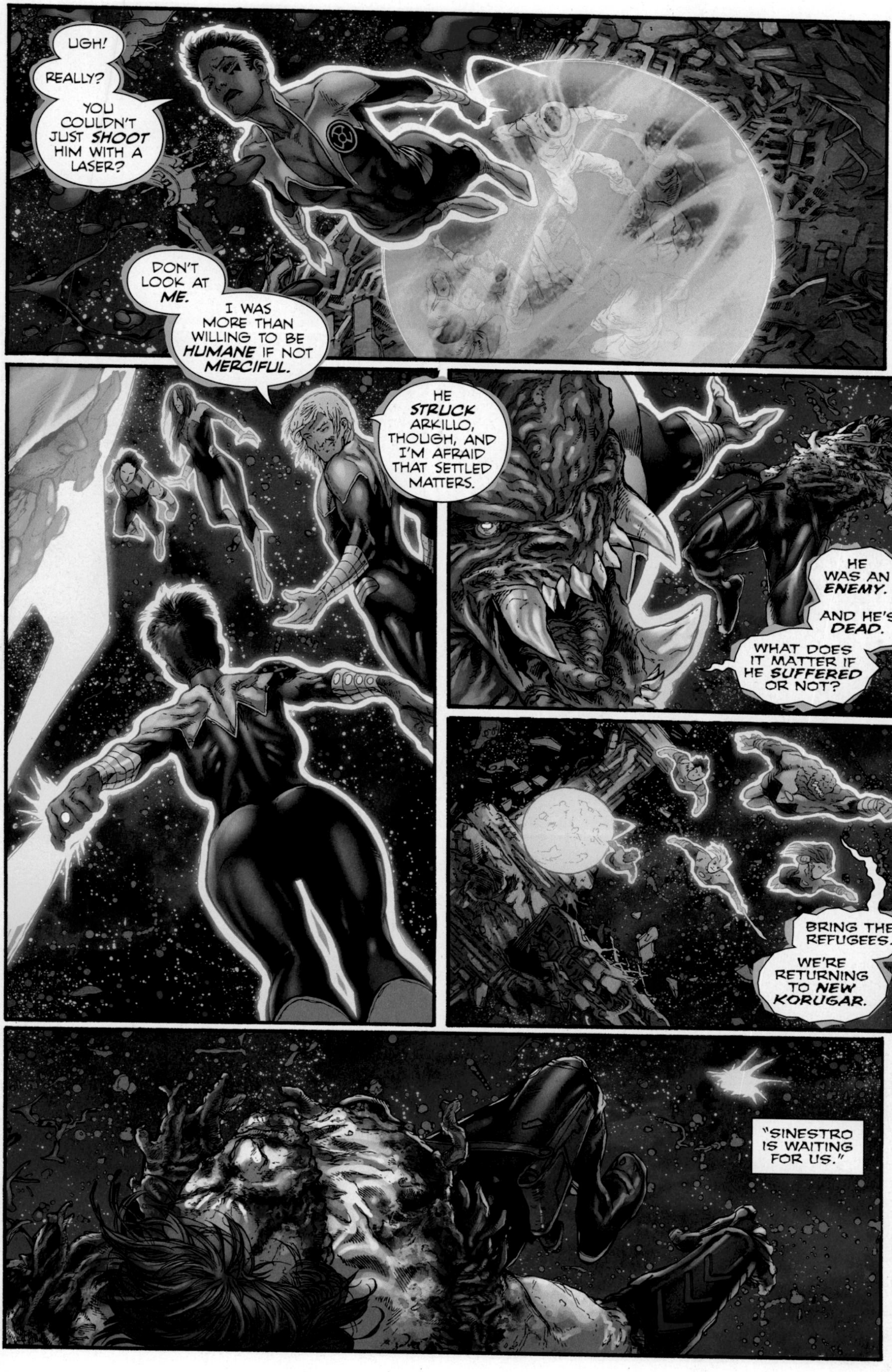
UGH!
REALLY?
YOU COULDN'T JUST SHOOT HIM WITH A LASER?
DON'T LOOK AT ME.
I WAS MORE THAN WILLING TO BE HUMANE IF NOT MERCIFUL.
HE STRUCK ARKILLO, THOUGH, AND I'M AFRAID THAT SETTLED MATTERS.
HE WAS AN ENEMY.
AND HE'S DEAD.
WHAT DOES IT MATTER IF HE SUFFERED OR NOT?
BRING THE REFUGEES.
WE'RE RETURNING TO NEW KORUGAR.
"SINESTRO IS WAITING FOR US."

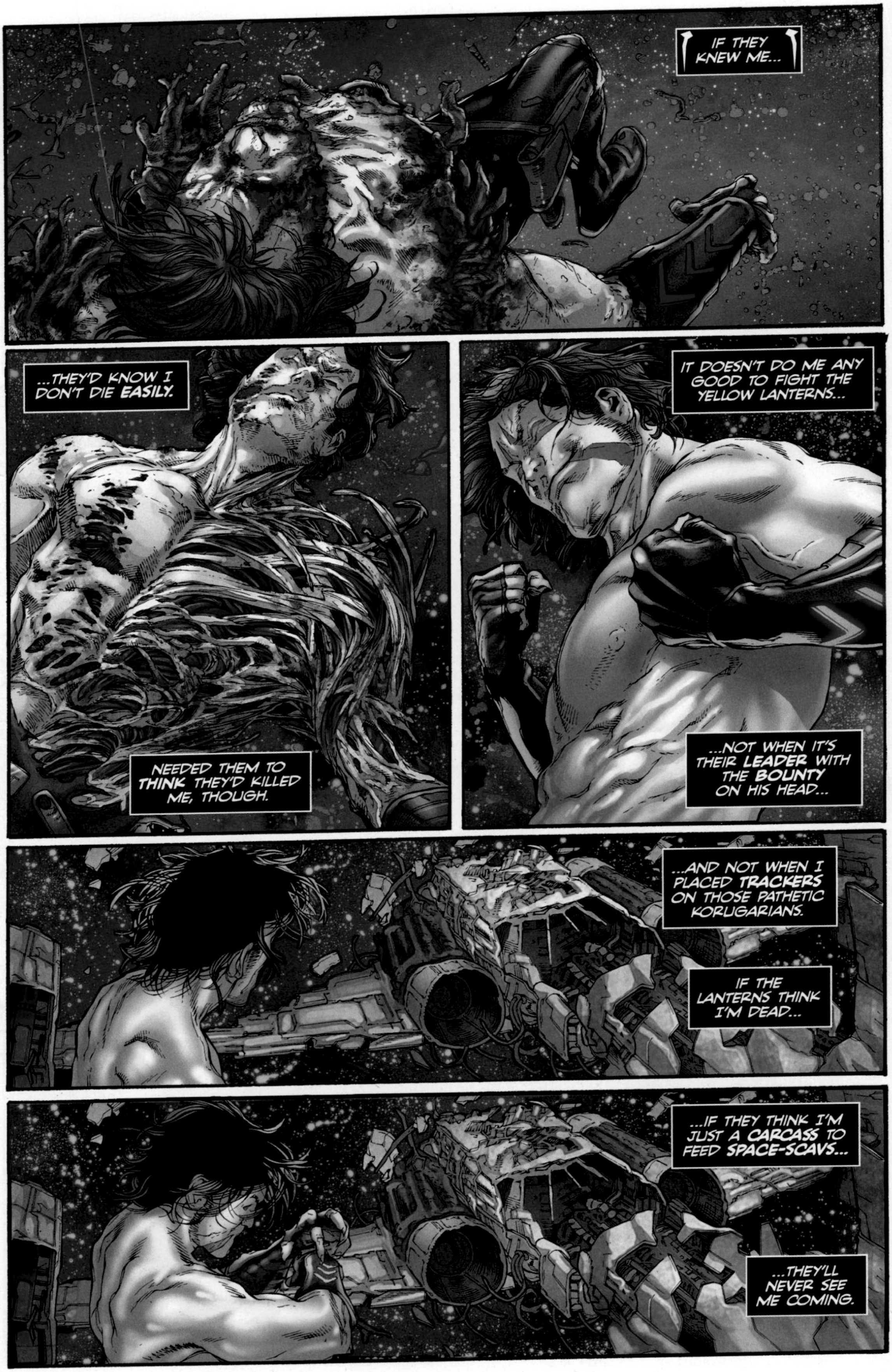
IF THEY KNEW ME...
...THEY'D KNOW I DON'T DIE EASILY.
NEEDED THEM TO THINK THEY'D KILLED ME, THOUGH.
IT DOESN'T DO ME ANY GOOD TO FIGHT THE YELLOW LANTERNS...
...NOT WHEN IT'S THEIR LEADER WITH THE BOUNTY ON HIS HEAD...
...AND NOT WHEN I PLACED TRACKERS ON THOSE PATHETIC KORUGARIANS.
IF THE LANTERNS THINK I'M DEAD...
...IF THEY THINK I'M JUST A CARCASS TO FEED SPACE-SCAVS...
...THEY'LL NEVER SEE ME COMING.

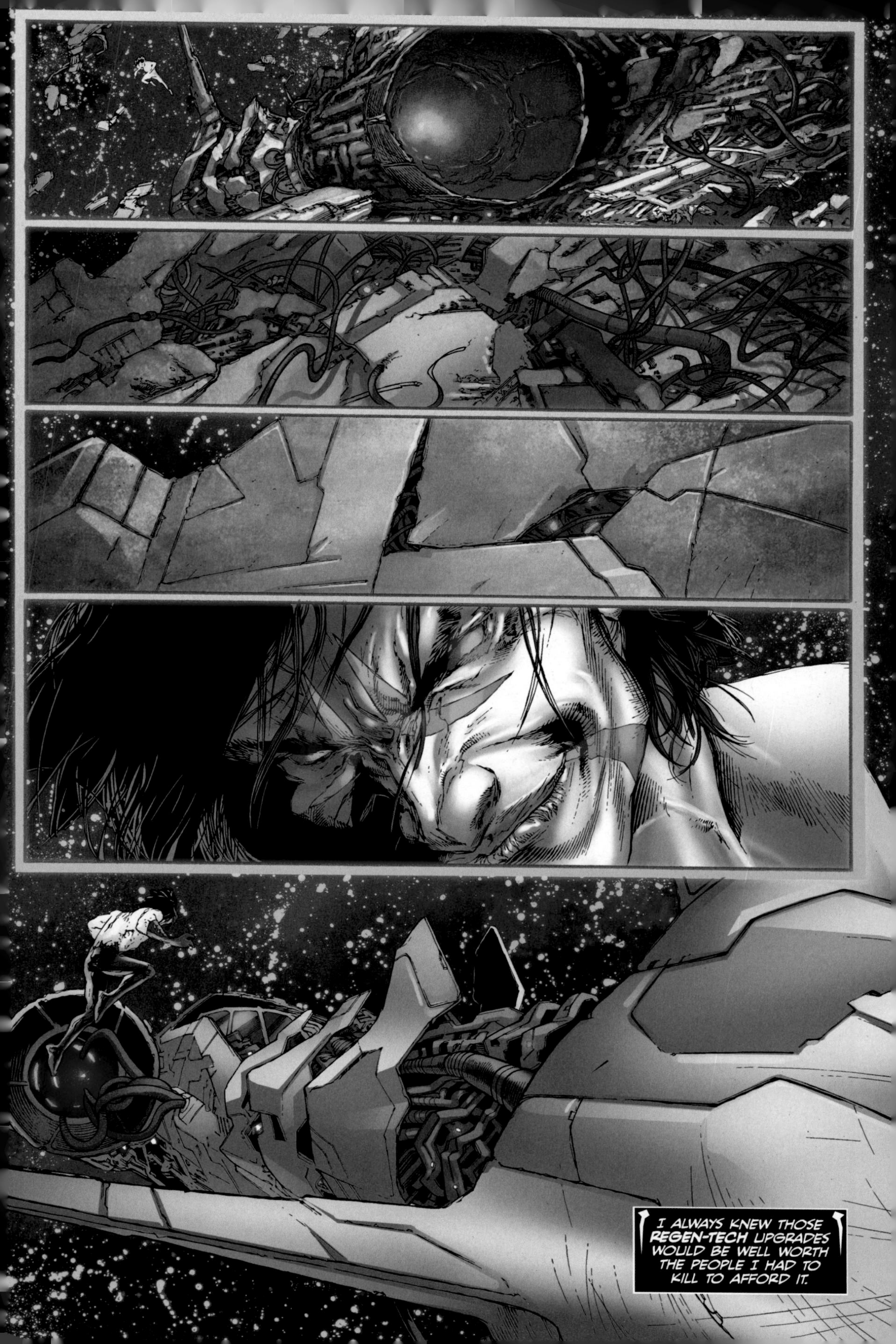
I ALWAYS KNEW THOSE REGEN-TECH UPGRADES WOULD BE WELL WORTH THE PEOPLE I HAD TO KILL TO AFFORD IT.

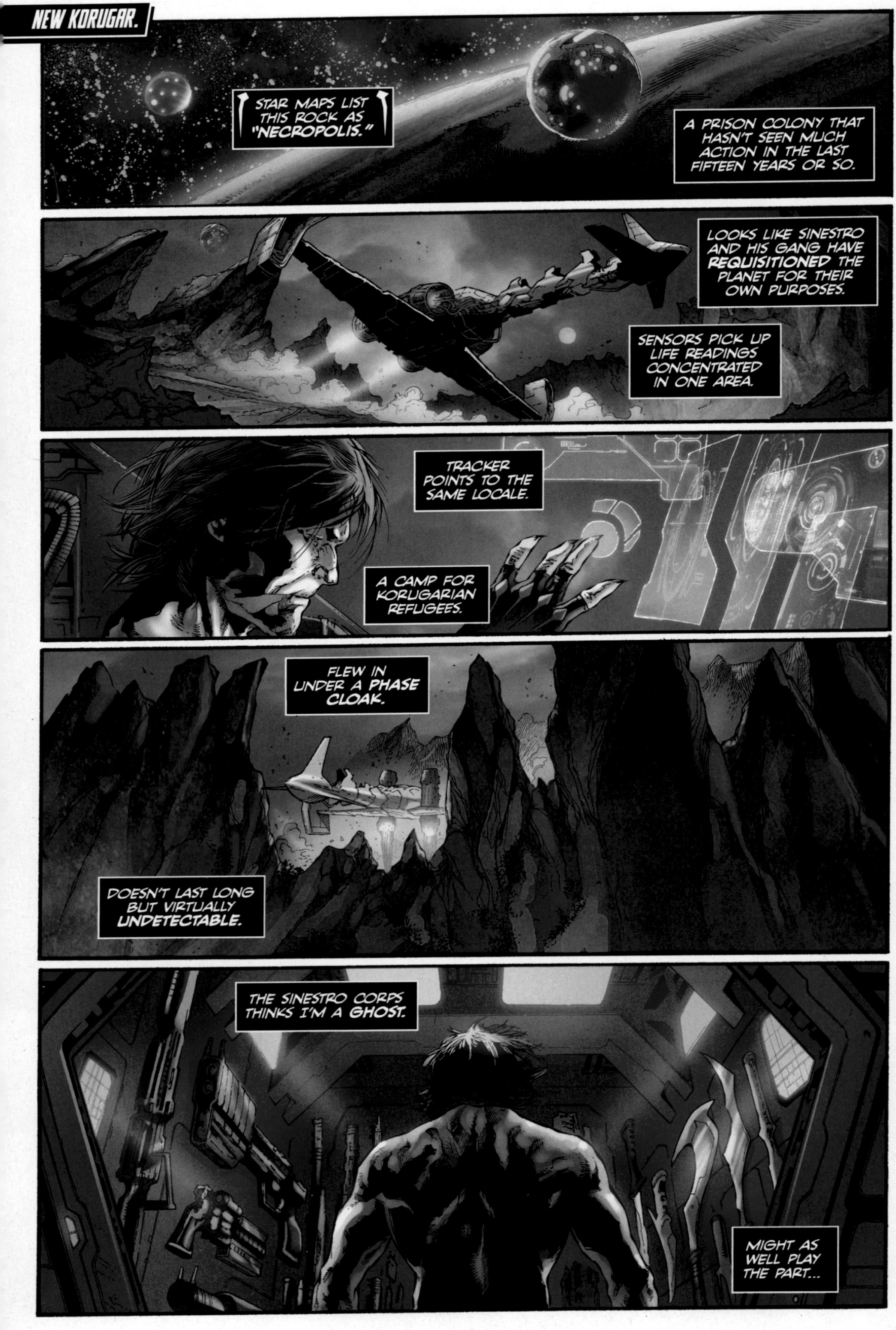
NEW KORUGAR.
STAR MAPS LIST THIS ROCK AS "NECROPOLIS."
A PRISON COLONY THAT HASN'T SEEN MUCH ACTION IN THE LAST FIFTEEN YEARS OR SO.
LOOKS LIKE SINESTRO AND HIS GANG HAVE REQUISITIONED THE PLANET FOR THEIR OWN PURPOSES.
SENSORS PICK UP LIFE READINGS CONCENTRATED IN ONE AREA.
TRACKER POINTS TO THE SAME LOCALE.
A CAMP FOR KORUGARIAN REFUGEES.
FLEW IN UNDER A PHASE CLOAK.
DOESN'T LAST LONG BUT VIRTUALLY UNDETECTABLE.
THE SINESTRO CORPS THINKS I'M A GHOST.
MIGHT AS WELL PLAY THE PART...

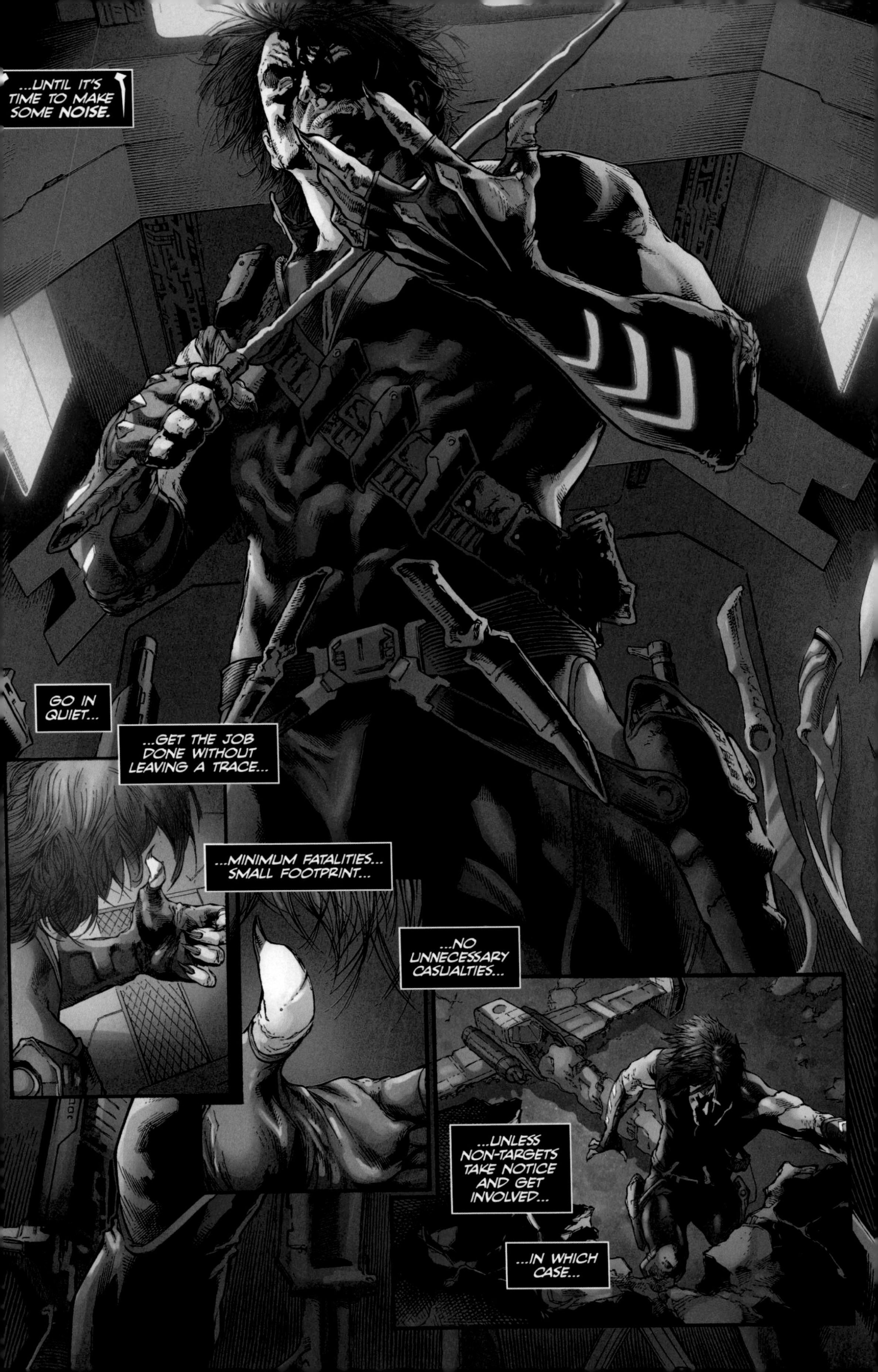
...UNTIL IT'S TIME TO MAKE SOME NOISE.
GO IN QUIET...
...GET THE JOB DONE WITHOUT LEAVING A TRACE...
...MINIMUM FATALITIES... SMALL FOOTPRINT...
...NO UNNECESSARY CASUALTIES...
...UNLESS NON-TARGETS TAKE NOTICE AND GET INVOLVED...
...IN WHICH CASE...

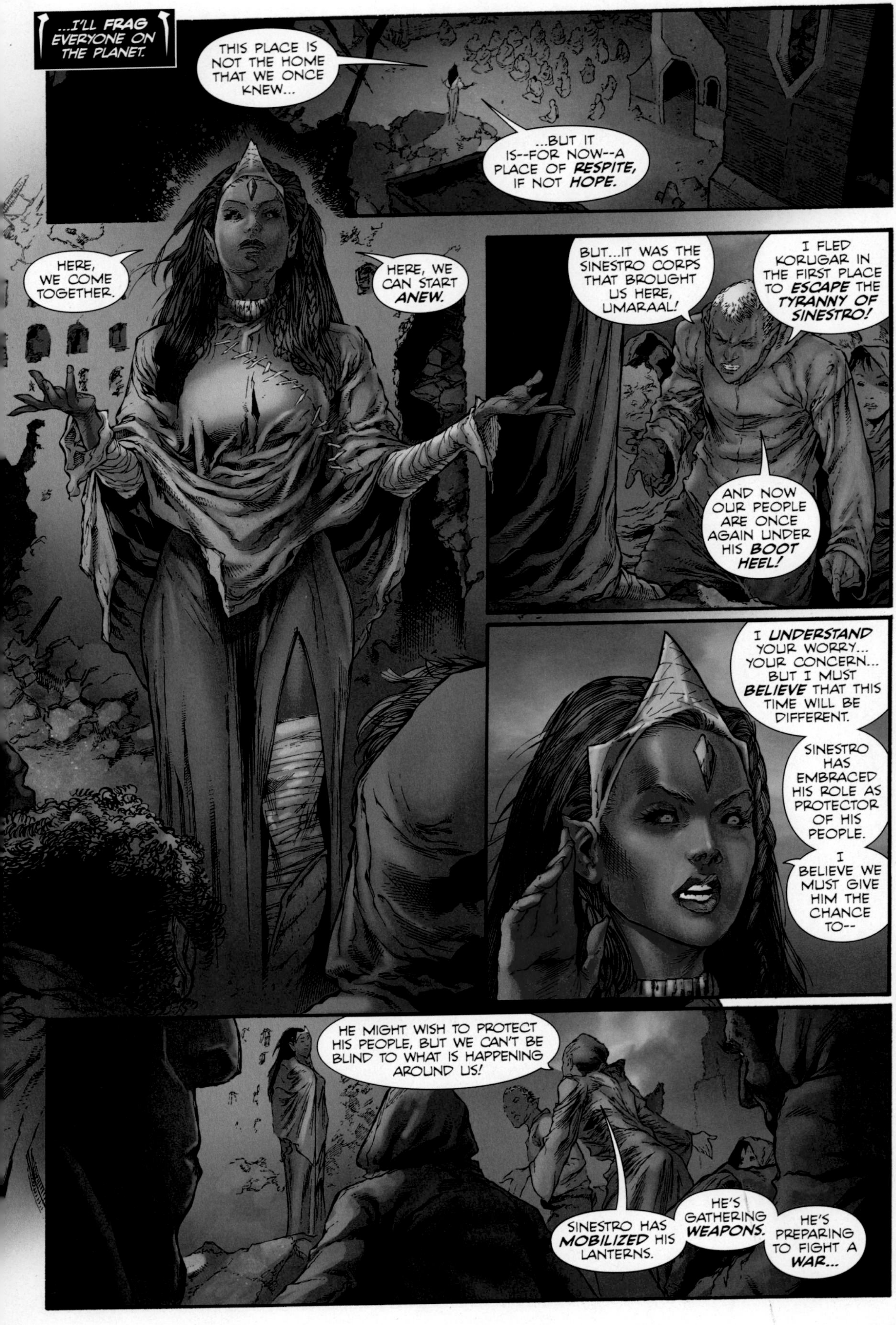
...I'LL FRAG EVERYONE ON THE PLANET.
THIS PLACE IS NOT THE HOME THAT WE ONCE KNEW...
...BUT IT IS--FOR NOW--A PLACE OF RESPITE, IF NOT HOPE.
HERE, WE COME TOGETHER.
HERE, WE CAN START ANEW.
BUT...IT WAS THE SINESTRO CORPS THAT BROUGHT US HERE, UMARAAL!
I FLED KORUGAR IN THE FIRST PLACE TO ESCAPE THE TYRANNY OF SINESTRO!
AND NOW OUR PEOPLE ARE ONCE AGAIN UNDER HIS BOOT HEEL!
I UNDERSTAND YOUR WORRY... YOUR CONCERN... BUT I MUST BELIEVE THAT THIS TIME WILL BE DIFFERENT.
SINESTRO HAS EMBRACED HIS ROLE AS PROTECTOR OF HIS PEOPLE.
I BELIEVE WE MUST GIVE HIM THE CHANCE TO--
HE MIGHT WISH TO PROTECT HIS PEOPLE, BUT WE CAN'T BE BLIND TO WHAT IS HAPPENING AROUND US!
SINESTRO HAS MOBILIZED HIS LANTERNS.
HE'S GATHERING WEAPONS.
HE'S PREPARING TO FIGHT A WAR...

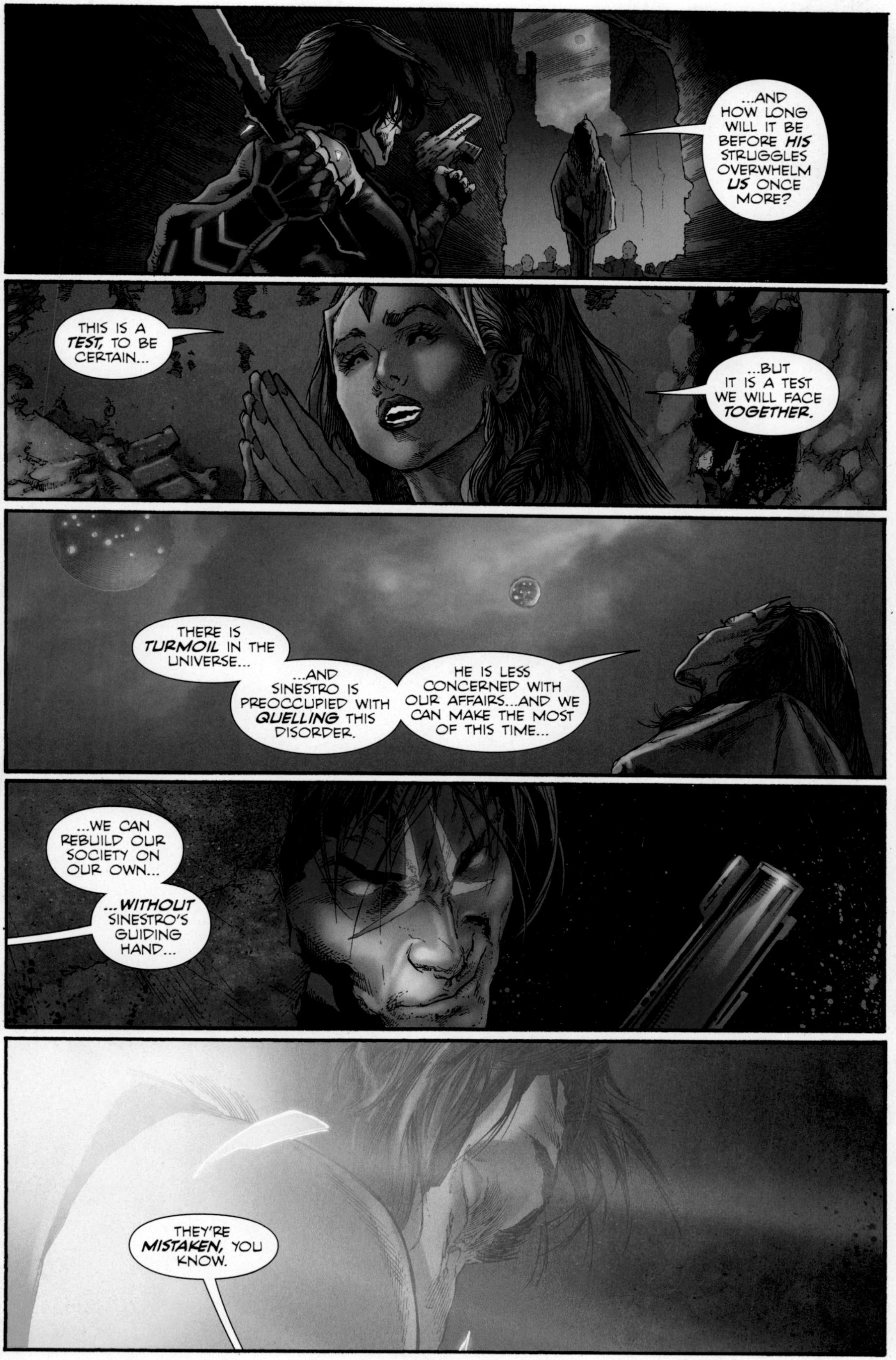
...AND HOW LONG WILL IT BE BEFORE *HIS* STRUGGLES OVERWHELM *US* ONCE MORE?
THIS IS A *TEST,* TO BE CERTAIN...
...BUT IT IS A TEST WE WILL FACE *TOGETHER.*
THERE IS *TURMOIL* IN THE UNIVERSE...
...AND SINESTRO IS PREOCCUPIED WITH *QUELLING* THIS DISORDER.
HE IS LESS CONCERNED WITH OUR AFFAIRS...AND WE CAN MAKE THE MOST OF THIS TIME...
...WE CAN REBUILD OUR SOCIETY ON OUR OWN...
...WITHOUT SINESTRO'S GUIDING HAND...
THEY'RE *MISTAKEN,* YOU KNOW.

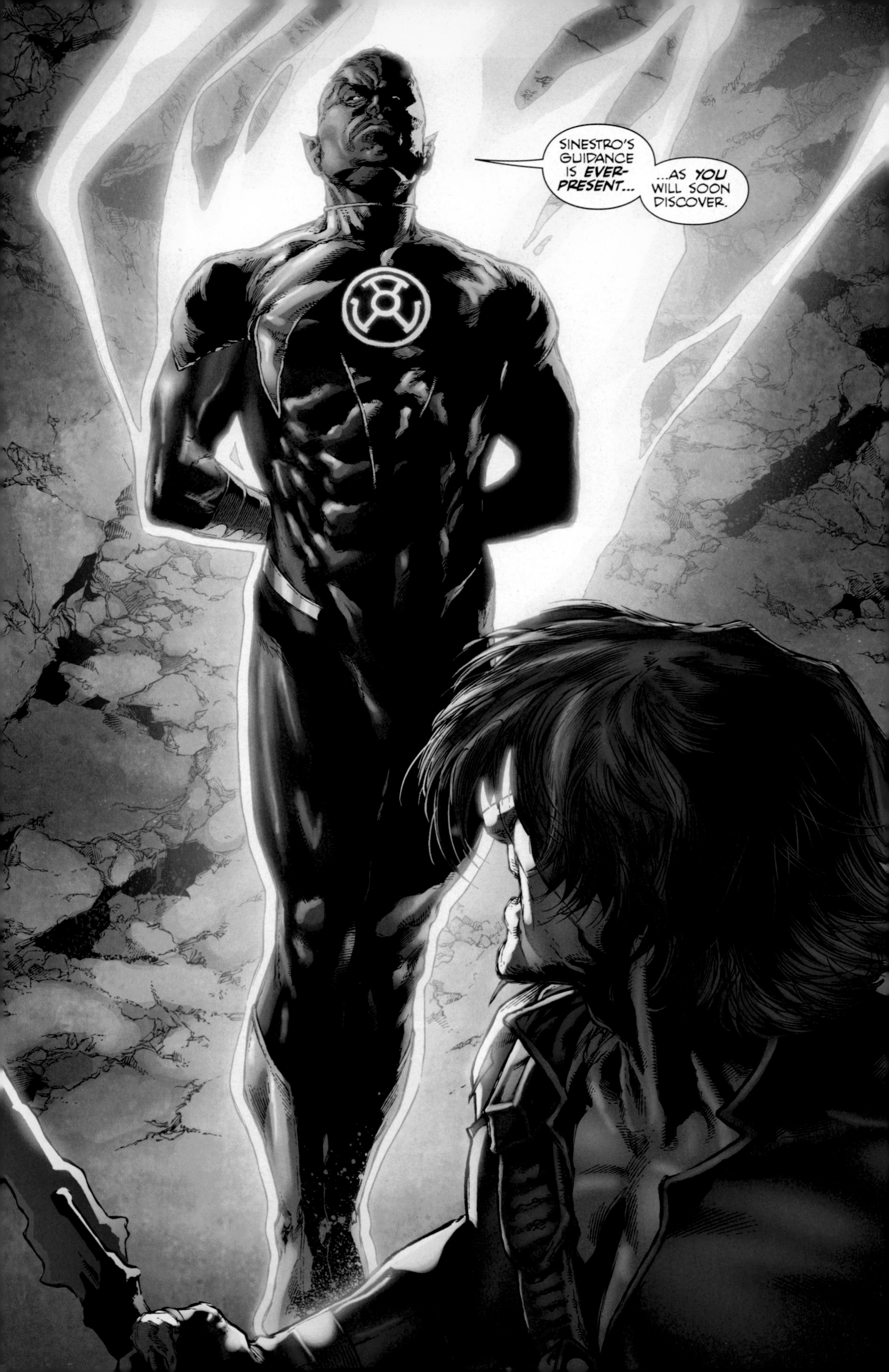
SINESTRO'S GUIDANCE IS *EVER-PRESENT...*
...AS *YOU* WILL SOON DISCOVER.

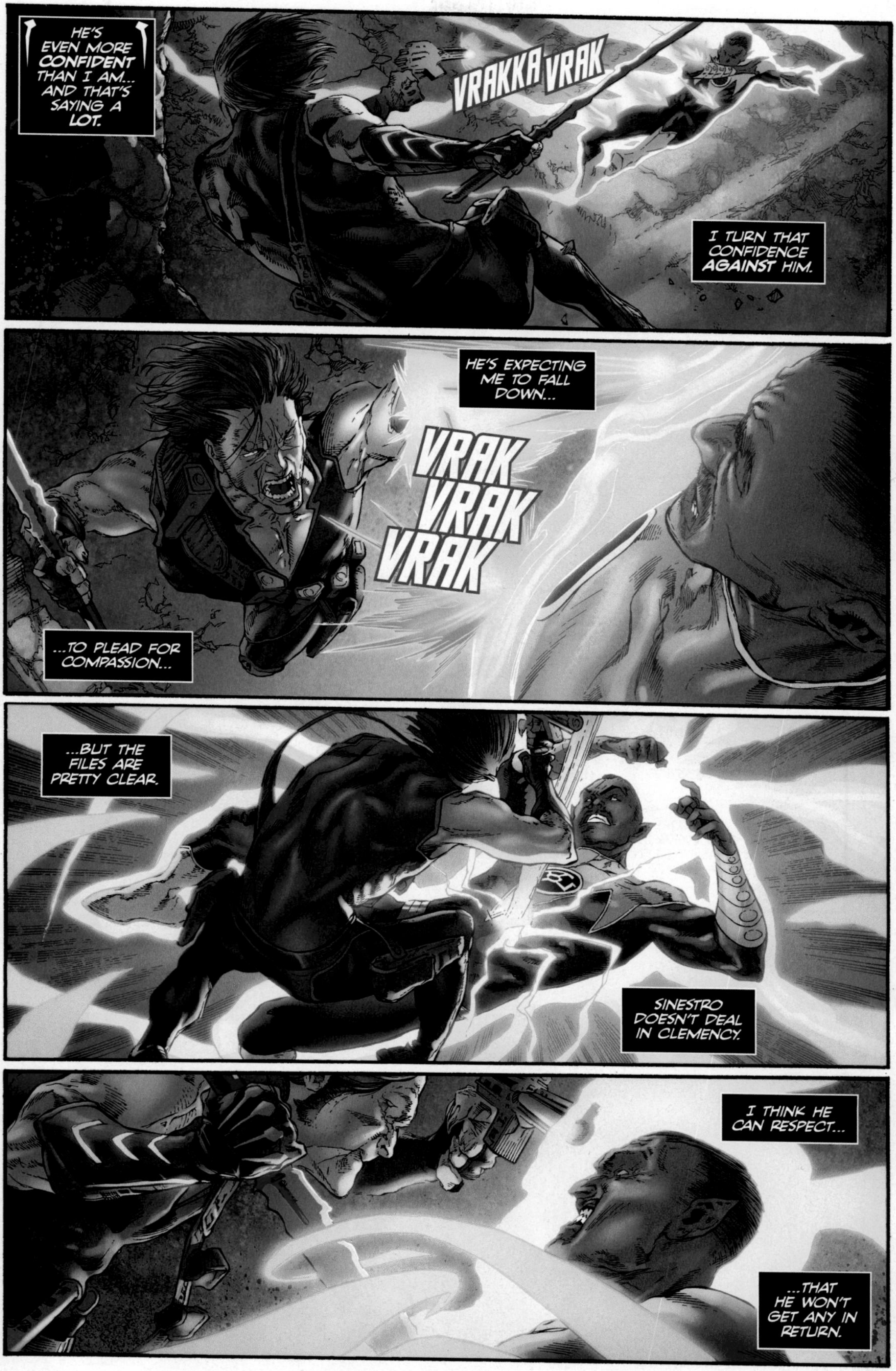
HE'S EVEN MORE CONFIDENT THAN I AM... AND THAT'S SAYING A LOT.
VRAKKA VRAK
I TURN THAT CONFIDENCE AGAINST HIM.
HE'S EXPECTING ME TO FALL DOWN...
VRAK VRAK VRAK
...TO PLEAD FOR COMPASSION...
...BUT THE FILES ARE PRETTY CLEAR.
SINESTRO DOESN'T DEAL IN CLEMENCY.
I THINK HE CAN RESPECT...
...THAT HE WON'T GET ANY IN RETURN.

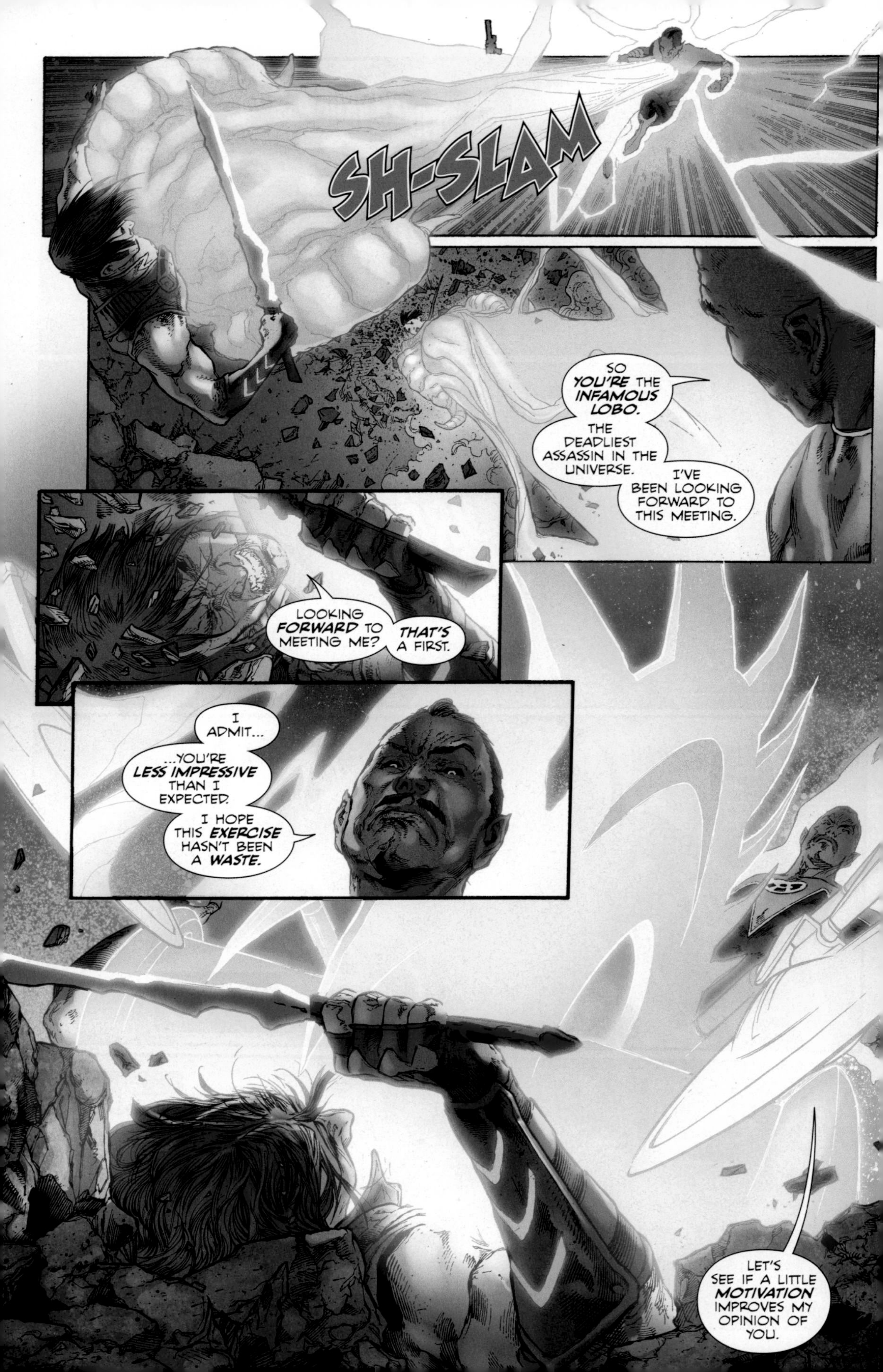
SH-SLAM
SO YOU'RE THE INFAMOUS LOBO.
THE DEADLIEST ASSASSIN IN THE UNIVERSE.
I'VE BEEN LOOKING FORWARD TO THIS MEETING.
LOOKING FORWARD TO MEETING ME?
THAT'S A FIRST.
I ADMIT...
...YOU'RE LESS IMPRESSIVE THAN I EXPECTED.
I HOPE THIS EXERCISE HASN'T BEEN A WASTE.
LET'S SEE IF A LITTLE MOTIVATION IMPROVES MY OPINION OF YOU.

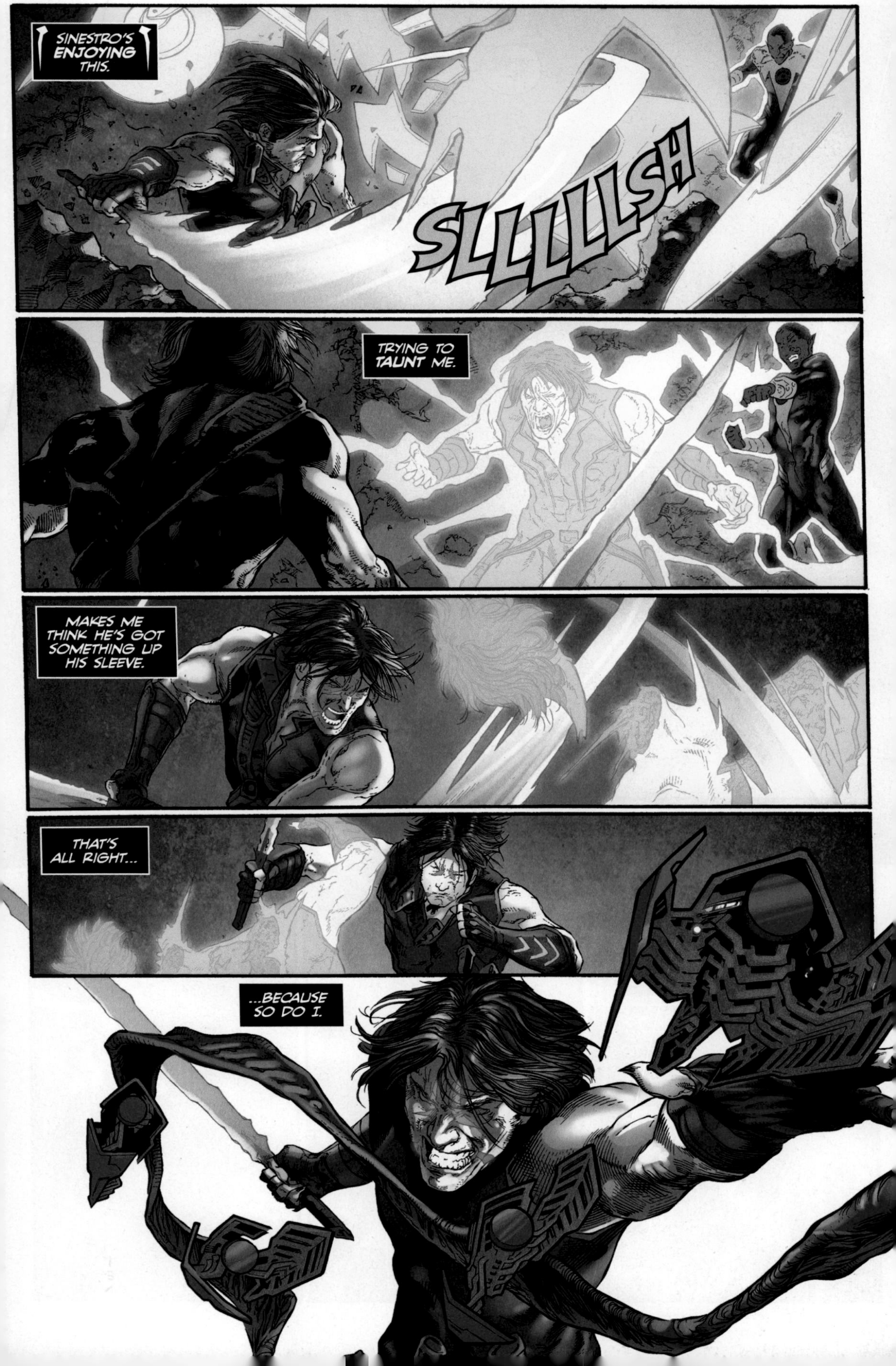
SINESTRO'S ENJOYING THIS.
SLLLLLSH
TRYING TO TAUNT ME.
MAKES ME THINK HE'S GOT SOMETHING UP HIS SLEEVE.
THAT'S ALL RIGHT...
...BECAUSE SO DO I.

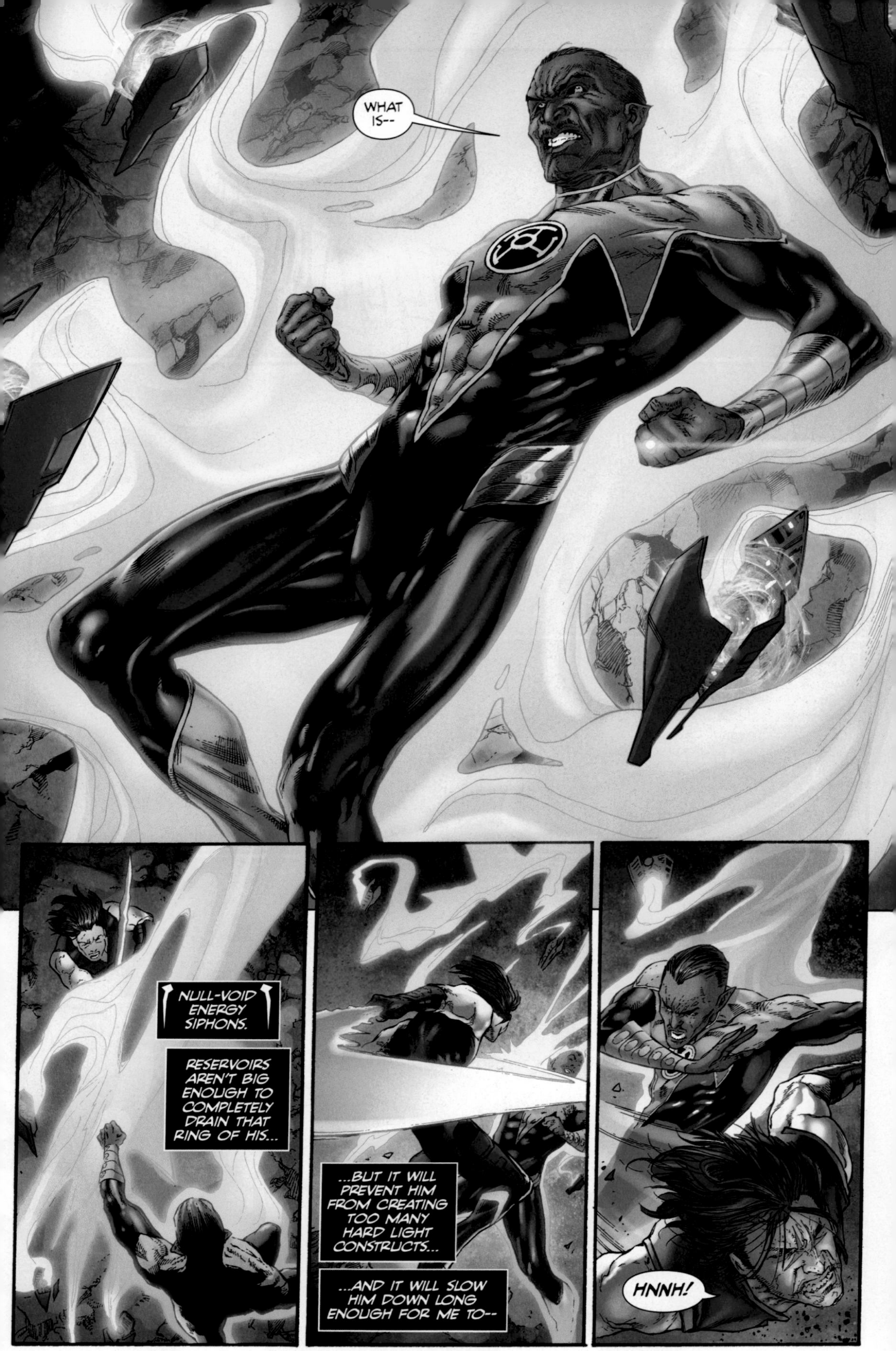
WHAT IS--
NULL-VOID ENERGY SIPHONS.
RESERVOIRS AREN'T BIG ENOUGH TO COMPLETELY DRAIN THAT RING OF HIS...
...BUT IT WILL PREVENT HIM FROM CREATING TOO MANY HARD LIGHT CONSTRUCTS...
...AND IT WILL SLOW HIM DOWN LONG ENOUGH FOR ME TO--
HNNH!

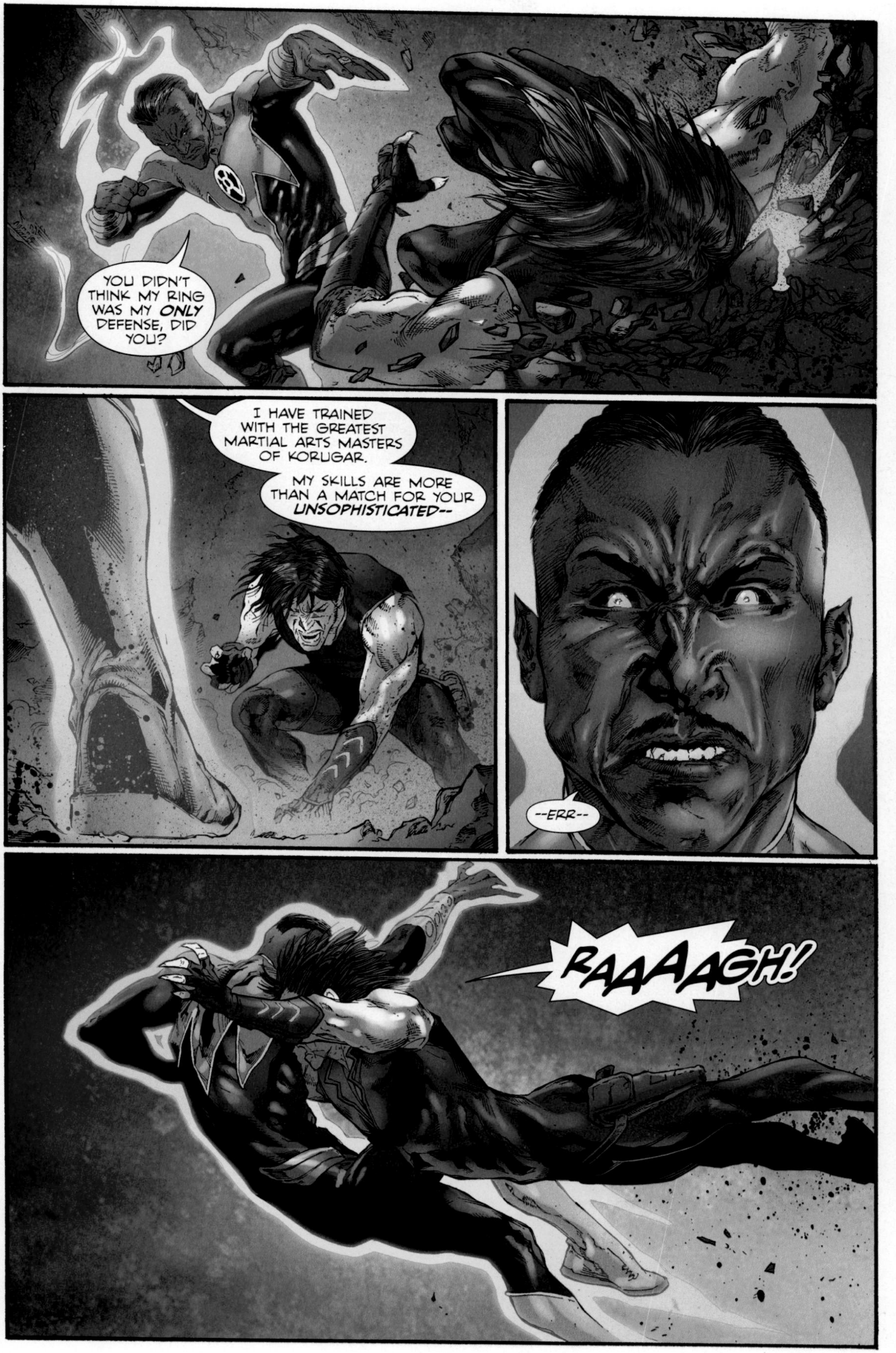
YOU DIDN'T THINK MY RING WAS MY ONLY DEFENSE, DID YOU?
I HAVE TRAINED WITH THE GREATEST MARTIAL ARTS MASTERS OF KORUGAR.
MY SKILLS ARE MORE THAN A MATCH FOR YOUR UNSOPHISTICATED--
--ERR--
RAAAAGH!

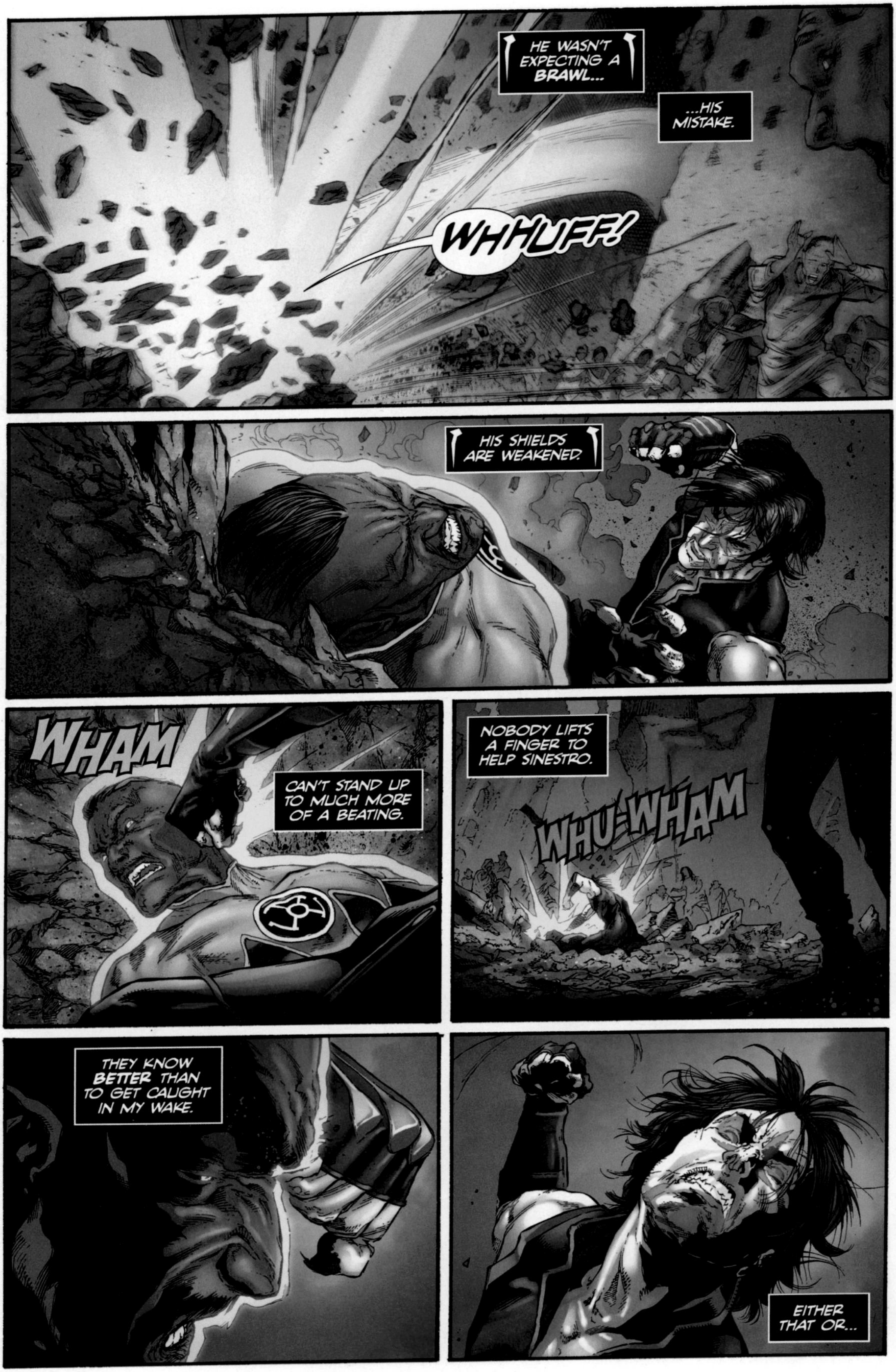
HE WASN'T EXPECTING A **BRAWL**...
...HIS MISTAKE.
WHHUFF!
HIS SHIELDS ARE WEAKENED.
WHAM
CAN'T STAND UP TO MUCH MORE OF A BEATING.
NOBODY LIFTS A FINGER TO HELP SINESTRO.
WHU-WHAM
THEY KNOW **BETTER** THAN TO GET CAUGHT IN MY WAKE.
EITHER THAT OR...

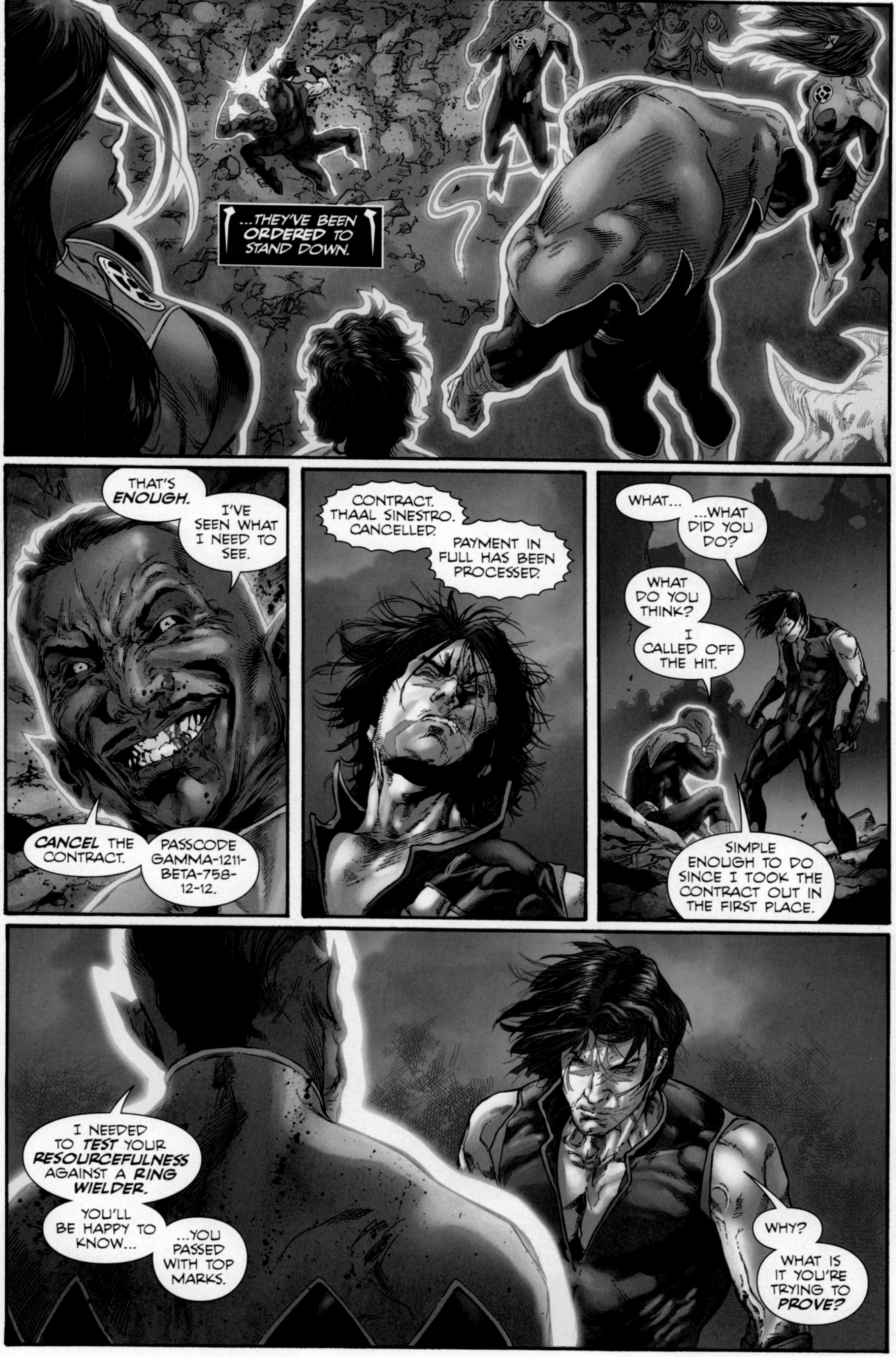
...THEY'VE BEEN ORDERED TO STAND DOWN.
THAT'S ENOUGH.
I'VE SEEN WHAT I NEED TO SEE.
CANCEL THE CONTRACT.
PASSCODE GAMMA-1211-BETA-758-12-12.
CONTRACT. THAAL SINESTRO. CANCELLED.
PAYMENT IN FULL HAS BEEN PROCESSED.
WHAT...
...WHAT DID YOU DO?
WHAT DO YOU THINK?
I CALLED OFF THE HIT.
SIMPLE ENOUGH TO DO SINCE I TOOK THE CONTRACT OUT IN THE FIRST PLACE.
I NEEDED TO TEST YOUR RESOURCEFULNESS AGAINST A RING WIELDER.
YOU'LL BE HAPPY TO KNOW...
...YOU PASSED WITH TOP MARKS.
WHY?
WHAT IS IT YOU'RE TRYING TO PROVE?

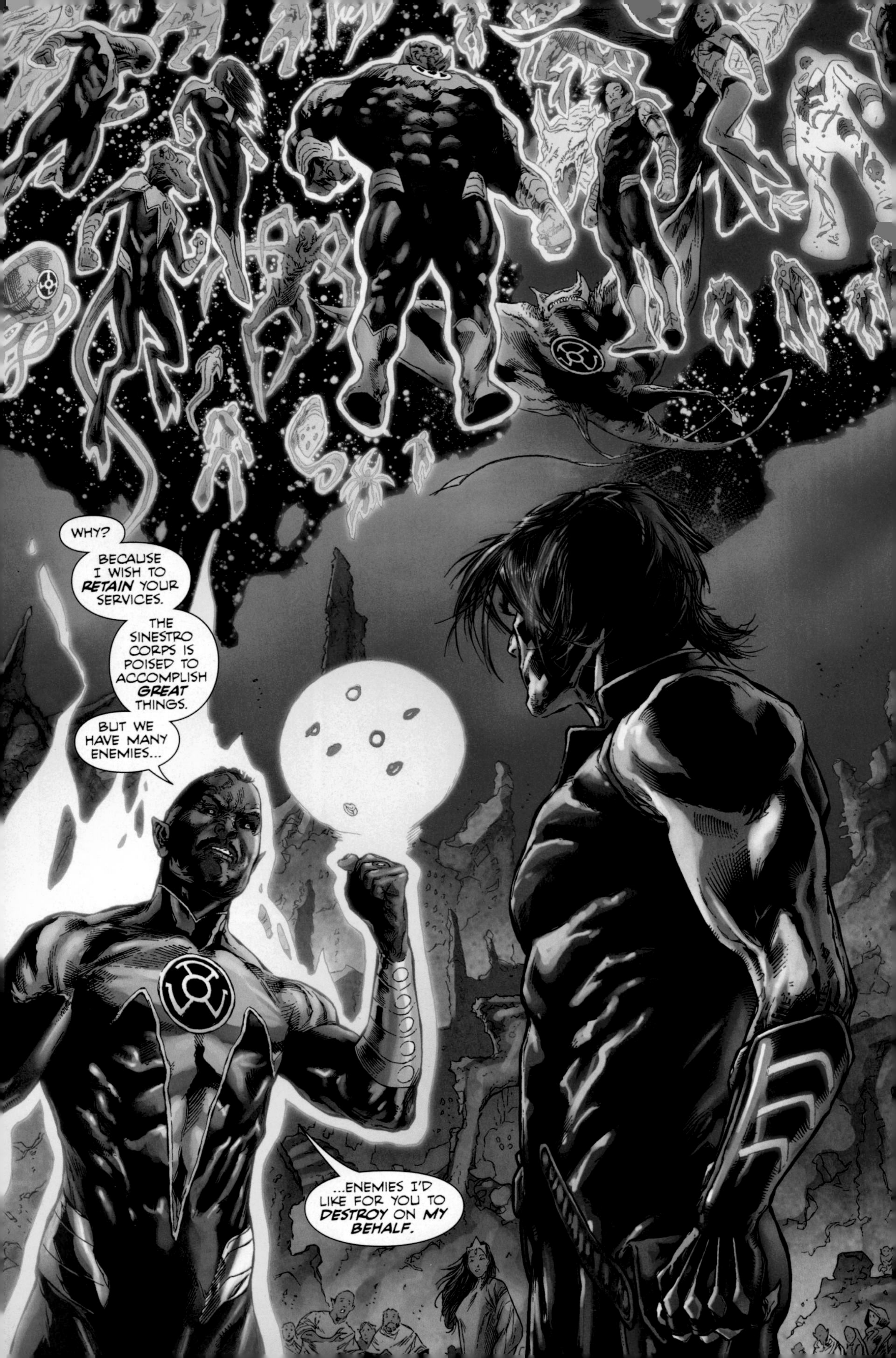
WHY?
BECAUSE I WISH TO *RETAIN* YOUR SERVICES.
THE SINESTRO CORPS IS POISED TO ACCOMPLISH *GREAT* THINGS.
BUT WE HAVE MANY ENEMIES...
...ENEMIES I'D LIKE FOR YOU TO *DESTROY* ON *MY BEHALF.*

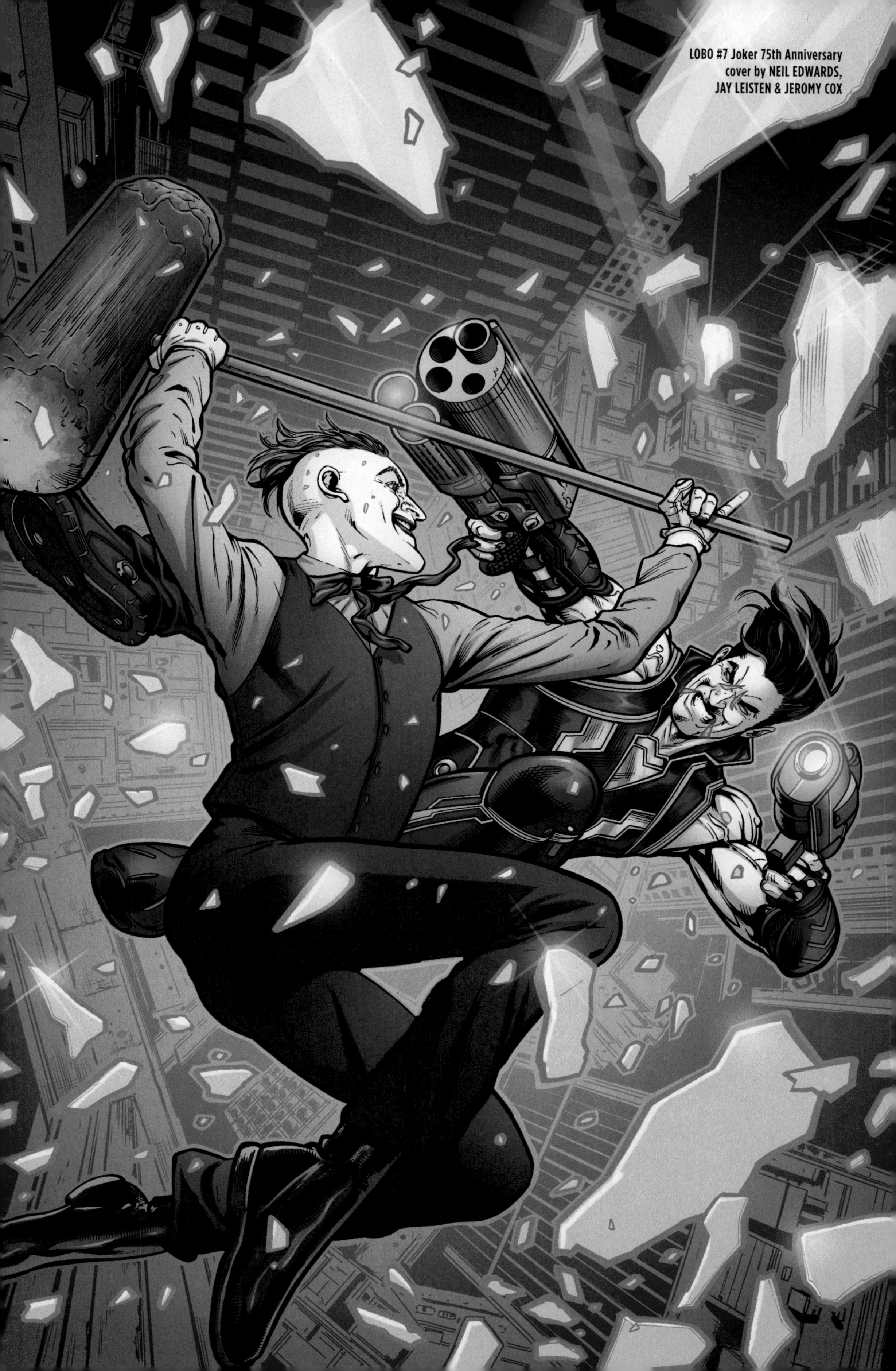

LOBO #7 Joker 75th Anniversary
cover by NEIL EDWARDS,
JAY LEISTEN & JEROMY COX

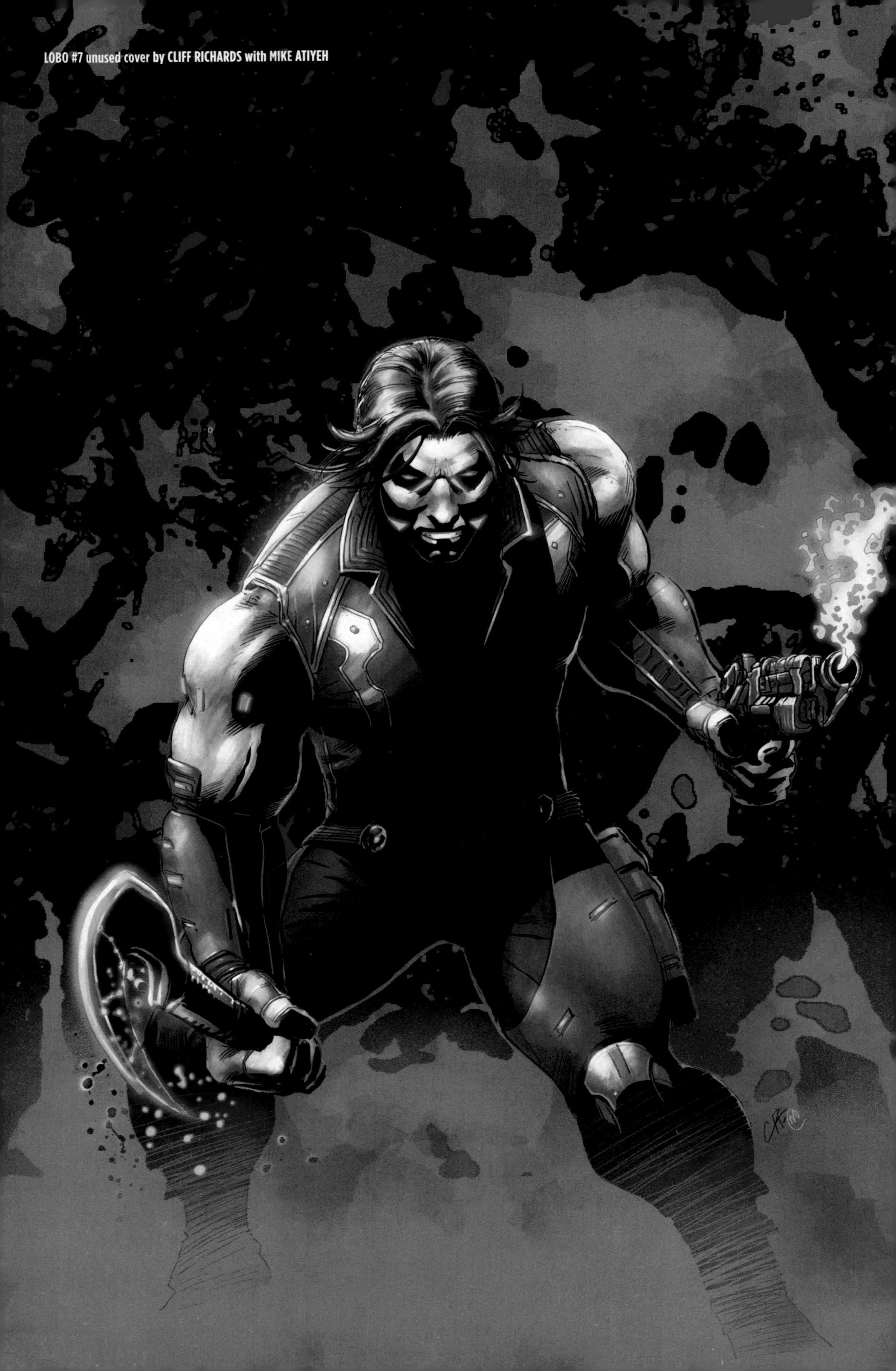

LOBO #7 unused cover by CLIFF RICHARDS with MIKE ATIYEH

LOBO #8 unused cover by CLIFF RICHARDS with MIKE ATIYEH

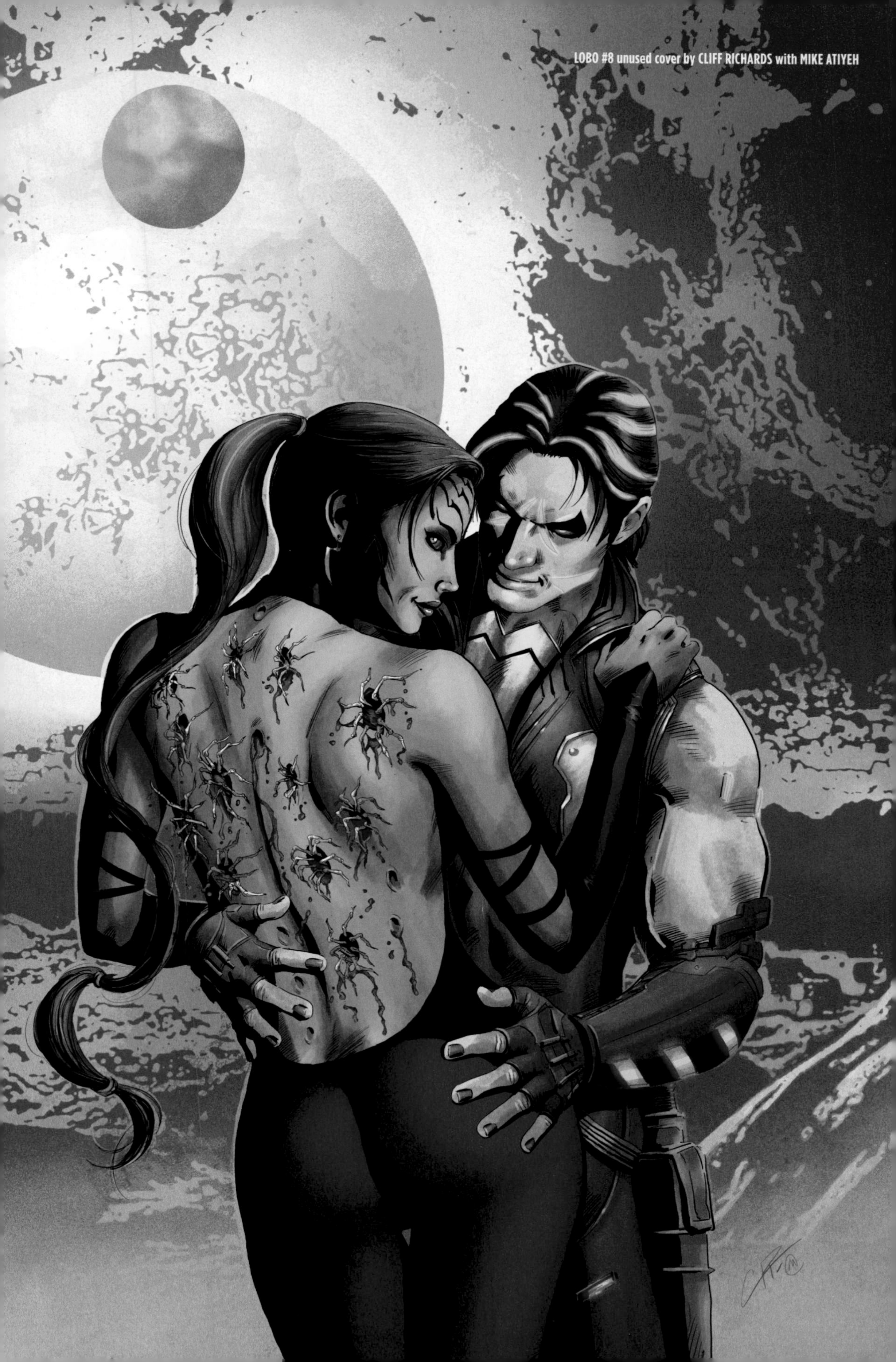

LOBO ANNUAL #1 unused cover by R.B. SILVA with MATT YACKEY

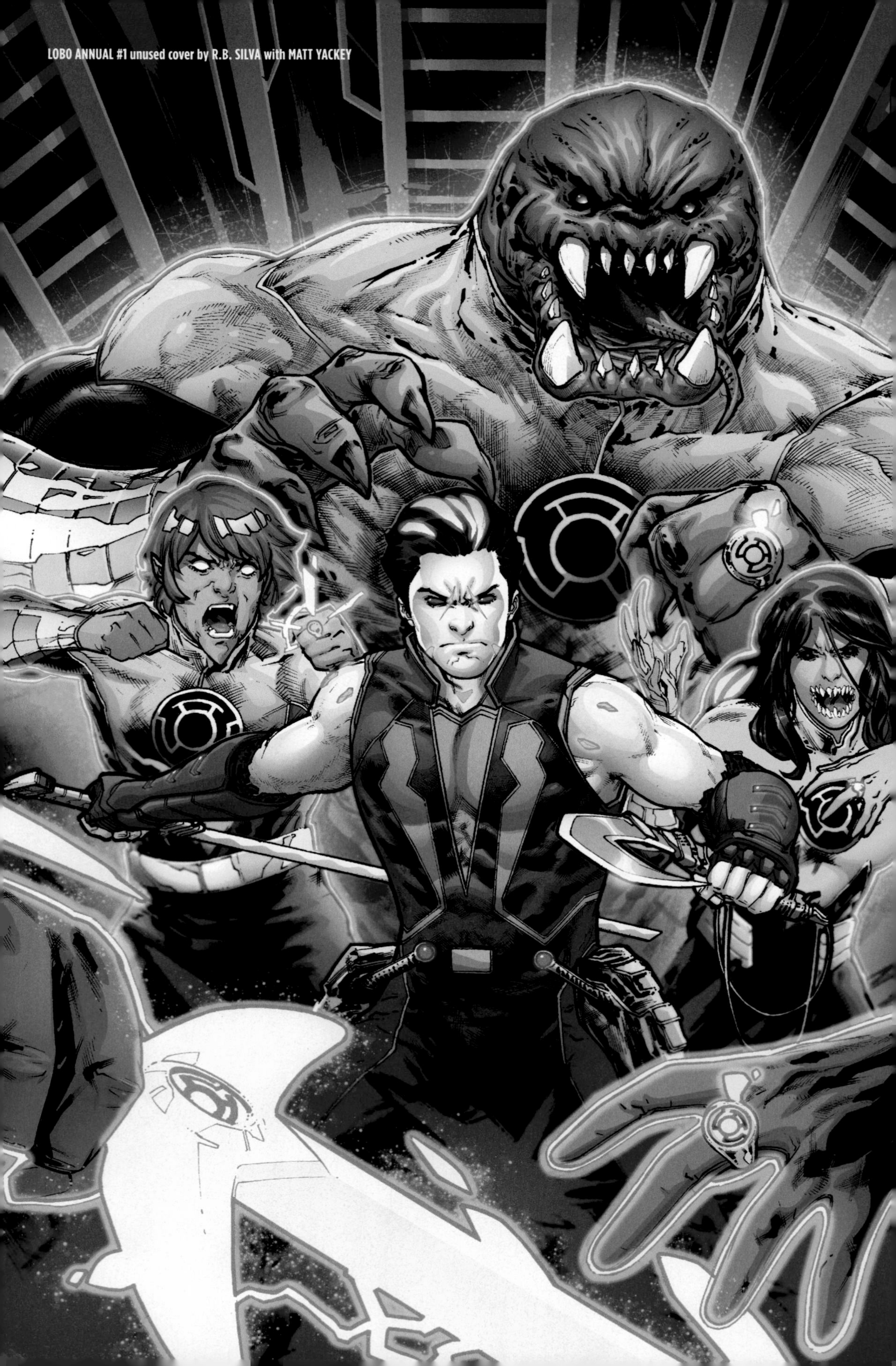

PENCILLER ROBSON ROCHA INKER PAGE# 01
TITLE LOBO-ANNUAL ISSUE # MONTH INTERIORS

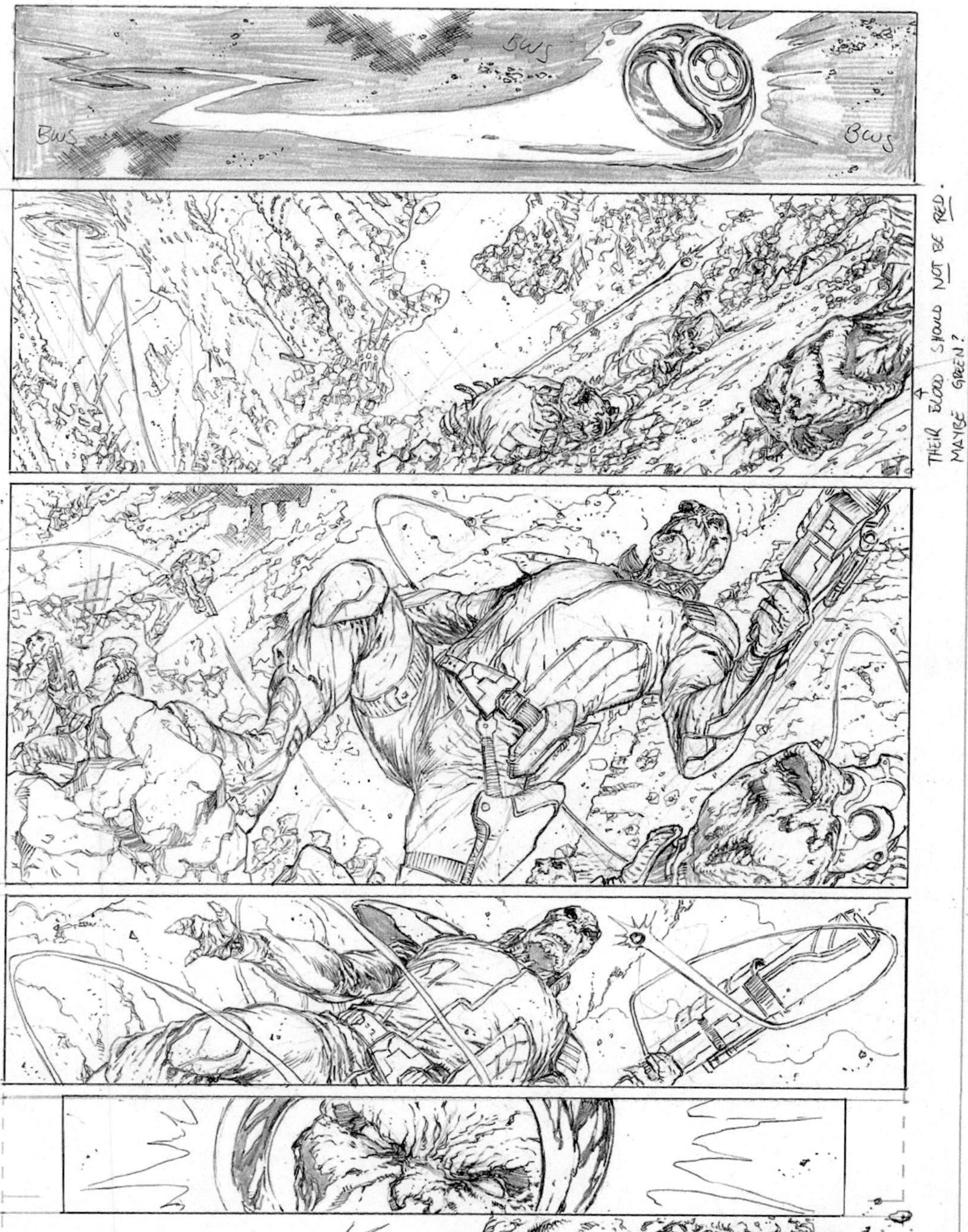
BWS
BWS
BWS
THEIR BLOOD SHOULD NOT BE RED. MAYBE GREEN?

LIVE AREA
CROP
BLEED
MINIMUM BLEED 1/4" ALL AROUND

CUT RIGHT-HAND PAGE AT THIS LINE
DOUBLE PAGE SPREAD: CUT AS SHOWN, ABUT PAGE EDGES, TAPE ON BACK, DO NOT OVERLAP
CUT LEFT HAND PAGE AT THIS LINE

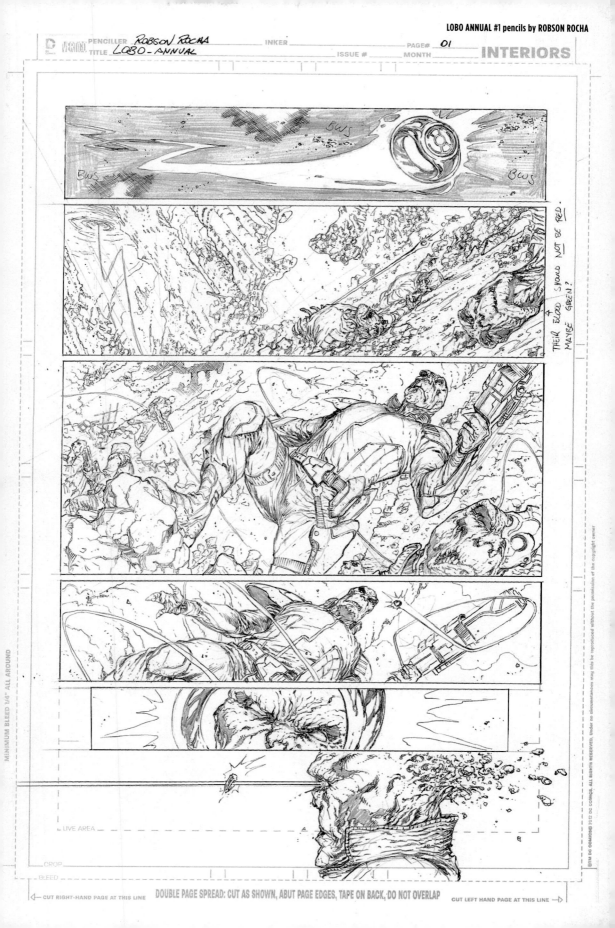

PENCILLER Robson Rocha INKER PAGE# 02
TITLE LOBO ANNUAL ISSUE # MONTH INTERIORS

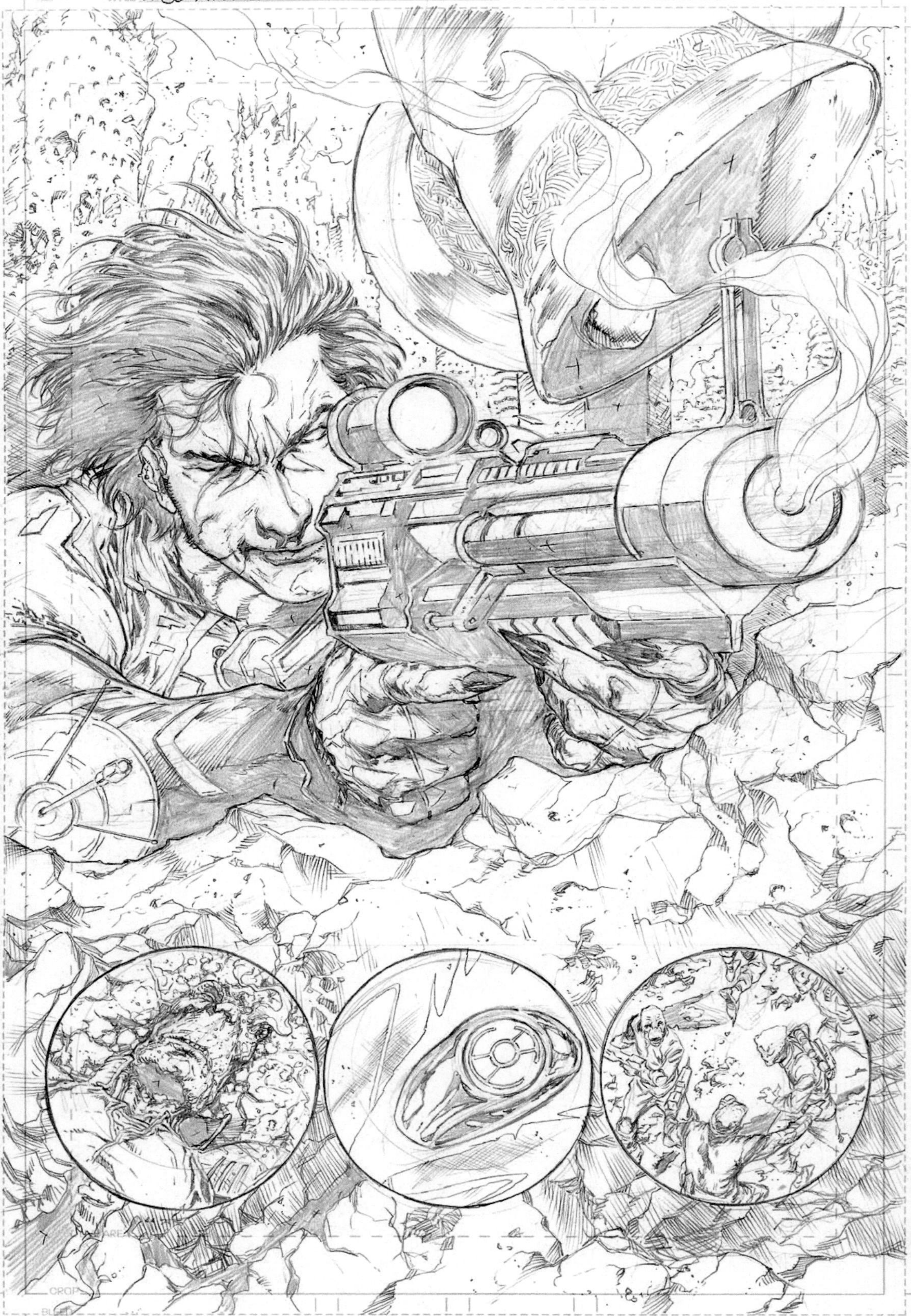

CUT RIGHT-HAND PAGE AT THIS LINE DOUBLE PAGE SPREAD: CUT AS SHOWN, ABUT PAGE EDGES, TAPE ON BACK, DO NOT OVERLAP CUT LEFT HAND PAGE AT THIS LINE

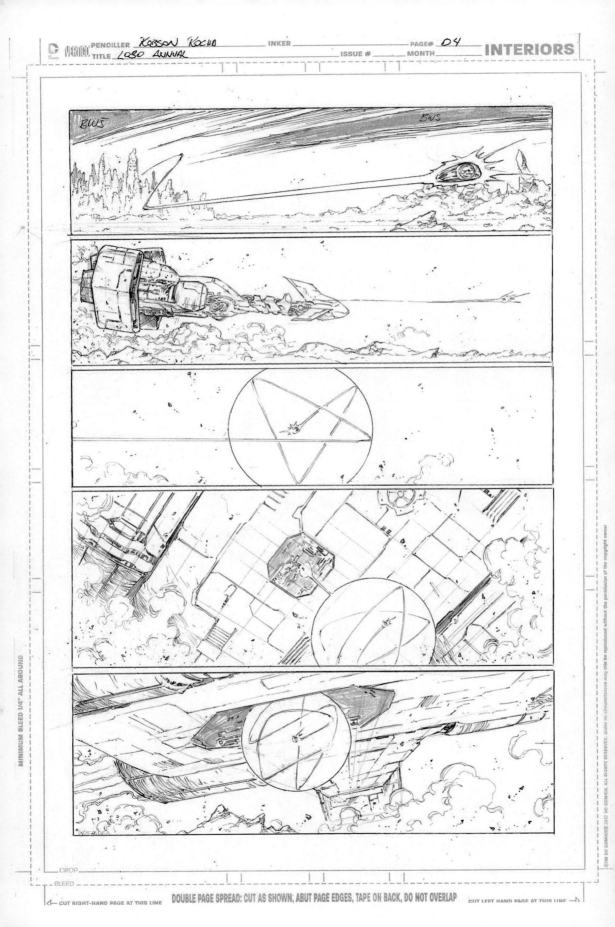

PENCILLER ROBSON ROCHA INKER PAGE# 05

TITLE LOBO ANNUAL ISSUE # MONTH

INTERIORS

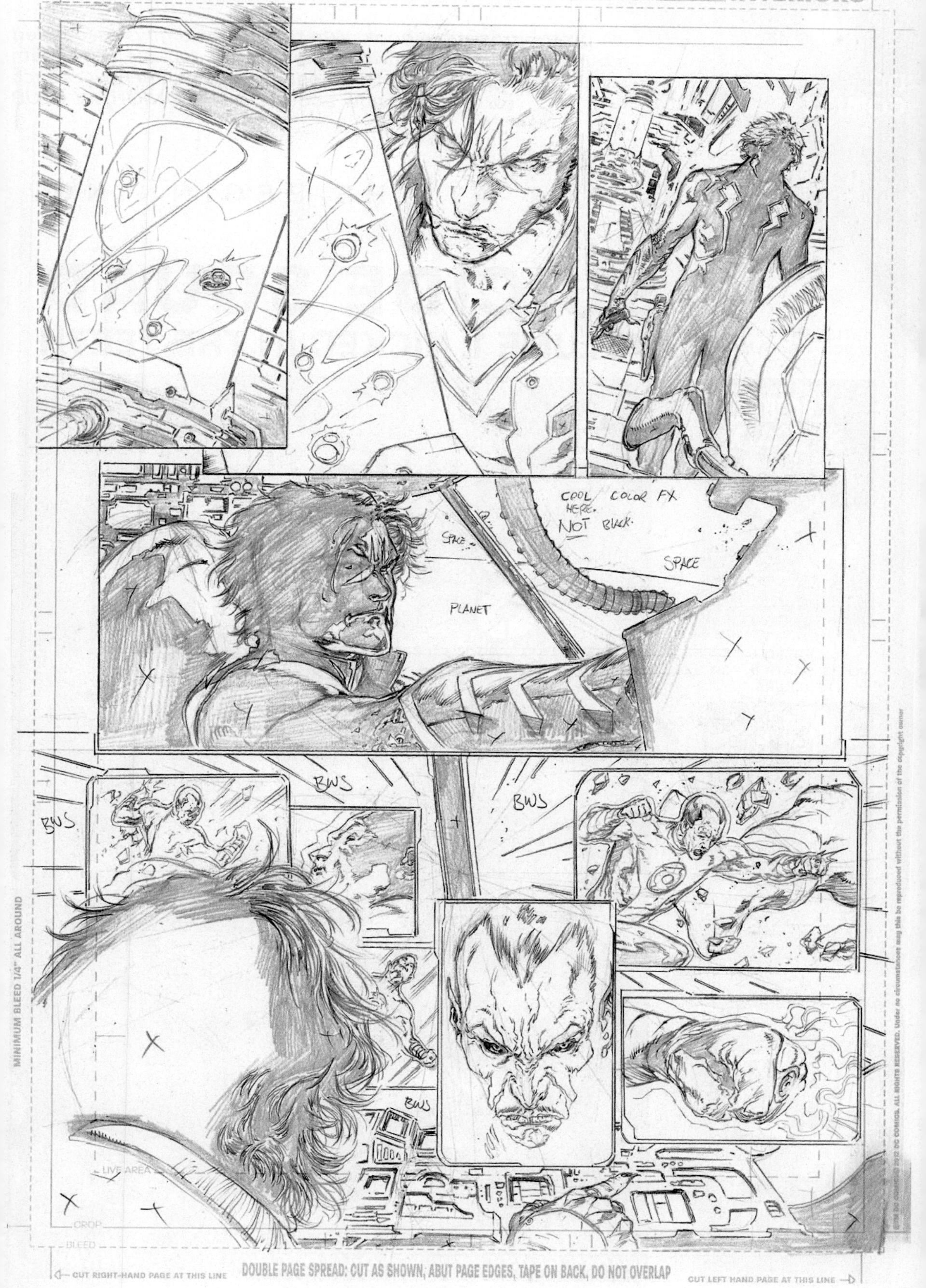
COOL COLOR FX HERE. NOT BLACK.
SPACE
SPACE
PLANET
BWS
BWS
BWS
BWS

MINIMUM BLEED 1/4" ALL AROUND

LIVE AREA

CROP

BLEED

CUT RIGHT-HAND PAGE AT THIS LINE

DOUBLE PAGE SPREAD: CUT AS SHOWN, ABUT PAGE EDGES, TAPE ON BACK, DO NOT OVERLAP

CUT LEFT HAND PAGE AT THIS LINE

DC COMICS™

"A pretty irresistible hook. What if the good guys assembled a bunch of bad guys to work as a Dirty Dozen-like superteam and do the dirty work traditional heroes would never touch (or want to know about)?"—THE ONION/AV CLUB

START AT THE BEGINNING!

SUICIDE SQUAD
VOLUME 1: KICKED IN THE TEETH

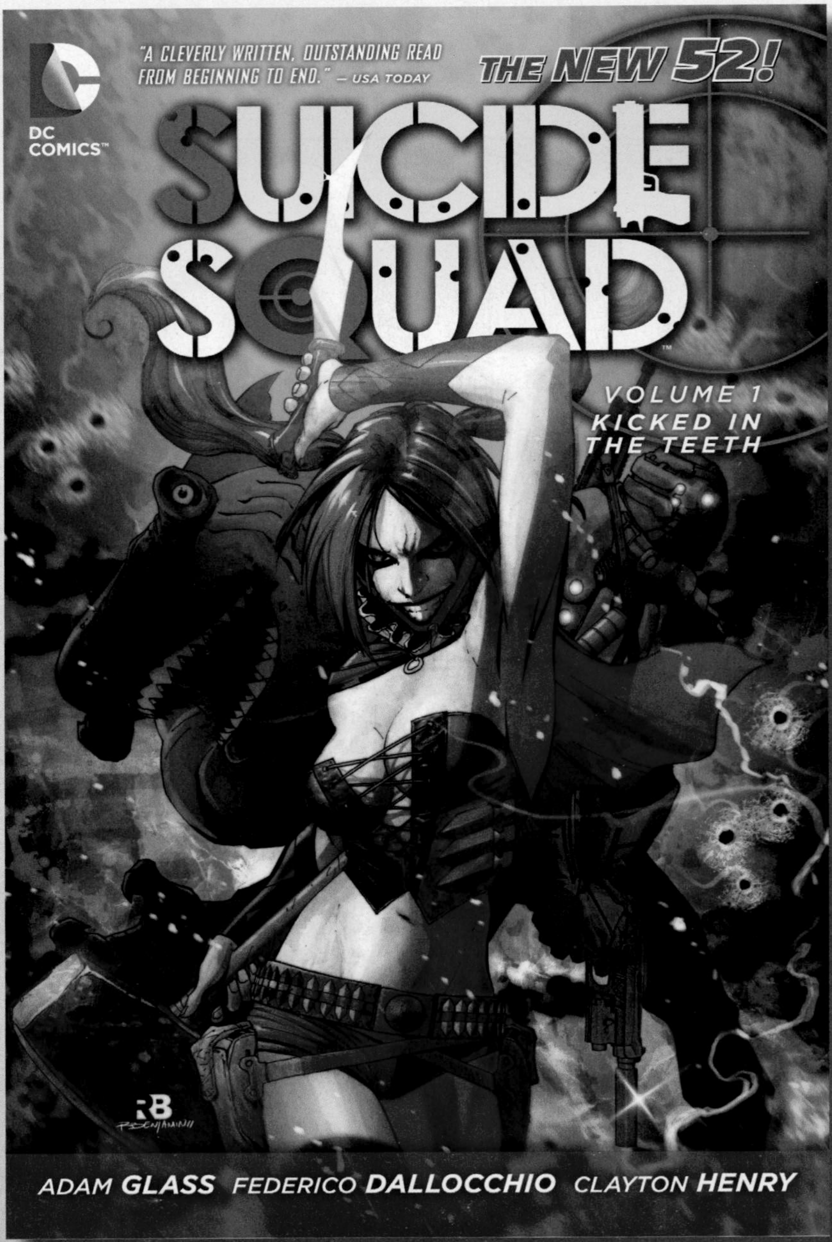
"A CLEVERLY WRITTEN, OUTSTANDING READ FROM BEGINNING TO END." — USA TODAY
DC COMICS™
THE NEW 52!
SUICIDE SQUAD
VOLUME 1 KICKED IN THE TEETH
ADAM GLASS FEDERICO DALLOCCHIO CLAYTON HENRY

SUICIDE SQUAD VOL. 2: BASILISK RISING

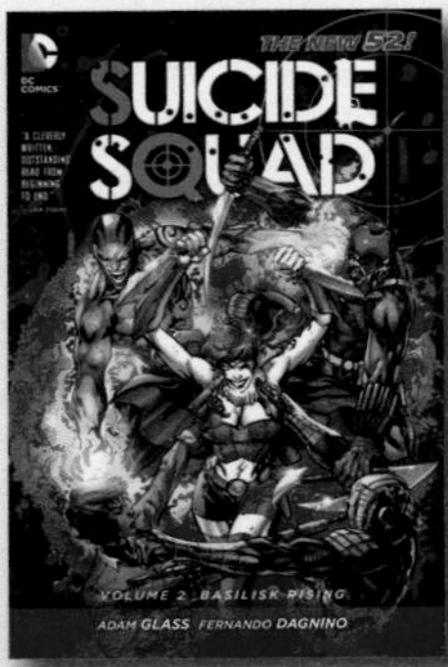
THE NEW 52!
SUICIDE SQUAD
VOLUME 2 BASILISK RISING
ADAM GLASS FERNANDO DAGNINO

SUICIDE SQUAD VOL. 3: DEATH IS FOR SUCKERS

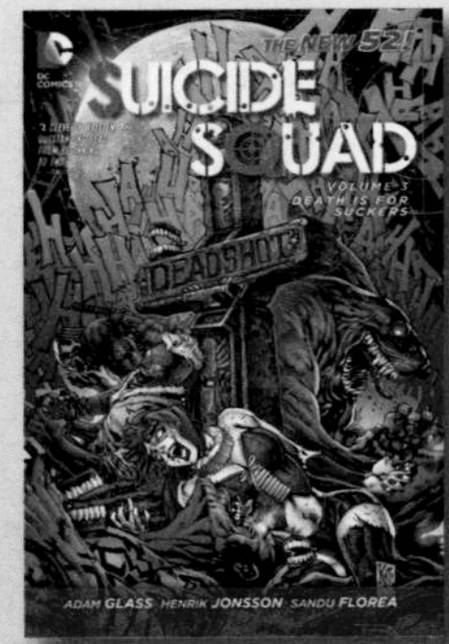
THE NEW 52!
SUICIDE SQUAD
ADAM GLASS HENRIK JONSSON SANDU FLOREA

DEATHSTROKE VOL. 1: LEGACY

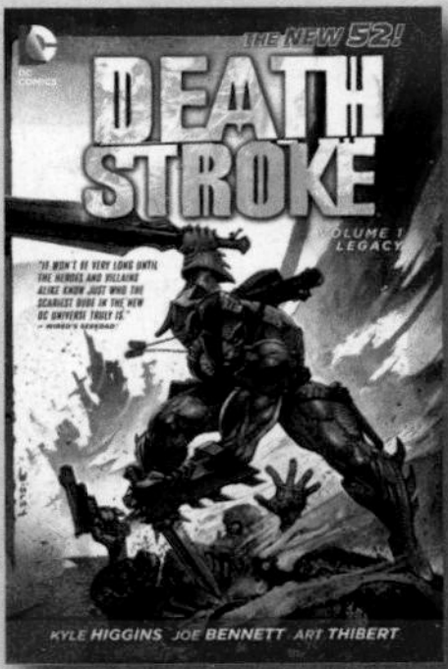
THE NEW 52!
DEATH STROKE
VOLUME 1 LEGACY
KYLE HIGGINS JOE BENNETT ART THIBERT